DOING YOUR
RESEARCH PROJECT

Fourth edition

DOING YOUR
RESEARCH PROJECT

A guide for first-time researchers
in education, health and social science

Fourth edition

JUDITH BELL

Open University Press

Open University Press
McGraw-Hill Education
McGraw-Hill House
Shoppenhangers Road
Maidenhead
Berkshire
England
SL6 2QL

email: enquiries@openup.co.uk
world wide web: www.openup.co.uk

and Two Penn Plaza, New York, NY 10121-2289, USA

First published 2005

A catalogue record of this book is available from the British Library

ISBN-13:   978 0335 21504 1 (pb)   978 0335 21505 8 (hb)
ISBN-10:   0335 21504 1 (pb)   0335 21505 X (hb)

Library of Congress Cataloging-in-Publication Data
CIP data applied for

Typeset by RefineCatch Ltd, Bungay, Suffolk
Printed in the UK by The Bath Press

CONTENTS

PREFACE TO THE FOURTH EDITION

The first edition of this book was written as a result of the accumulated experience of teaching research methods to undergraduate and postgraduate students in British and overseas universities and of writing distance learning materials for the British Open University and the University of Sheffield. Now, there are many good books on research methods on the market, but at that time, I had been unable to find one which quite covered the basic principles involved in planning research, but which was also an easy read and which made no assumptions about students' previous knowledge of research. *Doing Your Research Project* was intended to be a confidence builder, a starter book to provide new researchers with the necessary skills and techniques which would enable them to move on to more complex tasks and reading. I am told that it is now a set book for many undergraduate and postgraduate courses.

All the techniques and procedures described in the first edition were well tried and tested, but there are always ways of doing things better. The experience of teaching and supervising research students, and working through some of the procedures and techniques in research methods workshops suggested alternative approaches and the desirability of providing additional material. These were incorporated into the second edition in 1993, the third edition in 1999 and now further changes have become necessary for this fourth edition.

When the first edition was published in 1987, relatively few students were skilled in information technology (IT) and only the most advanced libraries provided general access to computer search facilities. By the time the second and third editions were published, times had changed so it became necessary to provide new material on access to libraries, search techniques, locating published materials, computer databases and the Internet. Other changes in this edition include more examples of research in a wider range of disciplines, additions to checklists and to further reading lists. All chapters in this edition have been updated and rewritten and new chapters have been included on ethical research, literature searching and literature reviews. However, the basic structure remains much the same as in the first, second and third editions.

ACKNOWLEDGEMENTS

I have been helped throughout the preparation of all four editions of this book by the interest of friends and colleagues who have given strong support in difficult times. I have been particularly grateful to Dr Ann Hanson and friends and former students from The Open University, Professor William Hoff, Emeritus Professor at the University of Manchester Institute of Science and Technology (UMIST) and to Dr Clive Opie, Deputy Head of the Northern Institute of Education at the Manchester Metropolitan University who all read drafts of this fourth edition, commented and made suggestions for changes. They were a great help.

I have particularly welcomed comments from research students who kindly (and sometimes gleefully) pointed out that they had found better ways of doing things than I suggested in the first three editions. I have been happy to incorporate their suggestions.

My continuing thanks to Michael Youngman, formerly of the University of Nottingham, who devised the question types in Chapter 8, which have eased the burden of many research students who are in the early days of designing questionnaires and interpreting the results. The generous assistance and support he invariably gave to many struggling PhD students, including me, made the difference between our dropping out altogether and actually finishing. My thanks also to Brendan Duffy and Stephen Waters, two outstanding Open University research students who

carried out investigations into aspects of educational management in their own institutions and developed a considerable
degree of expertise in research methods in the process. Both
generously allowed me to use some of their ideas and experiences.
Brendan, who already held a PhD in History before he embarked
on research into education management wrote 'The analysis of
documentary evidence' in the earlier editions of this book and has
extended and updated Chapter 7 for this edition.

I am grateful to Clara Nai and Gilbert Fan, Singaporean-based
former postgraduate students of the University of Sheffield, who
kindly permitted me to quote parts of their MEd literature reviews
in Chapter 6 and to John Richardson and Alan Woodley, both of
the British Open University, for permission to quote from their
journal article 'Another look at the role of age, gender and subject
as predictors of academic attainment in higher education'
(Richardson and Woodley 2003). My thanks also to Janette Gray
of Edith Cowan University in Western Australia for providing
material for the section on narrative inquiry in Chapter 1. Her
enthusiasm for and knowledge of this approach encouraged me to
read further but also to begin to understand what is involved in
narrative inquiry. I am similarly grateful to Katie Horne, once a
first-time researcher herself but now a professional researcher. She
kindly produced her Top Ten Guide to Searching the Internet at short
notice, which is included in Chapter 5.

Friends and colleagues have been particularly helpful in
arranging for me to have access to several excellent small specialist
libraries which are not normally open to outsiders. Linda Mealing,
friend, nurse and first-time researcher very kindly introduced me
to the librarians and the Director of Research of St Ann's Hospice
in Stockport and opened my eyes to the extent of ongoing
research into palliative care. Thanks also to the librarians in other
specialist libraries who allowed me to consult their library
catalogue and the range of journals on the shelves even though I
did not have a library card. I was not always so fortunate, so no
thanks at all to the few librarians who curtly refused to allow me
through the door. Well, we can only ask.

Fred Bell did his best to sort out a new computer which was
giving me unanticipated and ongoing grief, read all the scripts,
drew attention to typographical and other errors, winced at what

he regarded as some of my oversimplifications, which I usually ignored, and generally pointed out the error of my ways, as always.

Finally, I should like to thank two people who have been closely involved with all editions of *Doing Your Research Project*, namely Chris Madden, the artist who produced the maze on the front cover of each edition and Shona Mullen, formerly Publishing Director at Open University Press who saw me safely through each edition with great patience and good humour. Over the years, we have become friends and selfishly, I am sorry her new position as General Manager at McGraw-Hill will mean that we shall not be directly associated with any further publications.

Chris Madden and I have never met, but I have been delighted to work with an artist who appears to have the same weird sense of humour as me, but who also has the skill to put these ideas into practice. He had the original idea of a maze for the front cover of the first edition. The development of the maze theme over the following three editions has given me, and I hope him, a good deal of fun over the years as we thought of new ideas for including examples of distraught researchers who were going down blind alleys, losing patience and wondering why they ever started on the research in the first place. In the third edition, I especially liked the image of the student kicking his computer. I've felt like doing that myself on numerous occasions, particularly recently. However, the overall image is of students who managed to negotiate the maze and, having overcome the difficulties experienced by all researchers, are seen to be leaving it deliriously happy, in academic dress, holding their diplomas on high, throwing their mortarboards in the air and going forth to do more and even better research.

To you all, my grateful thanks.

INTRODUCTION

This book is intended for those of you who are about to undertake research in connection with your job, or as a requirement for an undergraduate, certificate or postgraduate course.

Regardless of the topic or the discipline, the problems facing you are much the same whether you are working on a small project, a Master's or a PhD thesis. You will need to select a topic, identify the objectives of your study, plan and design a suitable methodology, devise research instruments, negotiate access to institutions, materials and people, collect, analyse and present information, and, finally, produce a well-written report. Whatever the size of the undertaking, techniques have to be mastered and a plan of action devised which does not attempt more than the limitations of expertise, time and access permit. Large-scale research projects will require sophisticated techniques and, often, statistical and computation expertise, but it is quite possible to produce a worthwhile study without using computers and with a minimum of statistical knowledge. We all learn how to do research by actually doing it, but a great deal of time can be wasted and goodwill dissipated by inadequate preparation. This book aims to provide you with the tools to do the job, to help you to avoid some of the pitfalls and time-consuming false trails that can eat into your time allowance, to establish good research habits and to take you from the stage of selecting a topic through to the production of a well-planned, methodologically sound and well-written final report or thesis – ON TIME. There is, after all, little point in doing all the work if you never manage to submit. Throughout this book, I use the terms 'research', 'investigation', 'inquiry' and 'study' interchangeably, though I realize this is not acceptable to everyone. Some argue that 'research' is a more rigorous and technically more complicated form of investigation. Howard and Sharp discuss this issue in *The Management of a Student Research Project*:

> Most people associate the word 'research' with activities which are substantially removed from day-to-day life and which are pursued by outstandingly gifted persons with an unusual level of commitment. There is of course a good deal of truth in this viewpoint, but we would argue that the pursuit is not restricted to this type of person and indeed can prove to be a stimulating and satisfying experience for many people with a trained and enquiring mind.
>
> (Howard and Sharp 1983: 6)

They define research as 'seeking through methodical processes to add to one's own body of knowledge and, hopefully, to that of others, by the discovery of non-trivial facts and insights' (p. 6).

Drew (1980) agrees that 'research is conducted to solve problems and to expand knowledge' (p. 4) and stresses that 'research is a systematic way of asking questions, a systematic method of enquiry' (p. 8). It is the systematic approach that is important in the conduct of your projects, not the title of 'research', 'inquiry' or 'study'. Where collection of data is involved (notes of interviews, questionnaire responses, articles, official reports, minutes of meetings, etc.), orderly record keeping and thorough planning are essential.

No book can take the place of a good supervisor, but good supervisors are in great demand, and if you can familiarize yourself with basic approaches and techniques, you will be able to make full use of your tutorial time for priority issues.

The examples given in the following chapters relate particularly to projects which have to be completed in two to three months (what I have called the 100-hour projects), but I have been pleased to learn that numbers of Master's and PhD students have found them equally useful.

 **Part I**

PREPARING THE GROUND

● 1

APPROACHES TO RESEARCH

It is perfectly possible to carry out a worthwhile investigation without having detailed knowledge of the various approaches to or styles of research, but a study of different approaches will give insight into different ways of planning an investigation, and, incidentally, will also enhance your understanding of the literature. One of the problems of reading about research reports and reading research reports is the terminology. Researchers use terms and occasionally jargon that may be incomprehensible to other people. It is the same in any field, where a specialized language develops to ease communication among professionals. So, before considering the various stages of planning and conducting investigations, it may be helpful to consider the main features of certain well-established and well-reported styles of research.

Different styles, traditions or approaches use different methods of collecting data, but no approach prescribes nor automatically rejects any particular method. Quantitative researchers collect facts and study the relationship of one set of facts to another. They use techniques that are likely to produce quantified and, if possible, generalizable conclusions. Researchers adopting a qualitative perspective are more concerned to understand individuals' perceptions of the world. They seek insights rather than statistical perceptions of the world. They doubt whether social 'facts' exist and question whether a 'scientific' approach can be used when dealing with human beings. Yet there are occasions when qualitative researchers draw on quantitative techniques, and vice versa.

Classifying an approach as quantitative or qualitative, ethnographic, survey, action research or whatever, does not mean that once an approach has been selected, the researcher may not move from the methods normally associated with that style. Each approach has its strengths and weaknesses and each is particularly suitable for a particular context. The approach adopted and the methods of data collection selected will depend on the nature of the inquiry and the type of information required.

It is impossible in the space of a few pages to do justice to any of the well-established styles of research, but the following will at least provide a basis for further reading and may give you ideas about approaches you may wish to adopt in your own investigation.

Action research and the role of practitioner researchers

Action research is an approach which is appropriate in any context when 'specific knowledge is required for a specific problem in a specific situation, or when a new approach is to be grafted on to an existing system' (Cohen and Manion 1994: 194). It is not a method or a technique. As in all research, the methods selected for gathering information depend on the nature of the information required. It is applied research, carried out by practitioners who have themselves identified a need for change or improvement, sometimes with support from outside the institution; other times not. The aim is 'to arrive at recommendations for good practice that will tackle a problem or enhance the performance of the organization and individuals through changes to the rules and procedures within which they operate' (Denscombe 2002: 27).

Lomax (2002: 124) provides a series of useful questions for action researchers under the headings of purpose, focus, relations, method and validation. Under the 'purpose' heading, she asks:

• Can I improve my practice so that it is more effective?

- Can I improve my understanding of this practice so as to make it more just?
- Can I use my knowledge and influence to improve the situation?

Under 'method', she asks whether the action researcher can collect 'rigorous data' which will provide evidence to support claims for action. These and similar questions can serve as a starting point for action research but when the investigation is finished and the findings have been considered by all participants, the job is still not finished. The participants continue to review, evaluate and improve practice. The research involves 'a feedback loop in which initial findings generate possibilities for change which are then implemented and evaluated as a prelude to further investigation' (Denscombe 1998: 58). It implies a 'continuous process of research' and 'the worth of the work is judged by the understanding of, and desirable change in, the practice that is achieved' (Brown and McIntyre 1981: 245).

There is nothing new about practitioners operating as researchers, but as in all 'insider' investigations, difficulties can arise if dearly-held views and practices of some participants are challenged, as can happen if the research evidence appears to indicate that radical changes must take place if progress is to be made. Denscombe reminds us that:

> Because the activity of action research almost inevitably affects others, it is important to have a clear idea of when and where the action research necessarily steps outside the bounds of collecting information which is purely personal and relating to the practitioners alone. Where it does so, the usual standard of ethics must be observed: permissions obtained, confidentiality maintained, identities protected.
>
> (Denscombe 1998: 63)

Of equal, or perhaps even greater importance is that before the research begins, everyone involved must know why the investigation is to take place, who will see the final report, and who will have responsibility for implementing any recommended changes.

Case study

Even if you are working on a 100-hour project over a three-month period, the case study approach can be particularly appropriate for individual researchers because it provides an opportunity for one aspect of a problem to be studied in some depth. Of course, not all case studies have to be completed in three months, or even three years. For example, Korman and Glennerster's (1990) study of what led to the closure of a large mental hospital took seven and a half years to complete. Sadly, you will have to wait until you are head of research in your hospital, local authority, university or government department before you will be in a position to undertake and to obtain the funding for such a venture, so for the time being, be realistic about the selection of your case study topic. Yin reminds us that 'case studies have been done about decisions, about programmes, about the implementation process, and about organizational change. Beware these types of topic – none is easily defined in terms of the beginning or end point of the case.' He adds that 'the more a study contains specific propositions, the more it will stay within reasonable limits' (Yin 1994: 137). Good advice and worth following.

Case studies may be carried out to follow up and to put flesh on the bones of a survey. They can also precede a survey and be used as a means of identifying key issues which merit further investigation, but the majority are carried out as free-standing exercises. Researchers identify an 'instance', which could be the introduction of a new way of working, the way an organization adapts to a new role, or any innovation or stage of development in an institution. Evidence has to be collected systematically, the relationship between variables studied (a variable being a characteristic or attribute) and the investigation methodically planned. Though observation and interviews are most frequently used, no method is excluded.

All organizations and individuals have their common and their unique features. Case study researchers aim to identify such features, to identify or attempt to identify the various interactive processes at work, to show how they affect the implementation of systems and influence the way an organization functions. These processes may remain hidden in a large-scale survey but could be crucial to the success or failure of systems or organizations.

Critics of case study

Critics of the case study approach draw attention to a number of problems and/or disadvantages. For example, some question the value of the study of single events and point out that it is difficult for researchers to cross-check information. Others express concern about the possibility of selective reporting and the resulting dangers of distortion. A major concern is that generalization is not always possible, though Denscombe (1998: 36–7) makes the point that 'the extent to which findings from the case study can be generalized to other examples in the class depends on how far the case study example is similar to others of its type'. He illustrates this point by drawing on the example of a case study of a small primary school. He writes that:

> This means that the researcher must obtain data on the significant features (catchment area, the ethnic origins of the pupils and the amount of staff turnover) for primary schools in general, and then demonstrate where the case study example fits in relation to the overall picture.
>
> (1998: 37)

In his 1981 paper on the relative merits of the search for generalization and the study of single events, Bassey preferred to use the term 'relatability' rather than 'generalizability'. In his opinion

> an important criterion for judging the merit of a case study is the extent to which the details are sufficient and appropriate for a teacher working in a similar situation to relate his decision making to that described in the case study. The relatability of a case study is more important than its generalizability.
>
> (Bassey 1981: 85)

He considers that if case studies

> are carried out systematically and critically, if they are aimed at the improvement of education, if they are relatable, and if by publication of the findings they extend the boundaries of existing knowledge, then they are valid forms of educational research.
>
> (p. 86)

Writing about an education case study in 1999, he amends or rather adds to his 1981 thoughts. He recalls that

> Previously I had treated the concept of generalization (of the empirical kind, that is) as a statement that had to be absolutely true. This is the sense in which physical scientists use the term. It is the basis of their concept of scientific method . . . in which a hypothesis stands as a generalization (or law) only if it withstands all attempts at refutation. I argued that there were very few generalizations (in this absolute sense) about education – and even fewer, if any, that were useful to experienced teachers.
>
> (Bassey 1999: 12)

He makes it clear that he still holds to this view as far as scientific generalizations (of the absolute kind) are concerned but now acknowledges there can be two other kinds of generalization which can apply in the social sciences, namely statistical generalizations and 'fuzzy' generalizations:

> The statistical generalization arises from samples of populations and typical claims that *there is an x per cent or y per cent chance that* what was found in the sample will also be found throughout the population: it is the quantitative measure. The fuzzy generalization arises from studies of singularities and typical claims that *it is possible, or likely, or unlikely that* what was found in the singularity will be found in similar situations elsewhere: it is a qualitative measure.
>
> (p. 12)

The pros and cons of case study will no doubt be debated in the future as they have been in the past. It's as well to be aware of the criticisms but, as I said at the beginning of this section, case study can be an appropriate approach for individual researchers because it provides an opportunity for one aspect of a problem to be studied in some depth. You will have to decide whether or not it suits your purpose.

Survey

It would be nice to have a clear, short and succinct definition of 'survey' but as Aldridge and Levine (2001: 5) point out, 'Each survey is unique. Therefore, lists of do's and don'ts are too inflexible. A solution to one survey may not work in another.' Moser and Kalton (1971: 1) agree that it would be pleasant to provide a straightforward definition of what is meant by a 'social survey' but make it clear that 'such a definition would have to be so general as to defeat its purpose, since the term and the methods associated with it are applied to an extraordinarily wide variety of investigations . . .'. They continue by giving examples of the range of areas which might be covered by a survey:

> A survey may be occasioned simply by a need for administrative facts on some aspects of public life; or be designed to investigate a cause–effect relationship or to throw fresh light on some aspect of sociological theory. When it comes to subject matter, all one can say is that surveys are concerned with the demographic characteristics, the social environment, the activities, or the opinions and attitudes of some group of people.
>
> (Moser and Kalton 1971: 1)

The census is one example of a survey in which the same questions are asked of the selected population (the population being the group or category of individuals selected). It aims to cover 100 per cent of the population, but most surveys have less ambitious aims. In most cases, a survey will aim to obtain information from a representative selection of the population and from that sample will then be able to present the findings as being representative of the population as a whole. Inevitably, there are problems in the survey method. Great care has to be taken to ensure that the sample population is truly representative. At a very simple level, that means ensuring that if the total population has 1000 men and 50 women, then the same proportion of men to women has to be selected. But that example grossly oversimplifies the method of drawing a representative sample and if you decide to carry out a survey, you will need to consider what characteristics of the total population need to be represented in your sample to enable you to say with fair confidence that your sample is reasonably representative.

In surveys, all respondents will be asked the same questions in, as far as possible, the same circumstances. Question wording is not as easy as it seems, and careful piloting is necessary to ensure that all questions mean the same to all respondents. Information can be gathered by means of self-completion questionnaires (as in the case of the census) or by an interviewer. Whichever method of information gathering is selected, the aim is to obtain answers to the same questions from a large number of individuals to enable the researcher not only to describe but also to compare, to relate one characteristic to another and to demonstrate that certain features exist in certain categories.

Surveys can provide answers to the questions What? Where? When? and How?, but it is not so easy to find out Why? Causal relationships can rarely, if ever, be proved by survey method. The main emphasis is on fact-finding, and if a survey is well structured and piloted, it can be a relatively cheap and quick way of obtaining information.

The experimental style

It is relatively easy to plan experiments which deal with measurable phenomena. For example, experiments have been set up to measure the effects of using fluoridated toothpaste on dental caries by establishing a control group (who did not use the toothpaste) and an experimental group (who did). In such experiments, the two groups, matched for age, sex, social class, and so on were given a pre-test dental examination and instructions about which toothpaste to use. After a year, both groups were given the post-test dental examination and conclusions were then drawn about the effectiveness or otherwise of the fluoridated toothpaste. The principle of such experiments is that if two identical groups are selected, one of which (the experimental group) is given special treatment and the other (the control group) is not, then any differences between the two groups at the end of the experimental period may be attributed to the difference in treatment. A causal relationship appears to have been established. It may be fairly straightforward to test the extent of dental caries (though even in this experiment the extent of the caries could be caused by many factors not controlled by the experiment) but it is quite another matter to test changes in behaviour. As Wilson (1979) points out, social causes do not work singly. Any examination of low student attainment or high IQ is the product of multiple causes.

> To isolate each cause requires a new experimental group each time and the length and difficulty of the experiment increase rapidly. It is possible to run an experiment in which several treatments are put into practice simultaneously but many groups must be made available rather than just two . . . The causes of social phenomena are usually multiple ones and an experiment to study them requires large numbers of people often for lengthy periods. This requirement limits the usefulness of the experimental method.
>
> (Wilson 1979: 22)

So, experiments may allow conclusions to be drawn about cause and effect, *if* the design is sound, but large groups are needed if the many variations and ambiguities involved in human behaviour are to be controlled. Such large-scale experiments are expensive to set up and take more time than most students working on 100-hour projects can give. Some tests which require only a few hours (e.g. to test short-term memory or perception) can be very effective, but in claiming a causal relationship, great care needs to be taken to ensure that all possible causes have been considered.

It is worth noting at this point that there can be ethical issues associated with experimental research. Permission to conduct the research must be obtained from the heads of institutions or units concerned and from the participants themselves. All must be fully informed about what is involved. Proposals may have to be considered by ethics committees and/or research committees in order to ensure that subjects of the research will not be harmed by it. Particularly if children are involved, permission to participate must be sought from parents.

Cohen et al. (2000) particularly object to the principle of 'manipulating' human beings. They write that:

> Notions of isolation and control of variables in order to establish causality may be appropriate for a laboratory, though whether, in fact, a social situation ever *could become* the antiseptic, artificial world of the laboratory or *should become* such a world is both an empirical and moral question . . . Further, the ethical dilemmas of treating humans as manipulable, controllable and inanimate are considerable.
>
> (Cohen et al. 2000: 212)

Quite so, though ethical issues have to be considered in all research, regardless of the context. If you decide you wish to undertake an experimental study, ask for advice, consider any implications and requirements – and be careful about making claims about causality.

Ethnography and the ethnographic style of research

Brewer defines ethnography as

> The study of people in naturally occurring settings or 'fields' by methods of data collection which capture their social **meanings** and ordinary activities, involving the researcher participating directly in the setting, if not also the activities, in order to collect data in a systematic manner but without meaning being imposed on them externally.
>
> (Brewer 2000: 6)

Ethnographic researchers attempt to develop an understanding of how a culture works and, as Lutz points out, many methods and techniques are used in that search:

> Participant observation, interview, mapping and charting, interaction analysis, study of historical records and current public documents, the use of demographic data, etc. But ethnography centers on the participant observation of a society or culture through a complete cycle of events that regularly occur as that society interacts with its environment.
>
> (Lutz 1986: 108)

Participant observation enables researchers, as far as is possible, to share the same experiences as the subjects, to understand better why they act in the way they do and 'to see things as those involved see things' (Denscombe 1998: 69). However, it is time-consuming and so is often outside the scope of researchers working on 100-hour projects or on fixed-time Master's degrees. The researcher has to be accepted by the individuals or groups being studied, and this can mean doing the same job, or living in the same environment and circumstances as the subjects for lengthy periods.

Time is not the only problem with this approach. As in case studies, critics point to the problem of representativeness. If the researcher is studying one group in depth over a period of time, who is to say that group is typical of other groups that may have the same title? Are nurses in one hospital (or even in one specialist area) necessarily representative of nurses in a similar hospital or specialist area in another part of the country? Are canteen workers in one type of organization likely to be typical of all canteen workers? Critics also refer to the problem of generalization, but as in the case study approach, if the study is well structured and carried out, and makes no claims which cannot be justified, it may well be relatable in a way that will enable members of similar groups to recognize problems and, possibly, to see ways of solving similar problems in their own group.

The grounded theory approach

The grounded theory approach to qualitative data analysis was developed by Glaser and Strauss in the 1960s during the course of a field observational study of the way hospital staff dealt with dying patients (1965, 1968). So what does it involve? Strauss (1987) tells us that

> The methodological thrust of the grounded theory approach to qualitative data analysis is toward the development of theory, without any particular commitment to specific kinds of data, lines of research, or theoretical interests. So, it is not really a specific method or technique. Rather it is a style of doing qualitative analysis that includes a number of distinct features, such as theoretical sampling, and certain methodological guidelines, such as the making of constant comparisons and the use of a coding paradigm, to ensure conceptual development and density.
>
> (Strauss, 1987: 5)

He defines *theoretical sampling* as

> sampling directed by the evolving theory; it is a sampling of incidents, events, activities, populations, etc. It is harnessed to the making of *comparisons* between and among those samples of activities, populations, etc.
>
> (p. 21)

The theory is not prespecified. It emerges as the research proceeds (hence 'theoretical' sampling).

Over the years, there have been some adjustments to the original 1960s' approach to grounded theory, but the principles remain much the same, which are that theory evolves during actual research by means of the analysis of the data.

Punch considers that

> grounded theory is best defined as a research strategy whose purpose is to generate theory from data. 'Grounded' means that the theory will be generated on the basis of data; the

theory will therefore be grounded in data. 'Theory' means that the objective of collecting and analysing the research data is to generate theory. The essential idea in grounded theory is that theory will be developed inductively from data.

(Punch 1998: 163)

At first sight, this seems straightforward enough, but as Hayes makes clear,

The process of conducting grounded theory research isn't just a matter of looking at the data and developing a theory from it. Instead, it is what researchers call an **iterative** process – that is, a cyclical process in which theoretical insights emerge or are discovered in the data, those insights are then tested to see how they can make sense of other parts of the data, which in turn produce their own theoretical insights, which are then tested again against the data, and so on.

(Hayes 2000: 184)

She continues by reminding us that

The theory which is produced using a grounded theory analysis may sometimes be very context-specific, applying only in a relatively small number of situations; but because it is always grounded in data collected from the real world, it can serve as a very strong basis for further investigations, as well as being a research finding in its own right.

(p. 184)

Most grounded theory researchers will begin with research questions but they do not start with a hypothesis, nor do they begin their investigation with a thorough review of the literature relating to their topic. They build up theory from their data and they do not wait until all data are collected before they begin the analysis stage. Instead, analysis takes place as the data are collected. The researcher examines the findings of an interview or of participant observation and then proceeds to the analysis of those findings before any other data are collected. As the research proceeds, there will be more data collection and more analysis and so on until 'theoretical saturation' is reached, which is the stage at which 'new data are not showing any new theoretical elements, but rather confirming what has already been found' (Punch 1998: 167).

Miles and Huberman have some reservations about the principle that coding and recording are over when the analysis appears to have run its course, when all the incidents can be readily classified, when categories are 'saturated' and sufficient numbers of 'regularities' have emerged. They warn us to 'be careful here' because

> Fieldwork understanding comes in layers; the longer we are in the environment, the more layers appear to surface, and the choice of when to close down, when to go with a definitive coding system or definitive analysis can be painful. That choice may be dictated as much by time and budget constraints as on scientific grounds. When those constraints are relaxed, saturation can become a vanishing horizon – just another field trip away, then another . . .
>
> (Miles and Huberman 1994: 62)

Glaser (1992) has also expressed some concern at the way grounded theory has developed over the years, in particular the development and use of computer-assisted code and retrieval software which claims to generate theory on grounded theory lines. He considers that more subtle procedures are required in order to tease out the layers of meaning which emerge, and this cannot be achieved by any narrow analytical procedures.

The analysis of grounded theory data is, to me at least, quite complex. It requires the researcher to identify concepts, codes, categories and relationships in order to bring order to the data, and the time taken to become skilled at identifying and applying them is considerable. I confess that I find the level of abstraction and the language used which appear to be implicit in grounded theory difficult to absorb. However, that is no more than my perception of the difficulty of teasing out those layers of meaning. Many colleagues and former students whose views I respect and who have successfully completed research based on a grounded theory approach disagree with me. They tell me that the computer software can cope with the layers and the complexity perfectly well. So, all I can say is that before you decide to commit yourself to a grounded theory approach, read as widely as time permits and, as always, take advice before you finally decide how to proceed.

Narrative inquiry and stories

It is only relatively recently that I have become interested in the use and interpretation of narratives and in particular the acceptance of stories as valuable sources of data. Stories are certainly interesting and have been used for many years by management consultants and others who present examples of successful (and unsuccessful) practice as a basis for discussion as to how successful practice might be emulated and disasters avoided. What has always taxed me has been how information derived from story-telling can be structured in such a way as to produce valid research findings. It took an experienced group of postgraduate and post-doctoral students who had planned their research on 'narrative inquiry' lines to sort me out and to explain precisely what was involved. I was not even sure what narrative inquiry actually meant and so, always believing the best way to find out is to ask an expert, I asked one member of the group, Dr Janette Gray, to tell me. She wrote as follows:

> It involves the collection and development of stories, either as a form of data collection or as a means of structuring a research project. Informants often speak in a story form during the interviews, and as the researcher, listening and attempting to understand, we hear their 'stories'. The research method can be described as narrative when data collection, interpretation and writing are considered a 'meaning-making' process with similar characteristics to stories (Gudmunsdottir 1996: 295). Narrative inquiry can involve reflective autobiography, life story, or the inclusion of excerpts from participants' stories to illustrate a theme developed by the researcher. A narrative approach to inquiry is most appropriate when the researcher is interested in

portraying intensely personal accounts of human experience. Narratives allow voice – to the researcher, the participants and to cultural groups – and in this sense they can have the ability to develop a decidedly political and powerful edge.

(Gray 1998: 12)

Colleagues to whom I had earlier spoken and who had successfully adopted a narrative inquiry approach to one or more of their research projects had always made it clear that stories were not merely used as a series of 'story boxes' piled on top of one another and with no particular structure or connecting theme. The problem I had was in understanding how such structures and themes could be derived. Jan's explanation was as follows:

All forms of narrative inquiry involve an element of analysis and development of theme, dependent on the researcher's perspective. Stories share a basic structure. The power of a story is dependent on the storyteller's use of language to present an interpretation of personal experience. The skill of the narrative researcher lies in the ability to structure the interview data into a form which clearly presents a sense of a beginning, middle and an end. Even though the use of story as a research tool is a relatively new concept in the social sciences, historically story has been an accepted way of relating knowledge and developing self-knowledge. One of the major strengths of such a means of conducting inquiry is the ability to allow readers who do not share a cultural background similar to either the storyteller or the researcher to develop an understanding of notices and consequences of actions described within a story format. Narrative is a powerful and different way of knowing . . .

Data collection for narrative research requires the researcher to allow the storyteller to structure the conversations, with the researcher asking follow-up questions. So a narrative approach to the question of how mature-age undergraduates perceive their ability to cope with the experience of returning to study would involve extended, open-ended interviews with mature-aged students. This would allow the students to express their personal experience of the problems, frustrations and joys of returning to study. It might also involve similar 'conversations' with other stakeholders in their education – perhaps family members; their tutors and lecturers – to provide a multiple perspective of the context of the education of mature-aged undergraduates.

(Gray 1998: 2)

Jan added that 'the benefit of considerate and careful negotiation will be a story allowing an incredibly personal and multi-faceted insight into the situation being discussed'. I am sure this is so. I have become convinced of the value of this approach and that stories can in some cases serve to enhance understanding within a case study or an ethnographic study. However, narratives can present their own set of problems:

Interviews are time-consuming and require the researcher to allow the storytellers to recount in their own way the experience of being (or teaching) a student. This may not emerge in the first interview. Until a trust relationship has developed between researcher and storyteller, it is highly unlikely that such intimate information will be shared. Such personal involvement with the researcher involves risks and particular ethical issues. The storytellers may decide they have revealed more of their feelings than they are prepared to share publicly and they may insist either on substantial editing or on withdrawing from the project.

(Gray 1998: 2)

Problems of this kind can arise in almost any kind of research, particularly those which are heavily dependent on interview data, but the close relationship needed for narrative inquiry can make the researcher (and the storyteller) particularly vulnerable.

The fact that the narrative approach carries with it a number of potential difficulties, particularly for first-time researchers, and researchers operating within a particularly tight schedule, certainly does not mean that it should be disregarded when considering an appropriate approach to the topic of your choice. Far from it – but as is the case with all research planning, I feel it would be as well to discuss the issues fully with your supervisor before deciding what to do, and if possible to try to find a supervisor who is experienced, or at least interested, in narrative inquiry.

Which approach?

Classifying an approach as ethnographic, qualitative, experimental, or whatever, does not mean that once an approach has been selected the researcher may not move from the methods normally associated with that style. But understanding the major advantages and disadvantages of each approach is likely to help you to select the most appropriate methodology for the task in hand. This chapter covers only the very basic principles associated with different styles or approaches to research which will suffice – at any rate until you have decided on a topic and considered what further information you need to obtain.

Further reading is provided at the end of this chapter. As far as possible, I have tried to indicate books and journals which should be available in academic libraries or on the World Wide Web. However, always consult the library catalogue. If there is an online facility, the librarian will show you how the system operates. Then take advantage of what the library has in stock or is able to obtain from another library, preferably without cost.

Further reading

Aldridge, A. and Levine, K. (2001) *Surveying the Social World: Principles and Practice in Survey Research*. Buckingham: Open University Press.

Bassey, M. (1981) 'Pedagogic research: on the relative merits of the search for generalisation and study of single events', *Oxford Review of Education*, 7(1): 73–93. Also reproduced as Chapter 7 in J. Bell, T. Bush, A. Fox et al. (eds) (1984) *Conducting Small-scale Investigations in Educational Management*. London: Harper & Row.

Bassey, M. (1999) *Case Study Research in Educational Settings*. Buckingham: Open University Press.

Bassey, M. (2001) 'A solution to the problem of generalisation in educational research: fuzzy prediction', *Oxford Review of Education*, 27(1): 5–22.

Bassey, M. (2002) 'Case study research', Chapter 7 in M. Coleman and A.R.J. Briggs (eds) *Research Methods in Educational Leadership and Management*. London: Paul Chapman Publishing.

Bell, J. and Opie, C. (2002) *Learning from Research: Getting More from Your Data*. Buckingham: Open University Press. Part 5 discusses the way Tim Chan planned and carried out a survey of student evaluation of teaching effectiveness (SET) as part of his doctoral research (Chan 2000). If you are considering an experiment, then you may wish to consult Part 3 which discusses how Lim Cher Ping structured his experimental research into the effectiveness of a computer-based learning program (Lim 1997).

Bowling, A. (2002) *Research Methods in Health: Investigating Health and Health Services*, 2nd edn. Maidenhead: Open University Press. See pp. 410–15 for an account of action research.

Brewer, J.D. (2000) *Ethnography*. Buckingham: Open University Press.

Casey, K. (1993) 'The new narrative research in education', *Review of Research in Education*, 32: 211–53.

Clough, P. (2002) *Narratives and Fictions in Educational Research*. Maidenhead: Open University Press. Peter Clough provides interesting 'fictional' stories which demonstrate the use of narrative in reporting research, and discusses the potential merits and difficulties of such an approach.

Cohen L. and Manion, L. (1994) 'Case studies', Chapter 5 in *Research Methods in Education*, 4th edn. London: Routledge.

Darlington, Y. and Scott, D. (2002) *Qualitative Research in Practice: Stories from the Field*. Maidenhead: Open University Press (first published in 2002 by Allen & Unwin, Australia). Chapter 1 considers issues relating to quantitative and/or qualitative methods.

Denscombe, M. (1998) *The Good Research Guide for Small-scale Social Research Projects*. Buckingham: Open University Press. Chapter 2 provides a clear account of the advantages and limitations of case study. Chapter 3 deals with experiments, Chapter 4 with action research and Chapter 5 with ethnography. Helpful checklists are provided at the end of main sections.

Denscombe, M. (2003) *The Good Research Guide*, 2nd edn. Maidenhead: Open University Press. Part I, 'Strategies for social research' considers a number of approaches, including survey, case studies, Internet research, experiments, action research, ethnography, phenomenology and grounded theory. Checklists are again provided.

Fogelman, K. (2002) 'Surveys and sampling', Chapter 6 in M. Coleman and A.R.G. Briggs (eds) *Research Methods in Educational Leadership and Management*. London: Paul Chapman Publishing.

Goodson, I.F. and Sikes, P. (2001) *Life History Research in Educational Settings: Learning from Lives*. Maidenhead: Open University Press. This book explores reasons for the popularity of life history research in education, though many of the examples they consider are likely to have similar application to researchers in other disciplines.

Hammersley, M. (1989) *The Dilemma of Qualitative Method*. London: Routledge. On pages 172–7 and 198–204, Hammersley provides a well-argued critique of grounded theory, discusses its relationship to earlier studies of analytic induction and considers some of the criticisms sometimes levelled at Glaser and Strauss's (1967) approach. Quite a hard read but worth the effort.

Hammersley, M. (1990) *Classroom Ethnography: Empirical and Methodological Essays*. Buckingham: Open University Press.

Hart, E. and Bond, M. (1995) *Action Research for Health and Social Care*. Buckingham: Open University Press.

Hayes, N. (2000) *Doing Psychological Research: Gathering and Analysing Data*. Buckingham: Open University Press. Chapter 3, 'Experiments', provides useful information about causality in experiments.

Lomax, P. (2002) 'Action research', Chapter 8 in M. Coleman and A.R.J. Briggs (eds) *Research Methods in Educational Leadership and Management*. London: Paul Chapman Publishing.

Lutz, F.W. (1986) 'Ethnography: the holistic approach to understanding schooling', in M. Hammersley *Controversies in Classroom Research*. Milton Keynes: Open University Press. This is an excellent chapter which relates mainly to ethnographic research in education, but which has valuable advice about any type of qualitative research. The book is rather old now, but I hope will still be on the shelves of academic libraries or accessible via the Internet.

May, T. (2001) *Social Research: Issues, Methods and Process*, 3rd edn. Buckingham: Open University Press. See particularly Chapter 5, 'Social surveys: design to analysis'.

Moser, C.A. and Kalton, G. (1971) *Survey Methods in Social Investigation*, 2nd edn. London Heinemann. This book is rather old, but if there is a copy in your library, it is still worth consulting.

Opie, C. (2004) Chapter 5, 'Research approaches', in C. Opie (ed.) *Doing Educational Research*. London: Sage. This chapter considers case study, action research, experiments and grounded theory and includes interesting quotations from students' experiences.

Polit, D.F. and Hungler, B.P. (1995) *Nursing Research: Principles and Methods*, 5th edn. Philadelphia: Lippincott Company. Small but useful section on case study on pages 200–3.

Punch, K.F. (1998) *Introduction to Social Research: Quantitative and*

Qualitative Approaches. London: Sage. Pages 68–76 discuss some of the difficulties in designing experiments and give examples of a range of experiments and quasi-experiments. Pages 162–73 and 210–21 include excellent sections on the meaning and analysis of grounded theory.

Punch, K.F. (2003) *Survey Research: The Basics*. London: Sage. This 'How to' book is aimed at new researchers and is concerned mainly with small-scale quantitative surveys. Very useful.

Roberts, B. (2002) *Biographical Research*. Maidenhead: Open University Press. Chapter 6 considers oral history; Chapter 7 deals with narrative and in particular narrative analysis; Chapter 9 concentrates on ethnography and biographical research.

Thody, A. with Downes, P., Hewlett, M. and Tomlinson, H. (1997) 'Lies, damned lies – and storytelling: an exploration of the contribution of principals' anecdotes to research, teaching and learning about the management of schools and colleges', *Educational Management and Administration*, 25(3): July.

2

PLANNING THE PROJECT

Selecting a topic

Selecting a topic is more difficult than it at first seems. With limited time at your disposal there is a temptation to select a topic before the groundwork has been done, but try to resist the temptation. Prepare well and you will save time later. Your discussions and inquiries will help you to select a topic which is likely to be of interest, which you have a good chance of completing, which will be worth the effort and which may even have some practical application later on.

Many researchers in areas such as education, social science and health are directly concerned with the practical outcomes of research and in particular, the improvement of practice in their organization. The aim is not only 'to know facts and to understand relations for the sake of knowledge. We want to know and understand in order to be able to act and act "better" than we did before' (Langeveld 1965: 4).

This is not to deny the importance of research which may have no immediate practical outcome. Eggleston provides a timely reminder of the importance of longer-term objectives and of the need to look beyond current practices. To restrict research to current practices would, in his opinion, lay it 'open to the charge that its sole function was to increase the efficiency of the existing system in terms of accepted criteria and deny it the opportunity to explore potentially more effective alternatives' (Eggleston 1979: 5).

Clearly the need to explore potentially more effective alternatives to existing provision will always exist. After 100 hours of study, you are unlikely to be in a position to make recommendations for fundamental change in any system. However, whatever the size and scope of the study, you will in all cases be required to analyse and evaluate the information you collect and in some cases, you might then be in a position to suggest desirable changes in practice.

Discuss possible practical outcomes with your supervisor and ask whether the department has any guidelines for the selection of topics and the preparation of research briefs. Consider what the emphasis of your study is to be. Is applicability to be important or is your study to have different aims?

Getting started

You may be given a topic to research, but in most cases you will be asked to select a topic from a list or to decide on a topic yourself. You may have an idea or a particular area of interest that you would like to explore. You may have several ideas, all equally interesting. Write them down:

> *Something to do with mature students?*
> *Stress at work?*
> *The effectiveness (or otherwise) of the research methods/introduction to computing/ introduction to the library course?*
> *Supervision of research projects?*
> *Supervision of placements?*

These are all possible topics but before a decision can be made about which to select, some work needs to be done. Think about what might be involved in each one and which will be likely to maintain your interest. If you become bored with a topic, the time will drag unmercifully and the likelihood is that the quality of your research will suffer. Talk to colleagues and friends about your initial ideas. They may be aware of sensitive aspects of certain topics which could cause difficulties at some stage or they may know of other people who have carried out research in one or more of your topics who would be willing to talk to you. If you are hoping to carry out the research in your own institution, then another very good reason for discussing possible topics with colleagues is that you will probably be asking for their support and collaboration: early consultation is essential if you are to avoid difficulties later.

Try to bring the list down to a possible two – one likely to be of main interest and the second to fall back on if your preliminary investigations throw up problems. Let's say you decide you would be particularly interested in a mature students topic, but that stress comes a close second. It will have become clear to you that 'something to do with mature students' requires more focussing before you can proceed. So far, you have been thinking in general terms but now you need to start the process of trying out ideas and asking yourself questions.

Start with your first choice (mature students) and begin to write down your ideas on a sheet of A4 paper. I say A4 rather than the back of an envelope because you will need space. Write 'mature students' in the middle of the paper and link to it all the questions, doubts, theories and ideas you can think of. Brainstorm it. Insert arrows, if necessary, to link one idea or query with another. Write quickly and write as you think. If you decide to wait until your thoughts are in better order, you may (and probably will) have forgotten what you thought of first. It doesn't matter how illegible and disorganized your chart is as long as you can read your own writing. This first shot is for you, not other people.

The purpose of this exercise is to help you to clarify your thoughts and to try to decide what you actually *mean* by each statement and each question. It will give you ideas about refining the topic so that you will not be attempting to do research into everything there is to know about mature students, but into one precise aspect of the topic. It will give you clues as to whether this topic is likely to be too complex for you to complete in your timescale, or whether it might prove to be impossible because you would need access to confidential information which in all probability would be refused.

Your first shot will be a mess but that doesn't matter. Your second attempt will be far more focussed and you will be on the way to making a fairly firm decision about which aspect of your topic you wish to investigate. Incidentally, don't throw away your first or your second attempt/s until after your research is complete, examined and/or your work is published. You may need to refer to first shots and early drafts at some stage so start a 'reject' or a 'dump' file.

Consider your priorities. For example, if you have decided that you would be interested in investigating barriers to learning among mature undergraduates, draw together the various items on your first and second thoughts charts into a list of questions on your selected topics, eliminating overlaps or rejects, and adding any other thoughts which occur to you as you write. At this stage, the order and wording are not important. You are on the way.

Start with the purpose of the study. It might be difficult at this stage to provide the exact wording but it's rather important to know why you want to carry out this research. Think about it. Write down your ideas. Ask yourself questions and make a note of any prompts about the likely sub questions. Be critical. *The purpose of this is study is* . . . What?

- *to identify any barriers to learning for mature students?* Meaning of barriers'? Why do I need this information and how will I find it? Ask students? Ask a sample of students who started their degree course straight from school for comparison? Any differences? Any differences between mature students who experienced no barriers and those who did?
- *to identify any differences between the performance of mature and younger students?* How judged? Degree classification of former students? Should need access to statistics. Any data protection issues?

Each question raises other issues. Ask yourself:

- *What do institutions mean by 'mature'? What do I mean by 'mature' and 'older'?* Have to think of synonyms for 'mature'. Over 21, 25, 30, 60? Age at registration? Age at graduation?

Need to get this sorted. How will I find out? Will I be given access to records?

- *Which mature students?* Those who graduated since the university was established? In the last three years? All students in the university, in one department, in one subject area, one group? Need to think.
- *Which institutions/faculties/departments/groups are to be included in this investigation?* Need to ask supervisor's advice about how to go about obtaining permission. Is one institution/department/subject area/group sufficient – or feasible? Would it be acceptable for me to concentrate on mature students on my course?
- *Has any research been done already on this topic?* Need to get to the library to see what has already been written about mature students and see what those researchers did about the definition of 'mature' – and other things.

These questions will give you and your supervisor or tutor some idea of where you are heading. You're still at the *what* stage (the *how* stage comes later), but each stage continues to be a process of refining and clarifying so that you end with a list of questions, tasks or objectives which you can ask, perform or examine. These will become what Laws et al. (2003:97) describe as **researchable questions** which will take you a major step forward in the planning of your project.

Hypotheses, objectives and researchable questions

Many research projects begin with the statement of a hypothesis, defined by Verma and Beard as

> A tentative proposition which is subject to verification through subsequent investigation. It may also be seen as the guide to the researcher in that it depicts and describes the method to be followed in studying the problem. In many cases hypotheses are hunches that the researcher has about the existence of relationship between variables.
>
> (Verma and Beard 1981: 184)

This definition is taken a step further by Medawar, who writes:

> All advances in scientific understanding, at every level, begin
> with a speculative adventure, an imaginative preconception
> *of what might be true* – a preconception which always, and
> necessarily, goes a little way (sometimes a long way) beyond
> anything which we have logical or factual authority to
> believe in. It is the invention of a possible world, or of a tiny
> fraction of that world. The conjecture is then exposed to
> criticism to find out whether or not that imagined world is
> anything like the real one. Scientific reasoning is therefore at
> all levels an interaction between two episodes of thought – a
> dialogue between two voices, the one imaginative and the
> other critical; a dialogue, if you like, between the possible and
> the actual, between proposal and disposal, conjecture and
> criticism, between what might be true and what is in fact the
> case.
>
> (Medawar 1972: 22)

So, hypotheses make statements about relations between variables
and provide a guide to the researcher as to how the original hunch
might be tested. If we hypothesize, because our conjecture suggests it may be so, that age (one variable) has an influence on
degree results (another variable), then we can attempt to find out
whether that is so – at least amongst the subjects in our sample.
The results of the research will either *support* the hypothesis (that
age does have an influence on degree results) or will *not* support
it (age has no influence on degree results). As Denscombe points
out,

> the possibility of proof/disproof is built into the whole
> notion of an hypothesis. It takes the form 'if (theory X) is
> true, then (under conditions Y) we might expect to find
> (result X)'. The test of the hypothesis 'If . . . then . . .' lies in
> finding (or not finding) the expected outcome.
>
> (Denscombe 2002: 31)

Small-scale projects of the kind discussed in this book will
not require statistical testing of hypotheses often required in

large-scale sample surveys. Unless your supervisor advises otherwise, a precise statement of objectives and a list of researchable questions are generally quite sufficient. The important point is not so much whether there is a hypothesis, but whether you have carefully thought about what is, and what is not worth investigating. It may be permissible to make modifications to objectives or changes to the questions as the study proceeds, but that does not obviate the necessity of identifying exactly what you plan to do at the outset. Until that stage has been achieved, it is not possible to consider appropriate methods of data collection, so now's the time to check the following items.

Working title and the project outline

Select a **working title**. 'Barriers to learning', or 'Mature students'? Either will do for the time being. You're almost ready to produce the project outline for discussion with your supervisor, but just go through the stages once again:

- Are you clear about the *purpose of the study*? Are you sure about it? Do you think it's likely to be worth doing?
- Have you decided on the *focus of the study*?
- You have not yet *identified your sample*. Discussion with supervisor required and then permissions sought. You're not there yet.
- You've been through all your *key questions* (several times now) and know what your priorities are. There will almost certainly be adjustments as the research continues, but never mind.
- You have begun to consider *what information* you might need in order to be in a position to answer your questions. More work needed, but you've made a start.
- You have not yet begun to consider *how* you might obtain this information, but once the focussing is finished, you can begin to consider possible ways and means. Remember that you can't assume you will be allowed to interview people or give them a questionnaire to answer. You have to clear official channels and obtain permission.

There are still some decisions to be made, but you're ready to produce the first draft of your project outline for discussion with your supervisor. Before you do, think about your submission date. Think about *time*. What are your chances of completing your provisional plan in your allocated time? You are not going to be living in a cave with only a computer for company for the duration of your research, out of touch with work commitments, family responsibilities and holidays. They all need to be taken into account in your time plan. I make plans all the time and I live by the lists. I don't always succeed in keeping to them, but at least their presence is enough to remind me about what still needs to be done and to nag me when I am thinking about all the things I'd rather do than get back to the writing.

Timing

There is never enough time to do all the work that seems to be essential in order to do a thorough job, but if you have a handover date, then somehow the work has to be completed in the specified time. It is unlikely you will be able to keep rigidly to a timetable, but some attempt should be made to devise a schedule so that you can check progress periodically and, if necessary, force yourself to move from one stage of the research to the next.

If you have to complete more than one project in the year, it is particularly important to produce a list or a chart indicating the stage at which all data should have been collected, analysed and drafts produced. Delay on one project means that the timing for the second and third will be upset. It is immaterial whether you produce a list *or* a chart, but some attempt at planning progress should be attempted.

One of the most common reasons for falling behind is that reading takes longer than anticipated. Books and articles have to be located, and the temptation to read just one more book is strong. At some stage a decision has to be made to stop reading and start writing, no matter how inadequate the coverage of the subject is. Forcing yourself to move on is a discipline that has to be learnt. Keep in touch with your supervisor about progress. If things go wrong and you are held up on one stage, there may be other ways of overcoming the problem. Talk about it. Ask for help and advice *before* you become weeks out of phase with your timetable, so that you have a chance of amending your original project plan. The project outline is for guidance only. If subsequent events indicate that it would be better to ask different questions and even to have a different aim, then change while there is time. You have to work to the date specified by the institution, and your supervisor and external examiner will understand that.

Supervision

I can't emphasize enough the importance of establishing a good working relationship with your supervisor. Few researchers, inexperienced *and* experienced, can go it alone and expect to produce quality research. There are exceptions of course. Aren't there always? Somebody told me once about a PhD student who made it clear that he did not need a supervisor and had no intention of attending any research tutorials. He was advised that this would be very unwise and that his chances of succeeding without support were very slight. He persisted and eventually submitted a thesis which proved to be a work of outstanding quality and depth. His external examiner had no doubt in recommending that it was a clear pass. There is a problem with this approach, namely that few people can aspire to such single-mindedness and brilliance. Most of us really do need a supervisor in whom we have confidence, with whom we can share our thinking, who is willing to advise and to give an honest view about our drafts, and that applies regardless of whether we are working on a 100-hour project, an undergraduate or a postgraduate degree.

Student–supervisor relationships

I have occasionally heard students complain that they are getting a raw deal from their supervisors, and in some cases they may have been right – though not always. Supervisors are only human. Most will also be lecturing, supervising other students and carrying out their own research. Time is generally in short supply and some friends who are heavily committed with supervision have suggested to me that I give the impression that they should be available at all hours to see students on demand who might wish to discuss any aspect of their work, regardless of the time of day, the time involved and the frequency of such requests. Not so. A reasonable balance has to be struck, though I realize that the big question is what 'reasonable' means to both sides.

Perhaps not surprisingly, interviews with students and with supervisors reveal a wide variation in supervisory practice (Bell 1996; Phillips and Pugh 2000). The majority of students appear to have enjoyed very positive relationships with supervisors. Their comments were on the lines of 'very helpful'; 'taught me what research was all about'; 'could not have done this without her'; 'he made me believe I could do it, saw me through the bad times, read all my drafts carefully, was straight about what I had written and what more needed to be done'. However, when things went wrong, they went badly wrong, and students' comments were on the lines of 'could never get hold of him'; 'never returned my calls'; 'made me feel inadequate'; 'showed no signs of having read my drafts'; 'didn't seem to feel he had any responsibility for advising about my approach'; 'was only willing to see me once a term for a timetabled 20 minutes. He was always late but always finished on time. I had to travel 100 miles for these 10 minute meetings'; and 'went on study leave, never told me, and no-one was allocated to "take me over" at a crucial time in my research when I really needed help'.

Some of the supervisors put up a vigorous defence. Regular telephone calls at 11 p.m. or later in spite of repeated requests not to telephone after 9 p.m. so exasperated one supervisor that he refused to release his home telephone number to his next batch of tutees. There were complaints about students not turning up for arranged meetings; demands for drafts to be read overnight; the assumption that supervisors should always be in their room and available for consultation whenever they were needed, and so on.

The point of raising these issues here is not to lay blame one way or the other but rather to consider ways of avoiding conflict if at all possible, and, only if reason does not prevail, to consider ways of resolving difficult situations.

Codes of practice for supervision

All universities now have (or should have) a code of practice for supervision. However, providing such a code is one thing, and ensuring that everyone involved follows the guidelines may be quite another. You should certainly be able to see your university's or organization's code in order to know what your and your supervisor's rights and responsibilities are. Some universities automatically provide a copy for students; others do not.

Most codes advise that supervisors and students should at an early stage clarify what 'supervision' actually means and what it is reasonable for both to expect. Even where efforts are made to clarify rights and responsibilities, supervisor–student relationships do occasionally break down and if all efforts to improve the position fail, then the only thing to do is to request a change before depression and a feeling of hopelessness take over.

Change of supervisor

Achieving a satisfactory change may not always be as easy as it might seem. One part-time student who was not getting on with her supervisor was desperate to change but the department was unable to find another supervisor who was willing to accept her. Having drawn a blank after following all the laid-down procedures, she decided to take action herself. She stood at the door of the postgraduate students' common room one lunch time and shouted 'Is anybody here doing historical research?' When several hands went up, she asked what they thought of their supervisors and what their specialisms were. In desperation, she pleaded for an interview with the supervisor deemed by his students to be 'friendly, helpful, knowledgeable but tough' who eventually, though somewhat reluctantly, agreed to take her on. They got on well and three years later she trod he boards to receive her PhD. Her advice to students in a similar position was:

> If you have justifiable concerns, talk about them and try
> to sort them informally. If that approach fails, go through

the formal channels. In my case, neither approach produced the desired changes so I decided I had to take matters into my own hands. I didn't like doing what I did but I would never have completed with the first supervisor. He seemed to leave me feeling that I wasn't intellectually up to the research.

Most of the time, everything works well and supervisors are as anxious as their students that they should succeed, but if things go badly wrong, state your case clearly and fairly and don't give in.

Keeping records of supervisory tutorials

I firmly believe that records of supervisory tutorials should be kept by supervisors *and* by research students. Many of my colleagues disagree and claim this would be 'just another piece of unnecessary bureaucracy'. I am not speaking here of a large document which would require days, if not weeks to produce but a one-page pre-printed form which gives space for the date of the tutorial, a (very) brief note of issues discussed, targets set, if any, summary of comments given on drafts and on the general progress of the research, advice given and taken (or not taken) and the proposed date of the next meeting. Five minutes maximum at the end of the tutorial with a copy for the supervisor and for the student. This provides a useful record and reminder for both about what was said, promised and agreed (or disagreed) and acts as a log of progress. However, it now also serves another purpose. Disputes have increased and it is in the interests of supervisors and students that there should be such an agreed record. Keeping records is not just another attempt at imposing yet another level of useless bureaucracy. It is good professional practice. If your supervisor considers such a record is unnecessary, keep your own.

The research experience

The supervisor–student relationship at its best will ensure that your research experience will be demanding, but will also be valuable, enjoyable and will result in the successful completion of your investigation – on time. As I have suggested earlier, only isolationist geniuses with plenty of time and a first-class library at their disposal are likely to succeed – and there are not many geniuses around. Most of us need help, encouragement and supervisor expertise. As many first-time and experienced researchers have testified, a good supervisor is like gold dust, and by far the most valuable resource we have.

⊙ **Planning the project checklist**

1 Draw up a shortlist of topics.	Talk to colleagues, fellow students – anyone who will listen. Consult library catalogues, but briefly.
2 Decide on a shortlist of two.	Select your first choice and keep the second in mind in case your first choice proves to be too difficult or too uninteresting.
3 Make a list of first- and second-thoughts questions or produce a chart of ideas, thoughts, possible problems – anything you can think of.	This is for your eyes only. The purpose is to help you to clarify your thoughts about which aspects of the topic are of particular interest or importance.
4 Select the precise focus of your study.	You can't do everything, so you need to be clear about which aspect of the general topic you wish to investigate. Is your topic likely to be worth investigating? Think about it. The last thing you want is to be stuck with a topic that's going nowhere and which bores you to distraction.
5 Make sure you are clear about the purpose of the study.	Give some thought to your sample. You need to consult your supervisor about which individuals or groups might be included.

6 Go back to your charts and lists of questions, delete any items which do not relate to your selected topic, add others which do, eliminate overlap and produce a revised list of key questions.

You are aiming to produce **researchable questions.** Watch your language! Are you absolutely clear about the *meaning* of the words you use. Words can mean different things to different people.

7 Draw up an initial project outline. Check that you are clear about the purpose and focus of your study, have identified key questions, know what information you will require and have thought about how you might obtain it.

Check your submission date. Do you have enough time to carry out the research you have outlined – and to submit on time?

8 Consult your supervisor at the stage of selecting a topic and after drawing up a project outline.

You don't want to get too far down the research road before you check that all is well. Make sure you discuss a suitable sample and ask about who to approach for permissions.

9 It's best to know about your institution's code of practice for supervision and what to do if the relationship with your supervisor breaks down.

Do your best to clarify any unclear areas of supervisor/ student rights and responsibilities.

10 Keep a brief record of what has been discussed, and agreed, in supervisory tutorials.

It will help to remind you about what tasks and targets have been agreed.

11 Remember that a good supervisor is like gold dust and by far the most valuable resource you have, so don't make unreasonable demands. If you're asked not to phone after 9 p.m. because granny goes to bed at that time and the telephone disturbs her, please make sure you don't.

Unfortunately, very occasionally supervisor– student relationships break down. If you have justifiable concerns, try to talk about them and to sort out problems. If that fails, go through formal channels, state your case clearly and fairly and, if that fails, request a change.

> 12 From the start of your research, get into the habit of writing everything down.
>
> And don't throw away your drafts until your investigation has been submitted, assessed and/or published. You never know when you might need to refer to them.

Further reading

Cryer, P. (2000) *The Research Student's Guide to Success*, 2nd edn. Buckingham: Open University Press. Considers the roles and responsibilities of supervisors *and* of research students and provides guidance about what to do if things do not go well.

Delamont, S., Atkinson, P. and Parry, O. (2004) *Supervising the Doctorate: A Guide to Success*. Buckingham: Open University Press. This is a book written for supervisors, but it is full of helpful ideas and advice for students also.

Johnson, D. (1994) 'Planning small-scale research', Chapter 12 in N. Bennett, R. Glatter, R. Levačić (eds) *Improving Educational Management through Research and Consultancy*. London: Paul Chapman Publishing, in association with the Open University. This excellent chapter covers research planning, stages of carrying out an investigation, establishing the focus of a study, identifying the specific objectives of a study, arranging research access, developing the research instruments, collecting the data – and much more.

Laws, S. with Harper, C. and Marcus, R. (2003) *Research for Development: A Practical Guide*. London: Sage. Chapter 5 provides guidance about processes involved in planning research, writing the brief, defining the research process, setting the research questions and hypothesis testing. A useful checklist and list of further reading are provided. Well worth consulting.

Wolcott, H.F. (2001) *Writing up Qualitative Research*, 2nd edn. London: Sage Publications. Everything Wolcott has written is worth reading, his advice is excellent and if you can get hold of this second edition, read it all! He is particularly good, as the title of this book indicates, about writing but also about planning. He talks about his own practice, what he considers researchers should and should not do – and he can be funny at times. It all helps.

● 3

ETHICS AND INTEGRITY IN RESEARCH

At one time, it was possible to plan and carry out a small piece of research with the permission of a head of department, principal of a college, headteacher of a school or an administrator without having to go through formal channels. The informal route will still apply for many 100-hour studies as long as whoever is in charge is convinced of your integrity and of the worth of your research. However, times have changed. In most cases, your supervisor will be aware of any restrictions or legal requirements relating to your research and will ensure that you have appropriate advice about procedures well before you begin to plan your data collection. However, you may not always be able to rely on your supervisor's knowledge. For example, if you work in one organization but are supervised somewhere else, the supervisor may not know what your organization's requirements are. If you live in Singapore or Calcutta but are registered for a higher degree in an Australian or British university, your supervisor may have no idea at all about the local rules, so it will be up to you to find out what is required. Particularly if you have any doubts about the ethics of your proposal, make sure you consult as widely as you can, discuss your concerns and do not proceed if you or your advisers have any misgivings.

Research contracts, codes of practice, protocols and the principle of informed consent

There is nothing new about research contracts and ethical guidelines. They have all been used in a variety of ways for many years. They may have been called something different and their use was on a less formal basis than now, but they existed. Twenty years ago, Lutz, writing about ethnographic research, advised researchers that

> it is undoubtedly necessary for every ethnographer to establish some type of 'contract' with the society to be studied. Such a 'contract' may include specifications about what records may and may not be examined; where the ethnographer may or may not go, when, and under what circumstances; which meetings may be attended and which are closed; how long the researcher will stay in the field; who (if anyone) has access to field notes, and even who has the right to review and/or approve the ethnography and its analysis prior to publication, or under what circumstances they may or may not be published at all.
>
> (Lutz 1986: 114)

This is good advice, but it is 'advice', not a 'requirement'. These days, many organizations and professional bodies such as the Medical Research Council, the General Nursing Council, the British Sociological Association and others have gone a long way to formalize procedures and have produced their own ethical guidelines, research contracts, codes of practice and protocols, including such issues as deception concerning the purpose of investigations; encroachment on privacy; confidentiality; safety; care needed when research involves children – and much more.

Hart and Bond (1995: 198–201), writing about action research in health and social care, provide examples of different types of codes of practice or protocols which require researchers to ensure that participants are fully aware of the purpose of the research and understand their rights. Some are designed to be read out at the start of interviews, explaining that participation is voluntary, that participants are free to refuse to answer any questions and may withdraw from the interview at any time. Most promise confidentiality and anonymity, but as will be seen later in this chapter, it may be more difficult to fulfil such promises than might at first have been thought. Some suggest that respondents should be asked to sign a copy of the protocol form before the interview begins, indicating that they understand and agree to all the conditions. However, Hart and Bond argue that in their view:

> It is not sufficient for the interviewer simply to read it [the protocol] out and then expect the respondent to sign . . . The respondent might justifiably feel anxious about signing anything, particularly at an early stage when the interviewer may be unknown to him or her. In our view it would be better to give the respondent time to read and re-read the protocol for himself or herself at his or her own pace, and to negotiate any additions or changes to it with the researcher. We would also recommend that the respondent should have a signed copy of the form as a record.
>
> (Hart and Bond 1995: 199)

This is sound advice. In my view, subjects should never be expected to sign any protocol form unless they have had time to read and consider the implications. All researchers will be aiming at the principle of 'informed consent', which requires careful preparation involving explanation and consultation before any data collecting begins (see Gray 2000, reported in Bell and Opie 2002: 144–6; Oliver 2003: 28–30).

Bowling (2002: 157) also makes what to me is an important and rarely considered point, namely that in addition to ensuring that participants know exactly what will be involved in the research, the informed consent procedure 'reduces the legal liability of the researcher'. In these litigious days, it is as well to be sure we have done everything, not only to ensure participants' rights but also our own position.

Blaxter et al. (2001) summarize the principles of research ethics as follows:

> Research ethics is about being clear about the nature of the agreement you have entered into with your research subjects

or contacts. This is why contracts can be a useful device. Ethical research involves getting the informed consent of those you are going to interview, question, observe or take materials from. It involves reaching agreements about the uses of this data, and how its analysis will be reported and disseminated. And it is about keeping to such agreements when they have been reached.

(p.158)

Ethics committees

Ethics committees play an important part in ensuring that no badly designed or harmful research is permitted. Darlington and Scott consider they have

an important gatekeeping role in all research involving human subjects and are likely to be extra vigilant in their consideration of proposals for research concerning any potentially vulnerable groups of people. Ethics committees have a duty to consider all possible sources of harm and satisfy themselves that the researcher has thought through all the relevant issues prior to granting permission to proceed.

(Darlington and Scott 2002: 22–3)

Their gatekeeping is not always welcomed. Reason and Bradbury report some of the experiences of one of the researchers in the action research Midwives' Action Research Group (MARG). She felt that

the Ethics Committee not only seems to fulfil an ethical role but also a gate-keeping role in hindering would-be researchers whose work doesn't fit the empirical-analytic framework and also which might reveal unpleasant truths about the setting.

(Reason and Bradbury 2001: 295)

The researcher actually felt that the committee members were trying to block her research, and asked 'What gives them the right to tell me which women I can or cannot have a conversation with on a voluntary basis for my research? Do they have a legal right? Or is it assumed power?' Well, they certainly have a right to tell researchers what they can do and what they can't. I don't know whether they are legal rights but ethics committees are powerful and if your submission is rejected, you won't be allowed to do the research at all. Happily, I have never known or heard of reports of ethics committees trying to block research. It's possible that some committee members may sometimes appear to be . . . well, perhaps rather overzealous in their requirements – at least to researchers who have been required to resubmit, but they have a duty to ensure that no sloppy, damaging or illegal research is allowed to slip through and their requirements have to be met.

One complaint which is frequently levelled at ethics and research committees is the time taken to respond to submissions. Bowling (2002: 158) reports that researchers have been known to wait three to six months before receiving approval to proceed. Admittedly these delays have generally related to medical or other health-related topics where requirements are, and no doubt should be stringent, but few committees are speedy – at least, as far as anxious researchers are concerned. Sometimes, they meet infrequently. Dates of meetings are generally known beforehand but researchers will invariably have to submit applications well ahead of those dates. Everything takes time, so it's as well to be aware of dates, and of possible delays.

These requirements and delays may be alarming if you are working on a 100-hour project, but unless you are concerned with medical or health-related research, you may not always be required to go through the ethics committee procedures. However, you will still have to go through whatever vetting procedures your own organization, department and profession require, so make sure you know what they are.

Ethics and research committees often do their best to fast-track approval procedures for small studies but even so, they will never rubber stamp a badly prepared submission, nor should they, so do your best to get your submission right. It's unlikely your first draft will be good enough, so make sure your supervisor sees it, take advice, obtain any guidelines provided by the committees and conform to their requirements. Of course, there may be no requirements to submit anything to a committee. It may be quite sufficient if your supervisor gives you approval to proceed, but if you do find you have to wait for approval, there is a lot you can do such as reading about and around your topic, making notes, trying out different types of indexing and cataloguing systems and thinking about ways in which your findings might become part of your literature review. You might spend time familiarizing yourself with your institution's computer system, recording references, and, all being well, considering the possible design of some of your proposed data-collecting instruments. What you can't do is begin to collect data and contact participants before written approval is received.

Confidentiality and anonymity   ◉

Not surprisingly, all the 'informed consent' statements and ethical guidelines I have seen mention confidentiality and anonymity. We all know what they mean, don't we? Well, do we? Is my 'confidentiality' likely to mean the same as yours? I regret to say that I have come across many broken promises of confidentiality and anonymity in research projects and imprecision about what is meant by both terms can result in serious misunderstandings between researchers and participants. So, if you say that participants will be anonymous, then under no circumstances can they be identified. If you promise confidentiality . . . well, decide what you mean by that *in the context of your investigation*.

Sapsford and Abbott (1996: 318–19), writing about unstructured interviewing, remind us that 'interviewing is intrusive, but having your personal details splashed in identifiable form across a research project is even more intrusive'. They make it clear that in their view '*confidentiality* is a promise that you will not be identified or presented in identifiable form, while *anonymity* is a promise that even the researcher will not be able to tell which responses came from which respondent' (p. 319). These definitions are sound and, with appropriate acknowledgement, could well be adopted in your own research. However, the implications of each can be significant. I raise some of the issues in 'Selecting methods of data collection' in Part II of this book, but they are sufficiently important to raise also in this chapter. If you promise anonymity to questionnaire respondents, then, as Sapsford and Abbott point out, that means that no one, *including you* will know who has completed the questionnaire. As far as I am concerned, this means that no follow-up letters can be sent, no question-naires can have coded numbers or symbols so that responses can be identified and no other sneaky tricks of any kind can be used. If you feel you have to have the option of sending follow-up letters, then you must qualify your definition to respondents by saying something on the lines of 'By "anonymity" in the context of this study, I mean that no one will see (your completed questionnaire/ interview transcript) except me and all questionnaires and records will be shredded once the research is completed.' Is that what you mean? Think about it.

There can also be difficulties over confidentiality. If in your report you speak about the Director of Resources or the Head of English, you are immediately identifying the individuals con-cerned. If you invent a pseudonym or a code, it might still be easy for readers in the know to identify the individual or institution concerned. I recall the anger of one school principal who was guaranteed confidentiality for his school but the way the report was written made it clear to people in the area which school it was. No one minds being identified if the report is complimentary, but this particular principal was head of a school in a very poor area which for some years had had a reputation for truancy and indif-ferent examination results. Great strides had been made and many improvements achieved in the two years before the research but of course, long-term improvement takes time. His anger centred on the fact that he had been promised that the report would be written in such a way as to make it impossible for an individual school to be identified. His comment was that if any researcher came anywhere near his school in future, they would be shown the door. So, watch your language and don't promise anything you can't deliver.

Safeguarding confidentiality and anonymity if disseminating information by computer

In December 1997, the report of the Caldicott Committee on the review of patient-identifiable information was published (http://doh.gov.uk/ipu/confid/report/crep.htm). The review was commissioned because of concern about ways in which patient information was used in the National Health Service (NHS) in England and Wales and the use of information technology to disseminate information about patients. This is a very large, thorough and well-conducted review. Eighty-six flows of patient-identifiable information were mapped during the review and 16 recommendations for the improvement of practice were produced. It is easy to see how information stored on computers and transferred to other departments, hospitals or, for example, to general practitioner (GP) clinics might easily become available to individuals and organizations who have no right to that information. The same concern might also be expressed about the way firms, hospitals, universities and individuals disseminate information about employees, students and, in the case of research programmes, participants – unless steps are taken to ensure no individual can be identified. If you also have concerns about maintaining the confidentiality of your participants, I recommend that you read the report. I would also recommend that you consult the Data Protection Act 1998 (The Data Protection Registrar 1998), in particular the sections relating to individuals' right to privacy with respect to the processing of personal data (http://www.open.gov.uk/dpr/dprhome.htm). A great deal of additional secondary legislation has already been tabled and no doubt more will appear as time goes on.

Ethical research in practice and the problems of 'inside' research

Regardless of the requirements of your institution and of your supervisor, this will still be your research. Even if you are not obliged to conform to required codes of practice nor to the demands of ethics or research committees, you will need to satisfy yourself that you have done everything possible to ensure that your research is conducted in a way which complies with your own ethical principles. This is the approach adopted by Stephen Waters, a postgraduate diploma student and first-time researcher. At the time of the research, he was a teacher of English in a high school and decided that, if possible, he would undertake the research in his own school. He was interested in investigating the role of his own Head of English (called Director of English). The Director had expressed interest in and support for the study, and this convinced Stephen that the topic would be worthwhile and would have a good chance of being successfully completed in the time allowed (effectively three months). He decided to produce his own personal code of practice which made clear the conditions and guarantees within which he felt he must work, in order to ensure his own and his school's integrity. The preparation proceeded on the following lines:

1 Informal discussion with the headmaster to obtain agreement in principle.
2 Refinement of the topic, statement of the objectives of the study and preparation of a project outline.
3 Discussion with his tutor and further discussion with the Director of English.
4 Minor adjustments made to the project outline and a consideration of the methods to be used.
5 Formal submission of the project outline to the headmaster, together with names of colleagues he wished to interview and certain guarantees and conditions under which the research would be conducted.

The conditions and guarantees were presented as follows:

1 All participants will be offered the opportunity to remain anonymous.
2 All information will be treated with the strictest confidentiality.
3 Interviewees will have the opportunity to verify statements when the research is in draft form.
4 Participants will receive a copy of the final report.

5 The research is to be assessed by the university for examination purposes only, but should the question of publication arise at a later date, permission will be sought from the participants.
6 The research will attempt to explore educational management in practice. It is hoped the final report may be of benefit to the school and to those who take part.

So how did it go? This is what Stephen wrote after the project was completed.

I felt that presenting the guarantees formally was essential. As I was completely inexperienced in research, I had to assure the headmaster that the fieldwork would be carried out with integrity and convince him that he could place his trust in me.

With hindsight, I should have exercised greater caution. Condition 3 could not be met in full since I later found that, although a proper check could be made to verify statements participants had made while being interviewed, there was insufficient time for them to proofread a full draft. Condition 4 was fulfilled but the cost proved to be prohibitive and I decided to eliminate this condition when other case studies were undertaken. This experience certainly alerted me to the danger of promising too much too soon.

It was only when the time drew near for the findings of my research to be disseminated that I became aware of the two areas where the wording of my conditions of research was open to interpretation. The first was that, in promising confidentiality (Condition 2), I had not made it clear what the implications of releasing information would be. As there was insufficient time to release a draft report, no one could check whether my interpretation of what they had said was fair. In any case, as the headmaster was the only person to hold a written copy of my guarantees, the respondents could only interpret the conditions under which they had agreed to participate from my verbal explanation. In retrospect, it would have been better to have provided a duplicated explanation of the written outline of my intentions. Teachers are busy people and it was unreasonable to assume that they would be able to remember a conversation which had taken place some time before their services were formally required. As it was, whether or not they remembered the guarantees, they were totally dependent on my integrity to present their views in a balanced, objective manner.

More naïvely, until I was writing the report, I had not realized that identifying people by role may preserve the guarantee of anonymity for an outside reader, but it did not confer the same degree of obscurity for those within the school. Fortunately, my failure to clarify these points did not lead to problems – but it could have done.

Stephen Waters learnt a great deal from his first experience of conducting an investigation. He felt he had made some mistakes at his first attempt and was uneasy because he had not been able to fulfil all the conditions and guarantees. He had prepared the ground very well but had not fully appreciated the time and effort involved in reporting back to colleagues and in producing copies of reports. He was concerned at his lack of precision in defining exactly what he meant by anonymity and confidentiality, and made quite sure that in subsequent investigations he clarified the position. He found it harder to know what to do about role conflict. He was a full-time teacher and a part-time researcher – a not unusual combination – and on occasions found it difficult to reconcile the two roles. There were definite advantages in being an 'inside' researcher. For example, he had an intimate knowledge of the context of the research and of the micropolitics of the institution, travel was not a problem and subjects were easily reached. He knew how best to approach individuals and appreciated some of their difficulties. He found that colleagues welcomed the opportunity to air problems and to have their situation analysed by someone who understood the practical day-to-day realities of their task. On the other hand, he found interviewing some colleagues an uncomfortable experience for both parties. As an insider, he quickly came to realize that you have to live with your mistakes after completing the research. The close contact with the institution and colleagues made objectivity difficult to attain and, he felt, gaining confidential knowledge had the potential for affecting his relationship with colleagues. In the event, this did not seem to be the case, but he could foresee situations where problems might have arisen.

When he had successfully completed the diploma course, he was asked whether he felt it had all been worthwhile and whether he had any comments that might be helpful to others who were undertaking a research project for the first time. He wrote as follows:

> I may have given the impression that my research was so fraught with difficulties that it was counter-productive. If so, it is because I wish to encourage the prospective inside-researcher to exercise caution and to be aware of possible pitfalls. In reality, I enjoyed my research immensely and found that the experience of interviewing a cross-section of teaching staff provided me with a much greater working knowledge of the school's management practices. Indeed, my research was so absorbing that at times I found myself struggling to keep pace with my teaching commitments. I am certain, even without hindsight, that I could have done little to resolve this dilemma. I can honestly say that my research has made me more understanding of the problems con-fronting those responsible for running the school and has subsequently provided a great deal of thought about the educational issues. If my research had not been practically relevant I would have felt concerned about the extent of my commitment to it. As it was, several recommendations which appeared in my first report have been taken up by the school; my third report on the role of the governing body in the curriculum was placed on the agenda of a governors' meeting in spring and many colleagues have been complimentary about the content of the case studies in general. If I had to choose one strategy that I would encourage prospective inside researchers to adopt, it would be to relate the research report to the pragmatic concerns of the institution. That might perhaps help to persuade colleagues that participation in research will be as beneficial to them as it is to the researcher.

Whether or not you relate your research to the pragmatic con-cerns of the institution depends on the nature of your task and your own special concerns, but whether you are an inside or outside researcher, whether you are full-time or part-time, experienced or inexperienced, care has to be taken to make no promises that cannot be honoured. When Stephen carried out his first piece of research, guidelines, protocols and research contracts were less common than they are now. He had to devise his own guarantees and conditions. These days, most organizations will have their own set of rules, not only about the conduct of research, but also about who owns what.

Codes of ethical practice relating to intellectual ownership/property

At one time, relatively little was heard about intellectual property or ownership. It was and still is quite customary in scientific and technological departments for supervisors' names to appear on joint papers, the decision about the positioning of the names having been decided by the supervisor and/or in accordance with common departmental or institutional practice. Where research has been sponsored by government agencies or commercial organizations, institutions generally have an agreement in place about intellectual property rights about which students are, or should be, informed at the start of their research, particularly if they have been recruited specifically to carry out some pre-determined and pre-planned research. In some cases, students may be required to assign ownership of their intellectual property to institutions, to ensure that any potential patent or marketable findings are not lost, and so it is particularly important that everyone understands what this means. Is what students write the property of the institution or the organization or research council which funded it? Is it the property of the researcher alone, or the joint property of the researcher and the supervisor? If jointly owned, which name comes first in any published work? The question of the positioning of names may seem trivial, but the importance to all concerned cannot be underestimated. Universities in particular want their research students, and require their academic staff, to publish. Doing well in research assessment exercises brings not only recognition and prestige but also money – and all three count.

In hospitals and other health-related organizations institutional property guidelines and rules have been in place for many years and recently I have begun to see advertisements for the post of 'intellectual property adviser' for individual and for groups of hospitals which seems to me not only to indicate the importance of this issue in today's research and publishing worlds but also its complexity. Even where codes and guidelines are issued, disputes about ownership are still known to rage where students who consider they have done all the work find that their supervisor's and professor's names appear before theirs on published reports of the research.

The various codes of practice, guidelines and policies which are now frequently provided in academic institutions, departments, hospitals and funding bodies should go some way to eliminating unethical practice and misunderstandings over ownership, just as I believe codes and protocols can help to eliminate similar unethical practice in issues relating to informed consent. No codes of ethical practice can resolve all problems but they do at least clarify some of the major issues in this difficult area – and that is a start.

If you are a first-time researcher, the idea of asking to see your institution or organization's guidelines relating to intellectual property rights may seem irrelevant. Even so, it might be interesting to find out what the guidelines say. You never know, your research may be sufficiently outstanding and of sufficient interest to be considered for publication and it's as well to know what your rights would be in that happy eventuality. It's always a good idea to be prepared for success.

⦿ The ethics and integrity in research checklist

1 It's your responsibility to discover whether any restrictions or legal requirements relate to your research.

If you or your advisers have any doubts about the integrity of your proposal, don't proceed.

2 Many organizations now have ethical guidelines, codes of practice and protocols.

Make sure you know if such guidelines exist and conform to their requirements.

3 Always aim for the informed consent of your participants.

Remember that respondents should not be expected to sign any protocol form unless they have had time to read and consider the implications.

4 If all proposed research has to be vetted by the ethics committee in your organization, make sure your submission is well thought out. Find out when the committees meet and allow time for your submission to be considered.

Consult, show your draft to your supervisor, talk to any students who have had their submission to the ethics committed rejected – or approved.

5 Confidentiality and anonymity are generally promised to participants.

However, make sure you know what you, *and* your participants mean by each.

6 You must never break any promises to participants, so watch your language and never promise anything you can't deliver.

So if you promise anonymity, you can't send out follow-up letters. No tricks!

7 If you are using a computer, take care who is to see, or might see your text, particularly if it gives the names of participants at any stage.

Consult the Data Protection Act, particularly sections relating to individuals' right to privacy with respect to the processing of personal data.

8 Regardless of the requirements of your institution and of your supervisor, this will still be your research.	Even if you are not obliged to conform to required codes of practice, nor to the demands of ethics and research committees, ensure that your research is conducted in a way which conforms to your own ethical principles.
9 If you are carrying out research in your own institution or organization, do your best to let your colleagues know what you plan to do and how you hope they might be willing to help.	Don't be too ambitious. Consider how much time you are allowed in order to complete the research on time.
10 If you think you might wish to publish some of your findings at some stage, first make sure that you have obtained the permission of the people and institutions concerned.	And also make sure you have seen a copy of all your organization's and profession's codes of practice, protocols and guidelines, in particular ethical guidelines relating to informed consent and to intellectual property.
11 You may think you own what you have written and therefore, you can do as you like with any research report, article or book.	That might sometimes be possible, but not always, so check before you commit yourself.
12 No codes of ethical practice, protocols, guidelines and policies can solve all your problems, but they help.	They at least clarify some of the major issues.

Further reading

Aldridge, A. and Levine, K. (2001) *Surveying the Social World: Principles and Practice in Survey Research*. Buckingham: Open University Press. Pages 21–3 consider privacy, research ethics, informed consent, confidentiality and sensitivity.

Blaxter, L., Hughes, C. and Tight, M. (2001) *How to Research*, 2nd edn. Buckingham: Open University Press. Pages 157–61 deal with ethical issues in a clear and helpful way.

Brewer, J. D. (2000) *Ethnography*. Buckingham: Open University Press. Pages 88–99 discuss ethical issues relating to ethnographic research.

Busher, H. (2002) 'Ethics of research in education', Chapter 5 in M. Coleman and A.R.J. Briggs (eds) *Research Methods in Educational Leadership and Management*. London: Paul Chapman Publishing.

The Caldicott Committee (1997) Report on the review of patient-identifiable information. London: Department of Health.

Cohen, L. and Manion, L. (1994) 'The ethics of educational and social research', Chapter 16 in *Research Methods in Education*, 4th edn. London: Routledge.

Cohen, L., Manion, L. and Morrison, K. (2000) *Research Methods in Education*, 5th edn. Chapter 2, 'The ethics of educational and social research', provides 20+ pages of sound advice. London and New York: Routledge.

Darlington, Y. and Scott, D. (2002) *Qualitative Research in Practice: Stories from the Field*. Buckingham: Open University Press. See Chapter 13, 'Research ethics'.

Hart, E. and Bond, M. (1995) *Action Research for Health and Social Care: A Guide to Practice*. Buckingham: Open University Press. Pages 198–201 provide examples of ethics protocols.

Laws, S. with Harper C. and Marcus, R. (2003) *Research for Development*. London: Sage. Chapter 13 deals with ethics codes and responsibilities towards respondents. Well worth consulting.

Lutz, F.W. (1986) 'Ethnography: the holistic approach to understanding schooling' in M. Hammersley *Controversies in Classroom Research*. Milton Keynes: Open University Press. This is a very thorough chapter which, in addition to discussing issues relating to ethnographic research, also gives good advice about establishing a 'contract' for research, bias, and the importance of protecting the identity of every participant which 'leaves the particular person and place unnamed, unharmed, and unchanged' (p. 115).

May, T. (2001) *Social Research Issues, Methods and Process*, 3rd edn. Buckingham: Open University Press. Pages 59–68 consider ethical issues in social research.

Miles, M.B. and Huberman, A.M. (1994) *Qualitative Data Analysis*, 2nd edn. Thousand Oaks, CA: Sage. Chapter 11, pages 288–97 give excellent guidance about specific ethical issues, competence boundaries, informed consent, harm and risk, honesty and trust, privacy, confidentiality and anonymity, research integrity and quality, ownership of data, use and misuse of results, conflicts and dilemmas and tradeoffs. No matter how pressed for time you are, do your best to find time to consult this chapter.

Oliver, P. (2003) *The Student's Guide to Research Ethics*. Maidenhead: Open University Press. Oliver clarifies research terminology, discusses the moral justification of research, areas of research which raise ethical issues, issues relating to the principle of informed consent, anonymity and confidentiality – and much more.

Polit, D.F. and Hungler, G.P. (1995) *Nursing Research: Principles and Methods*, 5th edn. Philadelphia: J.B. Lippincott Company. Pages 118–35 include sections on ethical dilemmas in conducting research, codes, the principle of beneficence (freedom from harm), the right to fair treatment, the right to privacy, informed consent, and vulnerable subjects.

4

READING, REFERENCING AND THE MANAGEMENT OF INFORMATION

Reading

Ideally, the bulk of your reading should come early on in the investigation, though in practice a number of activities are generally in progress at the same time and reading may even spill over into the data-collecting stage of your study. If you're working to a strict time scale (and you will be, even if you have the luxury of being on a three-year full-time PhD programme), try to discipline yourself to ensure that reading doesn't take up more time than can be allowed. This is easier said than done because when you begin work on a topic, you're never sure what might be important and what might be irrelevant. Even if you're very disciplined about reading and resist the temptation to be led astray by some really interesting-sounding books or articles which may have nothing whatsoever to do with your topic, you'll still find it difficult to confine reading to precise time slots. It's rarely possible to obtain copies of all the books and articles at exactly the time you need them and there will always be new publications which may seem to be the answer to your prayers and which you consider just have to be read. The one thing we always have to accept is that we can't do everything. We have to do the best we can in the time available – and not to use 'more reading needed' as an excuse for not actually getting down to writing and what else needs to be done to progress the research!

Any investigation, whatever the scale, will involve reading what other people have written about your area of interest, gathering information to support or refute your arguments and writing about your findings. Reading as much as time permits about your topic may give you ideas not only about the research others have done but also about their approach and methods – and this is important, because everything you do from the start of your research will be preparation for the production of the final report.

Experience has shown that no matter how sophisticated we may consider ourselves to be as learners and researchers, we all need to be reminded about the importance of systematic recording. As soon as we begin to read, we begin to record and we have to include all the necessary detail. Next week, next month, 'one of these days', 'when I've got a minute' or 'when I've finished reading these 50 journal articles' won't do. We all think we shall remember, but after several weeks of reading, memory becomes faulty. After a few months, we may vaguely recall having read something some time about a particular topic, but when, where and by whom escapes us. After a longer period, the chances of remembering anything are remote.

Note-taking and guarding against plagiarism

As you read, make notes of what seem to you to be important issues and highlight them. You will be on the lookout for recurring themes, categories and keywords which will become increasingly important in your search for a structure or framework for your own research. Priorities (and issues) will inevitably change as your reading continues. You will in all probability abandon some of your early categories and identify others but keep a record, even of your early abandoned categories. You never know. They may crop up again in your later reading.

Take care with your note-taking. A particularly perceptive observation by an author may often illustrate a point you might wish to refer to, or even quote, at a later stage. Always make it quite clear in your notes which is the quotation and which is your paraphrase, or when you come to write up your project, you may find you are committing the sin of plagiarism.

Plagiarism is using other people's words as if they are your own. Remember that all sources have to be acknowledged, including paraphrases of other people's words *and* of other people's ideas. The issue of plagiarism has become a major issue in schools and in higher education, as a result of the availability of model answers to examination and assignment questions on the Internet – for a fee. It seems that large numbers of people are now prepared to pay for 'a guaranteed A grade essay' and blatantly submit the essay, or parts of it, as their own. The development of materials on the Internet has greatly increased the number of plagiarists who, apparently, can see nothing wrong in submitting such material as their own. This has become such an issue that plagiarism software has been developed and now is regularly used, particularly in universities, to check examination and assignment texts.

There have been some unfortunate well-publicized plagiarism cases recently which have brought discredit to the individuals concerned and now supervisors are on the lookout for any examples in your drafts. Most institutions now have guidelines on plagiarism, and make it clear that the penalties for infringement will be severe. These range from giving plagiarized work a fail grade to expulsion from the course. However, the final responsibility is yours, so take care. Guidelines are regularly updated, so make sure you have a copy of the latest version which in all probability will be provided in your institution's programme handbooks and in any codes of practice relating to academic standards. However, the best way to ensure you will never use other people's words or ideas as your own without acknowledgement is to be meticulous about your note-taking and in recording exact details of references.

If you are making an exact copy of wording, add inverted commas at the beginning and end of the extract. Record the chapter and page numbers, show clearly if you have left out any word or words in the text by adding three full stops, and file the extract where you know you will be able to find it, even if this requires some cross-referencing. If you have the facilities, it's an even better idea to photocopy the extract, adding details about the source in the usual way (library staff will advise about copyright regulations).

There's one more thing to bear in mind as you read and make notes, namely the need to ask yourself whether you can trust what you read. This is always difficult, but ask yourself whether any other sources corroborate a particular source. What does the research/report/document actually say, and what evidence is provided to support the findings? What is known about the author? Do you suspect bias? If so, why? Are sources fully referenced so that you can check them? Brendan Duffy considers all these questions and many more in the 'Critical analysis of documents' section of Chapter 7. Before you begin any concentrated period of reading, refer to this chapter and section and devise your own 'authenticity' checklist.

I keep a record of everything I read, even sources which have proved to be of no interest or use to me. Other people don't and have made it clear to me that as far as they are concerned it's stupid to keep records of useless sources and they are not going to clutter up their files with rubbish. They may well have a point and you may agree with them, but I tell myself there must have been some reason why I decided to look at the book or article in the first place. The title may have sounded interesting, or I might have read other works by the same author which impressed me. It would follow then that some time in the future, the title may still sound interesting and the author may still be remembered as having produced quality work in another context. I might come across the reference again, and ask to borrow the book again. I might have asked for a copy on inter-library loan, and there are costs involved with that. All this would be a waste of time and money, and in any investigation, whether small or large, there is never enough time to do everything that has to be done. A note to remind me why I decided the work was of no interest is enough to jog my memory and to enable me to abandon that particular line of enquiry. We all have our own ways of working and you will have to decide what your own particular practices are.

Referencing

In the early days of an investigation, it may seem enough to jot down a reference on the back of an envelope, but old envelopes thrown into a box will not provide a reliable resource, and the likelihood is that references will be incomplete and difficult to track down at a later stage. If you are only going to need half a dozen references, then scraps of paper may serve, but as your investigation proceeds, you will accumulate many sources of information and an orderly system of recording is essential *from the day you start reading.*

There are several perfectly acceptable ways of recording sources and other information. The Harvard method, i.e. author's surname and date, which I use in this book, has a number of advantages over other methods. It avoids footnotes, which are awkward to deal with and all sources mentioned in the text appear at the end of the report and not chapter by chapter. Most institutions will have a preferred 'house' style which you will be expected to adopt. If you are left to decide yourself, you will need to consider which of the available options suits you best. Different supervisors (and different publishers) adopt different styles. Look at the bibliographies or references sections at the end of several books. The likelihood is that you will find different approaches, though each will contain the following information.

For books

- Author's surname and forename or initials
- Date of publication
- Title (underlined or italics) and which edition, if appropriate
- Place of publication
- Name of publisher

For example:

May, Tim (2001) *Social Research: Issues, Methods and Process*, 3rd edn. Buckingham: Open University Press.

As you see, this is the third edition of a book first published in 1993 and so the number of the edition must be included. A new edition will incorporate a significant amount of upgrading and new writing, whereas a reprint is just what it says, namely the production of more copies of the original publication. Only new editions need to be noted.

A word about the punctuation. There is no reason why a full stop should appear after the title or '3rd edn'. You might prefer to use a comma or to leave a space. You might decide it would be better to indent the second line in order to make the author's name stand out more clearly. If you wanted to, you could put the author's name in capitals. Make up your mind and whichever approach you adopt, *every single reference you record from then on must be the same* – but remember, always check your organization's guidelines before you start.

Where there are three or more authors of a book, the same format will apply as for one author, but there are one or two things to note. When sources are referred to (cited) in the text of your report, there is no need to include the full reference. It is sufficient to write 'As May (2001: 42) says . . .'. I like to have page numbers because, without them, it becomes time-consuming and some-times impossible to find where the quotation appears in the book, though many authors do omit them.

If there are three or more authors, then it's customary to use '*et al.*' (and others) in the text for the second and subsequent names, though again, practice does vary. There is no full stop after 'et' because it is a complete word, but there is after 'al.' because that is an abbreviation for the Latin 'alia'. The full reference will appear in the alphabetic list of references at the end of your report. If an author or authors had more than one publication in the same year, then suffixes 'a' and 'b' should be added after the date of publication.

Let's move on. The referencing rules and regulations are not finished yet. There are certain differences if you are recording information about a journal article or a chapter in a book.

For journal articles

The author's surname, forename or initials and the date of publication are the same as for books but then, you are required to give

- the title of the article (sometimes in inverted commas, sometimes not);
- the title of the journal from which the article or chapter is derived (generally underlined or in italics, though again, not always);
- the volume number of the journal, the issue and page numbers.

For example, for a journal article:

Whitehead, N. (2003) 'Herbal remedies: integration into conventional medicine', *Nursing Times*, **99**(34): 30–33.

The volume number is generally in bold type and the issue number in brackets after the volume number. Page numbers of journal articles are always given.

For chapters in books

For a chapter in a book, something on the following lines would be appropriate:

Wragg, T. (2002) 'Interviewing', in M. Coleman and A.R.J. Briggs (eds) *Research Methods in Educational Leadership and Management*. London: Paul Chapman Publishing.

This is a chapter in a book which was edited by Coleman and Briggs and so (eds) is added after their names. After the 'in', the convention is that initials should be placed before rather than after the surname. However, follow whatever convention your institution requires.

Citing journal articles and other materials taken from CD-ROMs or the Internet

Remember that if you make a record of electronic journal articles, in addition to giving the full reference details as above, you also need to indicate that the sources were obtained from a CD-ROM or online. For example:

- Name of author
- Title of article (not underlined/italicized)
- [CD-ROM] or [Online] in square brackets
- Journal information (journal title underlined or italicized)
- Date of article
- Available from: or retrieved from: . . . name of service, URL of web site and date it was accessed. The URL (universal resource locator) is the unique address of the server on which the document is stored.

Practice may very slightly but the main point is that sufficient information must always be provided so that other researchers are able to retrieve the article from the database.

Some of the citations of electronic sources are quite complex so if your library provides guidance about how they should be recorded, follow that advice. However, if no guidance is given, it's best to check with Cite Them Right at http://www.unn.ac.uk/central/isd/cite/, produced by Richard Pears and Graham Shields at Northumbria University. This is an excellent, regularly updated (and at present free) site which gives guidance on how to cite a wide range of electronic and many other materials including email correspondence, computer programs, bibliographic databases, newspapers and electronic conferences.

Creating, editing and storing references electronically

Software such as EndNote, ProCite and Reference Manager has been available for some time now and new versions will no doubt continue to appear on the market. Bibliographic software has many advantages for researchers. For example, EndNote gives us the facility to create, store, organize, retrieve and cite references in our reports. Its library (database) holds more than 30,000 references and it allows us to search and manage the online bibliographic databases. Once we know how, we are able to produce our own bibliographies in various formats and, if we're clever enough, to insert graphics into text. Copyright and licensing restrictions may apply to some databases and electronic journals which restrict what we are permitted to print but others will allow us to download items direct into our own records. We may even be able to access summaries of journal articles, texts of newspapers, dissertations, abstracts of doctoral theses, books and conference proceedings.

You may find that your library will provide you with on-campus access to and support for one or more of the established systems. If so, you're lucky. Never ignore the facilities which are on the doorstep, particularly if they come free. However, many researchers are part-time, live or work some way from their main academic library (or are even based overseas), spend little or no time on campus and need to be able to access the software at home.

If you can provide evidence that you are an 'academic user' and wish to have access to your institution's databases and other facilities at home, that may be possible. Ask your supervisor what steps have to be taken. If she or he doesn't know, or says home access is not permitted, look further. Always look further. Ask one of the librarians. I always believe librarians know everything, and they generally do. They will know the rules and will tell you what is involved. However, even if permission for home use is given by your library, you need to be aware of one or two other requirements – and probably costs.

For example, you will discover that referencing and online search software take up quite a lot of space on your hard drive and require a great deal of available memory, so if you plan to work from home, you will not only need to be fairly computer-competent, but you will also need a computer that is up to the job. You may find you have to upgrade your computer or even buy a new one, as I did. That will cost, so before you commit yourself to anything, check the hardware requirements with one of the software suppliers.

When I decided I really had to become familiar with electronic referencing and to gain access to bibliographic databases, I optimistically thought it would be a straightforward and fairly quick matter. I read the helpful leaflets and attended the courses provided by the library and I practised. I have to confess it has taken me a lot longer than I thought it would and I am still learning. When I am working in the campus library, there is generally someone on hand to assist, but when I am at home and find I am not sure about or have forgotten some procedure, I am dependent on the EndNote manual. I really do wish it would stop telling me that the methods are 'simple' and that everything is 'made easy' when I find myself constantly asking what this, that or the other means. I had the same problem with the computer manual in the far-off days of venturing into computer use. Now manuals aren't generally provided with computers and I am dependent on what to me is the unhelpful computer help menu. I even find myself lamenting the lost days of the manual about which I once constantly complained.

I appreciate that not all people have these difficulties, and thank goodness for that. I have known people who, when they bought their first computer, sat down one Saturday and appeared to have mastered it by Sunday evening. Some of my former students have told me they found the bibliographic software similarly easy to understand and use and said they really enjoyed getting to grips with the techniques of electronic referencing. They found the instructions provided in the manual to be perfectly clear and they shook their heads in bewilderment at my inability to cope with something so simple. So, best not to listen to me. Best to listen the many students who have gone through the learning process, are now competent in the use of their selected software and who appreciate the amount of time the referencing facility saves them.

In an ideal world, the necessary process of familiarization and practice should take place *before* you start your research proper because once you begin, you have little time to spend time on unravelling the highways and byways of a new system. That's the theory, and it's good sense but not many of us live in an ideal world. Once your research starts, you will inevitably be short of time for the numerous things you have to do, so if you're working on a small project with relatively few references (say, 20 or fewer), you should perhaps ask yourself whether the time and effort involved in becoming familiar with a new electronic system warrant such a commitment.

There are a lot of 'may's and 'sometimes' in this section and it's difficult to avoid them. Organizations operate in very different ways, impose different conditions, regularly change their rules and I'm afraid it's up to you to find out which conditions apply in your own case. I do not wish in any way to imply that investing in and becoming competent in the use of bibliographic software are a waste of time, money and effort. Quite the reverse. Electronic referencing is magic and just what we all need, but you should be clear about what is involved.

If you decide to go ahead, work at it and never suffer in silence. If you're baffled, search out people who aren't, particularly if they are frequent users of the software you have selected. Ask for their advice – and don't be embarrassed at asking what you're afraid may seem like stupid questions. There are wizards everywhere if you can find them. Oh, and one more thing, as I always say. *Never* rely totally on your electronic magic. Keep back-ups of some kind. It's immaterial which, but something. Even magic can let you down sometimes.

The card index

I confess that in this electronic age, I still use cards as one method of keeping a record of references. These days, in libraries, I often seem to be in a minority of one by being laptop-less. Laptops may be portable but as far as I'm concerned, they are heavy to carry around all the time, and they're quite expensive to buy. Cards weigh, and cost, practically nothing; they fit comfortably into a pocket and as long as you always have a few on hand, you will always be in a position to make a full record of sources on the spot, wherever the spot might be. The cards are my back-up copy (or one of my back-up copies) and I transfer the information on to my computer as soon as I can. That provides the second copy *and* gives me the beginnings of a full list of references, in alphabetical order.

I still have memories of one terrible time when, somehow or another, almost fifty pages of script disappeared without trace from my computer. So now I do my best to cover all eventualities. After all, what if a power cut loses all my work, or, more probably, what if I press the wrong button one day and send ten chapters into oblivion? Back-up floppy disks and/or CD-ROMs of course and that's what I should have done or I wouldn't have lost 50 pages, would I? Ah, but what if a burglar takes my computer? It's happened before, hasn't it? Some of my colleagues think that my obsession for keeping copies in various forms is excessive and are not backward at telling me so. Perhaps they are right, but don't let anyone tell you there is only one way of doing things. It's immaterial which methods you select to make your copies as long as copies are made, so decide which ways suit you best and then keep to them.

The management of information

It will now have become clear that it isn't enough just to record the details of publications, on cards or on whichever electronic system you adopt. Even in a small project you will need to establish an indexing and cross-referencing system because there's no point in doing a large amount of reading if, at a later date, you can never find what you are looking for. As you read, get into the habit of examining how authors classify their findings, how they explore relationships between facts and how key issues emerge. Methods used by other researchers may give you ideas about how you might organize and categorize your own data.

Those of you who have created and stored references electronically will have had the opportunity to identify key words at the same time as you record your sources. This can be helpful, but whatever method of cross-referencing and indexing you select, the approach is fundamentally the same. Somehow or another, even in the very early stages of your research, you are thinking about ways in which you will be able to find who wrote what about different topics. The last thing you need is to spend days or even weeks looking for something you know you read, somewhere. You need to be able to go straight to it. Easy? Well not really. Orna reminds us that

> By the very fact of bringing items together in *one* way (by author, by main subject, by date of addition to the store for example), it separates items that have *other* things in common. The same author may have written articles on a number of quite different subjects, so while that arrangement makes it easy to find everything by a given author, it makes it hard to find items on a given subject.
>
> (Orna 1995: 49)

Well, life was never meant to be easy and we just have to do the best we can to ensure we have some sort of system which is easy to maintain and which is likely to give reasonable access to most of the source material and topics in your store. As Orna says, 'there is no "right way" of doing it and successful researchers use a wide variety of strategies' (p. 36). I keep to what have become habits of a lifetime, or at least of writing. As I've said earlier, I still record references on cards, and then transfer the information to the computer, but I start a cross-indexing system almost from the start of reading. The main card will include all the necessary referencing detail, but if that particular article or book raises interesting issues relating to 'grounded theory', 'literature reviews', 'women' or whatever, then another card with the heading of 'grounded theory', 'literature reviews', 'women' will include brief references (e.g. Bluebottle 2000: 46) indicating where I came across those topics and where I can find notes, books and journal articles. I start with general headings and only move to more detailed headings as the reading develops. For example, if I discover items relating to women chief executives in hospitals, I can add a sub-group to the general 'women' index.

If you are comfortable with computer-based indexing, then keep to that or devise your own cunning system which may defy logic for everyone else, but which works for you. But the one thing you can't do is do nothing.

Your system will enable you to group and sort your findings under headings, allow you to refer to notes, quotations and comments about items in books or articles which you might have read months earlier and in all probability would have forgotten without your indexing system. Moreover, the small effort involved in producing a system will be providing you with the bones of a future literature review – and that will resolve many problems when the time comes to write the review.

No system is absolutely guaranteed to be perfect, and you may still occasionally find yourself in the position of rummaging in box files or trying to dredge your memory about something you once read somewhere *but* your system will ensure that rummaging and dredging are reduced to a minimum. We don't have time to mess about in boxes, so get going with your cross-referencing.

A lot of fuss about nothing?

Well, no. Just acquiring the tools of the trade. Referencing can be irritatingly pernickety, but once you've established a routine, recording information becomes (or should become) automatic. If you assimilate the information in this chapter and if you record your sources accurately and consistently, you will have begun to establish good research habits and to lay the foundations of your own research. You will be rewarded for your hard work, if not in heaven, then certainly when you come to write your report. You will be able to locate information easily, to regroup and reclassify evidence and to produce referenced quotations to support your arguments.

Incidentally, if you were thinking of asking whether I always get references spot-on right every time, I should have to admit that I can't make such a bold claim. All I can say is that I do my best to check that I've noted and included everything because I know the grief errors and omissions will give me if I'm careless. I doubt whether any researchers, even the most experienced and the best, would be bold enough to claim they never made a mistake. The British Open University employs experienced course team writers and researchers to produce their course materials and readers. They are supported by expert, specialist course team librarians and have full access to the university library's print and online resources. Writing is their job, and yet Sally Baker, who is one of the specialist librarians recalls that

Unfortunately, from the number of whey-faced academics and researchers about to submit papers or theses who are found panicking in libraries as they desperately search for missing sources, page numbers, authors' initials and so on, it is apparent that even an occasional lapse in recording bibliographic details can result in hours of wasted time at the point when time is particularly short.

Trying to be kind, she continues:

It is inevitable that you will from time to time lack a similar detail from a reference – sometimes as a result of others' incorrect referencing – but if you adopt a disciplined approach to information management you will be able to minimize the number of occasions when this occurs.

(Baker 1999: 69)

She's right. So do your utmost to record every single detail at the time you read and record and that will go a long way to reduce stress and frustration to a minimum.

⊙   **Reading, referencing and the management of information checklist**

1 Read as much as you can about your topic in the time you have, and keep a record of what you read.

Try not to exceed your time limit. It's easy to read on and on in the search for enlightenment.

2 Decide on a system of referencing sources.

The Harvard method is probably the easiest to deal with, but check whether your institution has its own rules.

3 When you record sources, make sure you always note the author's name, forename or initials, date of publication, title, place of publication and publisher. Remember to keep more than one copy.

There are variations for books, articles in collections and journal articles. It's not easy to remember all the detail, so keep model cards until you are familiar with the requirements.

4 Make notes of what seem to you to be important issues. Look for and keep a 'first thoughts' list of categories and keywords.

Make it clear in your notes which are the authors' words and which are your paraphrases, though paraphrases also need to be cited.

5 Ask yourself whether you can trust what you read. Any sign of bias? Is referencing accurate?

What evidence do the authors provide to support their claims? Check Chapter 7 for information about sources, evidence and the analysis of documentary evidence.

6 Electronic referencing can be the answer to all our prayers. You may have access to online bibliographic databases at your own institution, so ask, and if familiarization courses are offered, make sure you attend.

But if you plan to work from home, consider the time it will take to familiarize yourself with the various techniques, the cost, whether your computer has the necessary space on the hard drive *and* sufficient memory.

7 Make sure you get usernames and passwords. Ask in your department, the library or the computer helpline – and don't take 'Not available for you' for an answer.

Because without them, you may not be able to get access to the material you want.

8 Establish a system of indexing and cross-referencing.

There's no point in doing a large amount of reading if, at a later date, you can never find what you are looking for.

9 If you record your sources accurately and consistently you will have begun to establish good research habits and to lay the foundations for your own research.

You will be rewarded, if not in heaven, then certainly when you come to write your report.

10 A lot of fuss about nothing?

Certainly not! Just getting to grips with the tools of the trade. If you decide you can't be bothered to deal with the detail or will sort it out 'later', then referencing will give you real grief later on in your research, so be warned. Keep those model cards to hand and check each reference to make sure everything is included. Well, all right. I suppose that even the most pernickety amongst us isn't perfect, so if you know you have an incomplete reference, at least give it an asterisk, colour-code it or do something to indicate that you need to get the detail sorted as soon as you can.

Further reading

Baker, S. (1999) 'Finding and searching information sources', Chapter 5 in J. Bell, *Doing Your Research Project: A Guide for First-Time Researchers in Education and Social Science*, 3rd edn. Buckingham: Open University Press. Sally Baker is an experienced and skilled librarian at the Open University and, as far as I am concerned, knows a great deal about literature searches. This chapter includes sections on literature searching, search structure, sources of information, citations, getting to know your library, selecting keywords, finding books, journal articles, theses and Internet resources and managing information. Finally, the example of a literature search is provided, as are numerous Web page addresses, many of which are still current.

Orna, E. with Stevens, G. (1995) *Managing Information for Research*. Buckingham: Open University Press.

Pears, R. and Shields, G. (2004) *Cite Them Right: Referencing Made Easy*. Newcastle upon Tyne: Northumbria University Press. This can be accessed via http://www.unn.ac.uk/central/isd/cite/ and is updated regularly by the authors. They give examples of new media, such as the Internet, text messages, virtual learning environments and provide advice relating to plagiarism, secondary referencing and common conventions. They plan to produce an updated electronic version of the book in the near future, but I still like to have the print version to hand.

I use it regularly. Obtainable from Northumbria University Press, Northumbia University, Ellison Place, Newcastle upon Tyne, NE1 8ST (tel. 0191 227 3700) or email: er.books@northumbria.ac.uk).

Rumsey, S. (2004) *How to Find Information: A Guide for Researchers.* Maidenhead: Open University Press. The section on referencing, plagiarism and keeping up to date with new developments is particularly useful.

5

LITERATURE SEARCHING

In Chapter 4, I emphasized the importance of accurate referencing. Now, if your references are in good shape and if you have
begun to establish an easy-to-manage system of cross-referencing,
your hard work will be rewarded. If you are also familiar with one
of the online search tools such as EndNote, you are likely to have a
head start in the literature searching trail. However, even with
these advantages, you will still need to develop a search strategy
and to acquire search skills so that, as far as possible, you are able
to identify only those items which relate directly to your topic and
which eliminate the many thousands which do not.

The library search

If you are involved in a 100-hour project, be realistic. You are
working to a very limited time scale, so start with what is available
in your own library. Remember to ask if there are specialist
librarians in your own area of study because if there are, they can
save you many hours of fruitless searching. I hope I am right in
assuming that you will already be familiar with the layout of the
library and will already have consulted your **library catalogue**
and the **library web page**. If not, make sure you do. Library
web pages vary, as always, but the best give information about

passwords, IT support, information about the databases and journals to which your university, college or organization subscribes, copyright regulations relating to the use of electronic resources and off-site use. Regardless of the size of your investigation, never overlook what your home institution can provide.

Books

Head for the stacks, scan the book titles in and around your topic area and if you see anything that might be of interest, find a chair and a table and set to work. Examine the contents lists. Book titles can be misleading, but the contents lists will give you a good idea of what the books are really about and the language used. Take a quick look at any chapters which might be relevant to your topic, examine the index and the list of references for each book. Photocopying facilities are generally available in libraries, for a fee, so buy a photocopying card, if that is the system in use in your library. Read the copyright regulations which are usually kept somewhere close to the photocopier. If you have any doubts about the regulations, consult library staff about what you can and cannot do, what is legal and what is not.

Photocopy the list of references/bibliographies at the end of books and chapters which seem to be of interest and flag or highlight any items which you think might need to be followed up at a later stage. These lists can often provide invaluable additional sources. Some researchers file the photocopies and only record highlighted items if they decide to consult chapters or books some time later. I'm a compulsive recorder and I add all highlighted items to my cards immediately and then transfer them to my biographical list as soon as I can. If you carry a laptop around with you all the time, you can record them on the spot and, as my colleagues repeatedly tell me, then you don't waste time by doing the job twice.

Note possible **keywords** *and* add a note to remind you where you found the book (library classification number, floor and shelf number, main library or annexe, in another library, another country – anything which will help you to find it again).

Journals

Your library catalogue will include a list of journals to which your institution subscribes. Journals are expensive, regardless of whether they are on library shelves or only available in electronic format. Either way, the library has to pay and as costs of books and subscriptions to online materials accelerate, many institutions have to make decisions about what they can afford.

There are hundreds and hundreds of journals and it can be difficult to know which are likely to produce the most useful information, but all disciplines have a core of 'quality' journals which include nationally or even internationally refereed articles. Researchers will often begin their search with this elite group. However, that is not to say that they are the only ones worth consulting. There are many others which might be equally useful, so ask your supervisor and fellow students about likely titles, check whether they are available in print format and, if so, once again head for the stacks.

As with books, look at the list of contents at the front (or sometimes at the back) of the journals, read abstracts at the start of articles and make a note of any interesting items and possible keywords. Take a photocopy of lists of references and, if copyright conditions permit, of any articles which are related to your topic – *and*, as with books, add a note to indicate where the journal was located.

When you reach the stage of deciding you have probably done as much as you can for the time being on library searching, go through the lists of references again. If you discover that the same research is cited time and time again in different books or articles, it seems reasonable to conclude that it is regarded by other researchers as being of quality and worth consulting, even if it is twenty or thirty years old. Resources over ten or more years old are not always included on the Web, so ask the library staff whether copies are still kept in the library and if so, where. Quite often, journals older than three or four years are removed from the shelves but that does not necessarily mean they have been destroyed. One library I often use keeps up to ten years of copies somewhere in the nether regions of the library and another hires a warehouse for older stock. Students (and staff) then have to place an order for the required books or journals.

All is not lost if your library does not hold the items you need, because it might be possible to ask for copy of a book on inter-library loan from another library or to obtain a photocopy of the journal articles you need – sometimes for a fee. Library staff will know what services are available and how to get hold of what you want, so ASK.

Computer literature searching

It always helps to be a computer wizard, but it's still perfectly possible to carry out a computer literature search even though you may consider yourself to be technologically challenged. Take advantage of whatever guidance your supervisor, department, friends or library staff provide about searching. Find out whose job it is to help inexperienced computer literature searchers and always ask for help if you are stuck. Don't suffer in silence and never believe you are the only one who appears to be incapable of solving all search problems ten minutes after sitting down at a computer. You won't be. Many libraries provide courses on computer literature searching where you will be able to try out approaches and ask any questions. No matter how pressed for time you are, make sure you attend – even if you come into the wizard category. Literature searching involves special techniques and know-how and before you can begin to think about starting your search, you have some work to do.

Passwords, usernames and working from home

In many computer literature searches, you will need a **password** or **passwords, username** and sometimes, **authorization codes**, particularly if you wish to gain access to full-text items. Passwords may be allocated automatically by the library, your department, your departmental IT officer and/or computer centres, but prac-tices vary, so if nothing is said or done, ask in the library about who issues what.

You may find you need more than one password and username in order to be able to access some of the databases you need. For example, many large libraries subscribe to the ATHENS system which is designed to simplify database access for higher education students and which requires specific ATHENS passwords and usernames. Library staff will give you information about how to obtain them.

If you wish to work from home or from a different country, your passwords and username may give you the same access as if you were working in your main library, but not always. You may need new passwords and authorization codes or, as I mentioned in Chapter 4, you may even need an off-site licence. Your institution may or may not pay for the licence so, as always, ask library staff or the computer/IT officer in your department what has to be done.

Search engines

If any 'How to . . .' or 'Easy Searching Guides' are available in the library, they will take you step by step through the requirements of some of the search engines and databases to which your institution subscribes. Study the instructions, keep them to hand for further reference and add them to the 'Favourites' list on your computer so that you can refer to them in future rather than typing in the webpage address (URL) every time. However, even with the assistance of such guides, at some stage you may need to consult other search engines in order to obtain access to a wider range of materials.

Search engines trawl very large numbers of databases, looking for sources which mention your keywords/index terms/phrases and which provide access to thousands of web sites, a few of which are listed at the end of this chapter. They will vary in quality and in content and it can take time to try out several so ask your supervisor, friends, fellow students and specialist librarians which, in their view, are the most user friendly.

It's possible to obtain information on just about anything through the Internet, ranging from where to buy a hat to how to find a six-bedroom house in central London. At present, I am not in the market for either but if ever I were, I might well log on to Google (http://www.google.com/) which happens to be my first-choice search engine and I'm sure it will provide me with all the information I need. However, the problem with these huge databases is that there can be too much information for our purposes and the time taken to sift findings can be considerable.

Literature searchers have been using Google for many years, but now, the development of Google Scholar (http:/www.scholar.google.com/) is proving to be a considerable bonus for academic users. It follows the Google format by allowing us to search by keyword, subject or author and contains an extensive range of peer-reviewed papers, information about theses, reports, books and citations (the number of times an item is cited in other publications). I like books, to be able to handle books and read them in bed so I rather like the information that if I wish to consult a particular book, Google Scholar will tell me which libraries in Britain stock it.

Search tools

Irritatingly, search engines are a law unto themselves. Some will accept Boolean operators (AND, OR and NOT) between each keyword or phrase but many do not. If you undertake a Google search, you will be told that 'The "AND" operator is unnecessary – we include all search terms by default'. Other search engines just ignore them or may require a comma, brackets, question marks, plus and minus signs – or something else. A question mark can sometimes replace a single letter so that WOM?N will find 'woman' or 'women'. Depending on the search engine, an asterisk placed in the middle of a word (middle truncation) will deal with different spellings, as in COL*R, which will find 'color' and 'colour'. This may seem to be unnecessary, but remember that your keyword wording has to be precise and if you are searching an American database, 'colour' may not be recognized. If the asterisk is placed at the end of a word (right truncation), as in CHILD*, then 'child', 'children' and 'childhood' will be found.

The problem is that search engines and databases may use all, some or none of the above operators. Fortunately, on-screen help, the database helpline, fellow students who are skilled searchers and your library 'How to . . .' leaflets will generally let you know what is required. If not, then I'm afraid it is a case of trial and error.

Devising a search strategy

When the first edition of this book was published in 1987, relatively few researchers were skilled in computer searches. Now, many will regard the World Wide Web as their first and sometimes only line of inquiry. However, the basic procedures involved in literature searching are much the same now as they were in 1987, namely defining the parameters of the study and refining and focussing keywords which will allow you to identify relevant sources and, if possible, to eliminate most of the irrelevancies.

Defining the parameters of your search (search limiters)

Ask yourself the following questions:

1 *Are you only interested in materials in English?* Do you want worldwide sources or UK or . . .? Take care. Be realistic. If you ask for too much at the start of your search, you may be over-whelmed by the amount of material you identify.
2 *Do you want information about literature from 1800 to the present day?* You don't have unlimited time on a 100-hour study, nor on a much larger investigation, so *for a start*, start small. Limit yourself to what has been published in the past 5 or 10 years and only look earlier when you need more information or when your supervisor says you should expand your search. Not all supervisors agree with the 5–10 years suggestion. Two experienced supervisors of scientific research who read drafts of this chapter made it clear that even in a short project, they would expect researchers to cover a wider range of literature. They pointed out that if researchers ignored earlier quality research and what they described as 'standard texts', they would not be in a position to present a balanced picture of the development of knowledge in their topic area over a period of

time. I understand their concerns. In a large investigation such as a PhD, researchers will almost always be required to produce a full literature review but the amount of time a 100-hour researcher has to spend on searching is necessarily very limited, so ask your supervisor for guidance about literature review requirements. Try not to close the literature search door too soon, but always keep a check on the amount of time you allow for searching and do your best not to exceed it.

3 *Where do you plan to concentrate your study?* Hospitals, schools, universities, colleges, prisons, adult education centres? Try including your location in your keywords and see what is produced.

4 *Are you only interested in one discipline area?* If you are only concerned with barriers to learning for mature students in nursing, it might be reasonable to include 'nursing' in your keywords.

5 *Do you wish to identify only research carried out in Scotland, Singapore, Australia, the USA – or worldwide?* Does it matter?

6 *Does it matter whether members of your sample are in higher education or not?* If it's of no concern where they are, leave 'higher education' out of your keywords.

7 *Have you thought about alternative terminology?* Your keywords are 'mature students', 'barriers (to learning)' and 'higher education'. In computer searches, database indexers may not use the same terminology or spelling as you so make a list of synonyms and alternatives. Consult a dictionary and a thesaurus such as *Roget's Thesaurus of English Words and Phrases*. Sometimes, databases actually provide a thesaurus which enables you to adopt the keywords used in the database. If so, use it.

Individual and grouped keywords

Your purpose in conducting the literature search is not to identify sources which relate specifically to each of your keywords in turn because what you really want to discover is whether mature students (or older students) in higher education (or universities, or colleges) experience any barriers (or hurdles) which impede their learning (or success) and that means you have to include all keywords in your search request.

Some search engines may accept phrases; others will not, but before you become too tied down to focussing on your particular requirements, see what two of the very large search engines make of your topic title. Start with Yahoo (http://search.yahoo.com/). Key in 'barriers to learning for mature students in higher education'. You are told there are 57,900 results and clearly more focussing is required (numbers may change on different dates, but this at least gives an idea of the number of findings which are likely to be identified from the topic title on any date).

If you do the same with Google Scholar (http://www.scholar. google.com/) you discover there are 4,500 results. Far more promising, but still a very large number. Note the URL and add it to the 'Favourites' list in your computer so you can find it again, if necessary. Scroll down a few pages, make a note of anything which might possibly be worth following up, but don't get carried away.

Copyright and licensing restrictions

It's always helpful to skim through complete articles and reports to see if they are as useful as they appear to be *but* if you want to download web pages to a file and to use extracts from them at a later date you have to be really careful about copyright and licensing restrictions. Database helplines should inform you what you can download, print and use, and what you can't. If they don't, and if you have any doubts, ask for help from your supervisor and/or specialist librarian. Some institutions' web pages provide fairly full statements about what in legal terms is 'fair dealing' and what is not, so it's worth while seeing if yours is one of them. It's very easy now to cut and paste from web pages and I imagine we all do it from time to time, *but* if you are careless and fail to give full details of where items come from, when they were retrieved and whose words you are pasting into your own records, you could be in real trouble because you could find yourself involved in a plagiarism case. These days, plagiarism is a disciplinary issue in institutions of higher education and this could be very serious indeed. In the past, I think some researchers were caught in this particular spider's web because of genuine ignorance rather than deliberate attempts at deceit but now, so many verbal and printed warnings are given to students that institutions have little patience with the 'Well, I didn't know that was wrong' excuse. *So take care.*

Focusing your keywords

In the early stages of your search, you can't afford to spend too much time scrolling down very large numbers of pages, so begin to focus your requirements more sharply to eliminate more of the irrelevant items. Look back at the 'Defining the parameters' section and check whether you are clear about your answers to each item. Sometimes, if you are not finding useful results, it might be advisable to try alternative keywords. What about 'hurdles' instead of 'barriers to learning'? You might also have decided that 'higher education' wasn't important but 'post-graduate' might be, so see what Google Scholar makes of 'students+hurdles+postgraduate+nursing'. Now, you discover that only 26 results are found and even those of you who are working on 100-hour projects can probably find time to scroll down all 26 pages. You find there are some likely sources, but as usual, only two lines are provided for each item and it's difficult to know whether they are really useful until you've seen the full text. You may be able to 'View as HTML' and if you decide to follow this route, you will be directed to the materials you need to consult. Some will give you free access to full texts but others will require a password or even involve a fee. If some items relate to journal articles, the name of the journals are generally given. Make a note of them and later, see if they are available on the library shelves or in electronic format. A word of warning here. Some web sites won't let you go back, so experienced Internet searchers tell me they open web links in a new window to keep track of findings. Others have different systems, so ask around. Find out which approach computer wizard fellow students adopt and ask how they keep their web records so they can speedily refer back to them and go from one to another when necessary.

Time – yet again!

Sorry to repeat myself, but literature searching and particularly computer searching can become compulsive and easily overlap into the time allocated for other essential tasks, so at some stage you have to tell yourself that 'Enough is enough for the time being. Get on with the rest of the research'. No prevaricating. Be disciplined and remember that you can't search for ever and you can't know everything, even if you are working on a very large investigation.

The critical examination of evidence

As far as possible, it is your job as a researcher to consider the worth of the research you have identified in your searches. Ask yourself whether, in your opinion, it was well designed and whether the data-collecting instruments were suitable for the purpose. In Chapter 7, Brendan Duffy reminds us, amongst other things, that 'writers will rarely declare their assumptions so it is the task of the researcher to expose them if possible. Ask yourself whether there are any signs of bias and partisanship.' He asks 'Does the evidence supplied convincingly support the author's arguments?' He was writing about the analysis of documentary evidence, but his advice is equally valid in considering the worth of research reports. Of course, it's not always easy to answer his questions. We may have few problems about identifying obvious signs of bias in another researcher but we need to be equally watchful about our own. For example, we may agree so strongly with an author's conclusions that we fail to question whether those conclusions are fully justified. Then there is the problem about insufficient information on which to make a judgement. If you are carrying out all your searches on the Web, you may find that information about research design is not always provided in sufficient detail. All you can hope to do is to examine reports of research as thoroughly and objectively as time and your impartiality allow.

To conclude

I can't emphasize enough the importance of using the facilities provided by your own institution. For example, as long as you have a password and username, it's usual for large academic libraries to give free on-site access to Internet resources, and to the search engines, databases and full-text e-journals to which they subscribe. If you know you are not a sophisticated Internet user, remember to ask what skills training and IT support are available and if the response is 'None', then ask someone else, because not everyone knows what is on offer.

Institution web pages are almost always kept up to date, so check every time you log in, in case any changes have been made to regulations and availability of services.

Top ten guide to searching the Internet

A few weeks ago I asked Katie Horne, a friend and professional researcher, if she had any particular tips on literature searching. She consulted her colleagues and together they came up with the following Top Ten Guide to Searching the Internet (Horne 2004), which acts here as a summary for the chapter instead of the usual checklist. In item 7, you will see that she urges us to take steps to avoid spam. I never thought of that, so it just shows that you can always learn something useful by talking to other people!

1 Give yourself plenty of time. It isn't called the World Wide Web for nothing! There are massive quantities of information and massive amounts of blind alleys and it is important to allocate enough time for the search within the project plan. Conversely, it is also important to set yourself a limit. Web searching can be addictive and it is difficult to know where to draw the line. Although there may be some sites you wish to return to throughout the project to check for updates it is important that you keep web searching in proportion with the other aspects of your literature review.

2 Be optimistic! Start by typing in exactly what you are looking for e.g. 'barriers to learning for mature students in higher education'. You might get lucky, and if not, it can often be interesting to see what the search engine thinks is relevant.

3 Be prepared with search limiters. Before you start, think about how you are going to frame your search just as you would with a journal search. What other search terms could be used e.g. 'adult participation in learning'? Think through whether you want to limit your search to UK sites only (most search engines will let you specify this). It is also worth setting yourself parameters in terms of the age of articles referenced or the sector.

4 Know your search engines. Different search engines have different sponsored links so it is important to try a variety. Amongst the best known are Google and Yahoo but there are several others. There are also specialist sites such as Google Scholar so it is worth spending some time to see which of these sites is bringing up the most relevant hits for your search.

5 When you find something don't lose it! It is worth writing down the exact URL of the page you have found as sometimes a lot of time can be wasted trying to retrace your steps, especially as links from search engines change depending on the number of hits sites get and new sites being created. Making a note of the site may not always be enough though, as sometimes web sites are so complicated it can be difficult to relocate the exact page you were looking for. You can save web pages as well which is also a handy way of making the information available off line. Try to get in the habit of opening web links in a new window as some sites won't let you go back.

6 Don't underestimate the news. Sites such as the Guardian and the BBC have dedicated education and other specialist sections. Not only can these provide current stories which can help to bring your research right up to date; they will also contain links to any reports referenced or to relevant organizations.

7 Avoid spam. Many sites will ask you to register before you can access information, in many cases just to help them by

monitoring who is using their site. Registering will often mean entering your email address and unfortunately this can mean your name gets onto email lists and you will start receiving spam emails. One way to get round this is to set up a dedicated email address for your research at one of the free sites such as Yahoo and Hotmail. This way you can monitor the address for useful emails and then close the account once you have finished so you don't receive unwanted emails to your main address.

8 Networking – the old-fashioned type. Your best route to finding the most relevant sites and search engines is to talk to your contacts. See what search engines your colleagues recommend or if they have stumbled over any relevant web sites. With so many routes to accessing information, word of mouth can save a lot of time but don't just limit yourself to other people on your course. It is worth speaking to anyone who uses the Internet on a regular basis.

9 Referencing. With the increased use of cutting and pasting directly from the Internet it can be difficult to keep track of where information is coming from so whenever you paste information, paste the weblink too. It is worth pointing out you will also need to reference the exact time and date you accessed the site because of the transient nature of Internet content.

10 Patience and persistence! The Web is an invaluable tool for researchers because of the vast amount of information available. It is also an incredibly frustrating tool because of the vast amount of broken links and, in all honesty, rubbish that is out there. Web searching can be very frustrating and often feels like searching for a needle in a haystack but once you find that needle, everything becomes worthwhile.

Electronic sources of information

The World Wide Web contains millions of items of information and therein can lie the problem. You are not interested in millions. Only those which relate to your topic. The following web page addresses (URLs) may give you a start if you are new to online searching, but as I've said earlier in this chapter, ask friends, colleagues, your supervisor and your specialist librarian which search engines and databases are likely to provide user-friendly access to the information you need.

Search engines

Remember that your search engine and/or database helpline can often give useful tips on shortcuts, so use both wherever possible.

1 **Google** is said to be the most popular search engine in use today (http://www.google.com/) and many literature searchers have depended on it for years. However, the development of **Google Scholar** has been a valuable addition for academics. Unless you are advised otherwise, you might wish to try this first via http://www.scholar.google.com/. It includes useful sections on 'Frequently asked questions' under the headings of 'Searching and indexing', 'Accessing and citing' and 'About Google Scholar' (http://scholar.google.com/scholar/about.html). Well worth consulting.

2 **Yahoo** (http://search.yahoo.com/) is another very large search engine which seems fairly easy to use and which accepted our keywords without difficulty.

3 **AltaVista** (http://www.altavista.com), like Google, Google Scholar and Yahoo, contains millions of pages. I didn't find the helpline as helpful as some of the others but the searches seem to produce reasonable results. We are told that if we enter www.altavista.com into the browser, this clever search engine will know we're in the UK and will 'serve us' www.altavista.co.uk. This 'provides local content' and allows us to search the UK Web in English. That seems to be quite useful and if we plan to get everything from everywhere, we can always click the Worldwide button below the search box.

4 **Metacrawler** (http://www.metacrauler.com) is 'meta' because it allows us to search different search engines and databases – and to select which to use. It's busy though and I find it quite complicated. However, don't listen to me. I'm no computer wizard.

Internet gateways

These are directories or catalogues which select and evaluate sites and arrange resources in a systematic way, rather like a library. They provide alphabetical and annotated sources under your specified headings which is helpful because this can give you ideas about which aspect of your topic might be worth pursuing.

The **Social Science Information Gateway (SOSIG)** (http://sosig.ac.uk/) is a useful gateway which identifies good quality sites in Social Science, Education and Research Methods. Sources are contributed by librarians and subject specialists.

Databases, books, journal articles (and a few other resources)

1 The *Index to Theses with Abstracts Accepted for Higher Degrees by the Universities of Great Britain and Ireland*, is in print and also online at http://www.theses.com/.

2 **Whitaker's** *Books in Print* is generally available for consultation in the reference section of libraries but can also be searched via http://www.whsmith.co.uk/uhs/Go.asp This was formerly via the Internet Book Shop but if you try the Internet Book Shop (http://www.bookshop.co.uk) you will be referred to the W H Smith webpage.

3 **REGARD** is the Economic and Social Research Council database containing information funded by the ESRC and accessed online via http://www.regard.ac.uk/.

4 **ERIC US Department of Education** is a huge education database which can be accessed direct at http://www.eric.ed.gov or via OCLC FirstSearch (http://www.oclc.org/support/documentation/firstsearch/databases/dbdetails/details/ERIC.htm). It includes indexes, abstracts, conference proceedings, reports and many of the journals listed in the *British Education Index*. I have found their online thesaurus very useful, amongst other things in reminding me about the various differences between English and American spelling. You will need an ATHENS password and username.

5 **WorldCat** is also accessed via OCLC FirstSearch (http://www.oclc.org/firstsearch/content/worldcat/default.htm). This is an amazing database of several million bibliographic records contributed by 50,540 libraries. It includes full text electronic books and journals, webpage articles and audio and video recordings. It can even tell you about collections in your own library. It's amazing.

6 **Journal articles** are likely to produce more up-to-date references than books and if for any reason you can't find what you are looking for from WorldCat, you could go to http://www.scre.ac.uk/is/webjournals.html and see what is on offer. Some publishers and information providers will give you free access to the full text of articles.

7 **Statistical database on education and literacy worldwide**, based on UNESCO figures is available via http://www.unesco.org/en/about

8 **UK Official Statistical Publications** are available at the Office for National Statistics web site at http://www.statistics.gov.uk/

9 **Department for Education and Science (DFES)** statistics may be accessed via http://www.dfes.gov.uk/index.htm

10 **The Stationery Office** (http://www.tso.co.uk/) includes the full text of some official documents.

Libraries

1 **Academic libraries' conditions of use throughout the UK** can be found by checking individual library web sites via The University of Wolverhampton UK Sensitive Map located at http://.scit.wlv.ac.uk/ukinfo/uk.map.html. This gives free access to information about individual libraries in higher education in the UK and to their catalogues. This is particularly useful for those of you who do most of your searching away from your main campus, and who hope to be given access to a library nearer home. It gives useful information about what specialist stock is held and even provides details about opening and closing times in term time or during

vacations. Best to check before you go though in case the rules have changed.

2 **Public library catalogues.** Many public libraries have their catalogues online and holdings can be checked at http://dialspace.dial.pipex.com/town/square/ac940.

3 **COPAC** (Consortium of University Research Libraries Online Public Access Catalogue) via http://copac.ac.uk/copac gives access to the catalogues of the largest university research libraries in the UK and Ireland.

4 **The British Library Online Public Access Catalogue** holds almost 10 million records of material, including books, journals and conference proceedings in the Humanities (1975–), Science, Technology and Business (1974–), Retrospective (Pre-1975), Music (1980–) and Music (Pre- 1981). It also has links to environmental, healthcare and social sciences. Perhaps rather more than we shall need for our research, but real riches are here. Access is now free online via http://www.bl.uk/catalogues/blpc and is available 24 hours a day and seven days a week.

Citations and references

In Chapter 4, I mentioned that when sources were referred to (that is 'cited') in the text of your report, the full details must be given in your list of references or in your bibliography. A bibliography in this sense would include all, or at least many of the sources you consulted during the course of your research whereas a list of references at the end of your report would include every source you cited. A bibliography is not generally required in research reports but follow the procedures recommended by your institution and department.

1 Providing full details of books, journal articles and chapters in books is straightforward enough once you know how, but knowing how to reference material from newspapers, the World Wide Web, the Internet, online journals, radio reports and a good many other information sources can be more problematic. If you are drawing on any of these sources, it will

be as well to check with 'Cite Them Right' at http://www.unn. ac.uk/central/isd/cite/.

2 **Web of Knowledge (WoK)** is hosted by MIMAS (http://www.mimas.ac.uk/) run by Manchester Computing at The University of Manchester. It includes three very large databases, namely the Science Citation Index, the Social Sciences Citation Index and the Arts and Humanities Citation Index. If you are a member of a UK higher education or further education institution, you are entitled to obtain access to most MIMAS services free of charge. You may need to register online with your ATHENS password and username to search most sites and some are only available via site subscription.

You can search by topic, place, person or full search. Indexes, references or citations that are listed at the end of journal articles are included.

MIMAS provides a helpdesk service (by telephone on 0161 275 6109 (ask for ISI Web of Knowledge support) or by email at wok@mimas.ac.uk.

3 **EndNote**: www.endnote.com (manuals are usually available for consultation in your library). Your academic library may have purchased a site licence for EndNote, Reference Manager and/or Pro-Cite and one or all will usually be available at PC centres for on-campus use. As I mentioned in Chapter 4, it may be possible for you to purchase an off-site student licence in order to be able to use the software at home. Your library, computer centre or IT department will give you advice and, I hope, support and training, if necessary.

Health and ethics

1 **Royal College of Nursing (RCNONLINE):** www.rcn.org.uk.
2 **Health Education Research** is a journal published by Oxford University Press assisted by Stanford University Library's High Wire Press. Allows you to search for articles and to browse the archive via http:/www.her.oupjournals.org/.
3 **Department of Health research and development** includes information of interest to researchers and to public health and

social care workers, via http://www.doh.gov.uk/research/index.htm.

4 **Department of Health statistics** may be found at http://www.doh.gov.uk/public/stats1.htm.

5 *The Caldicott Report: Report on the Review of Patient-identifiable Information*. December 1997, Department of Health. Recommendations may be seen via http://www.doh.gov.uk/ipu/confiden/report/recs.htm.

6 *Data Protection Act 1998: An Introduction*. The home page is available at: http://www.doh.gov.uk/ipu/confiden/report/report/recs.htm

7 *Ethical Principles for Conducting Research with Human Participants* published by the British Psychological Society (BPS), is available at http://bps.org.uk/documents/code/pdf. This is particularly useful in relation to consent and confidentiality.

6

THE REVIEW OF THE LITERATURE

Hart considers a review of the literature is important because

> without it you will not acquire an understanding of your
> topic, of what has already been done on it, how it has been
> researched, and what the key issues are. In your written
> project you will be expected to show that you understand
> previous research on your topic. This amounts to showing
> that you have understood the main theories in the subject
> area and how they have been applied and developed, as well
> as the main criticisms that have been made of work on the
> topic.
>
> (Hart 1998: 1)

In Hart's view, 'the review is therefore a part of your academic
development – of becoming an expert in the field' (p. 1). A critical
review of the literature will be required in most cases for a PhD
but a project lasting two or three months will not require anything so ambitious. If your supervisor agrees, you may decide to
omit an initial review altogether. However, evidence of reading
will still be required and the procedures involved in producing
that evidence will be much the same, regardless of the size of the
task.

The 'critical review' of the literature

The main point to bear in mind is that a review should provide the reader with a picture, albeit limited in a short project, of the state of knowledge and of major questions in the subject. In principle, that sounds easy enough but in practice it can prove to be anything but easy. Haywood and Wragg wryly comment that critical reviews are more often than not uncritical reviews – what they describe as:

> The furniture sale catalogue, in which everything merits a one-paragraph entry no matter how skilfully it has been conducted: Bloggs (1975) found this, Smith (1976) found that, Jones (1977) found the other, Bloggs, Smith and Jones (1978) found happiness in heaven.
>
> (Haywood and Wragg 1982: 2)

They remind us that it requires discipline to produce a review which demonstrates 'that the writer has studied the work in the field with insight' (p. 2). It's easy to produce a furniture sale catalogue, to collect facts and to describe what is, but not so easy to produce this 'critical' review. It involves questioning assumptions, querying claims made for which no evidence has been provided, considering the findings of one researcher compared to those of others and evaluating. All researchers collect many facts, but then must select, organize and classify findings into a coherent pattern. Verma and Beard agree that literature reviews must identify and explain relevant relationships between facts, but they also consider that

> the researcher must produce a concept or build a theoretical structure that can explain facts and the relationships between them . . . The importance of theory is to help the investigator summarize previous information and guide his future course of action. Sometimes the formulation of a theory may indicate missing ideas or links and the kinds of additional data required. Thus, a theory is an essential tool of research in stimulating the advancement of knowledge still further.
>
> (Verma and Beard 1981: 10)

This raises a number of issues relating to the meaning of 'theory' and of 'theoretical structure' and so before we look at extracts from some successful literature reviews, perhaps I should make sure we all mean the same thing when we speak about 'theory'. And that presents a few little problems because different people have slightly different views about meaning.

Theory and theoretical (or conceptual) frameworks

'Theory' has been explained as being 'a set of interrelated abstract propositions about human affairs and the social world that explain their regularities and relationships' (Brewer 2000: 192), as 'a proposition about the relationship between things' (Denscombe 1998: 240) or '*theory* at the lowest level can be an *ad hoc* classification system, consisting of categories which organise and summarise empirical observations' (Bowling 2002: 139). She continues that:

> It can be a taxonomy which is a descriptive categorical system constructed to fit the empirical observations in order to describe the relationships between categories (e.g. in a health care budget: spending on acute services, non-acute services, health promotion activities and so on).
>
> (p. 140)

However, it can be and often is merely taken to refer to the current state of knowledge in a subject derived from the published literature – what Wolcott (1992: 3–52) described as 'theory first' rather than 'theory after'. Punch clarifies the difference between the two as follows:

> In theory-first research, we start with a theory, deduce hypotheses from it, and design a study to test these hypotheses. This is theory verification. In theory-after research, we do not start with a theory. Instead, the aim is to end up with a theory, developed systematically from the data we have collected. This is theory generation.
>
> (Punch 1998: 16)

Care has to be taken before embarking on a 'theory after' approach, mainly because it requires the collection of a great deal of data which is inevitably well beyond the time scale and scope of most small (or smallish) studies. Not impossible for a PhD but still difficult.

Cohen, Manion and Morrison point out that 'model' is sometimes used instead of or interchangeably with 'theory':

> Both may be seen as explanatory devices . . . though models are often characterized by the use of analogies to give a more graphic or visual representation of a particular phenomenon. Providing they are accurate and do not misrepresent the facts, models can be of great help in achieving clarity and focusing on key issues.
>
> (Cohen, Manion and Morrison 2000: 12–13)

I particularly like Miles and Huberman's admirably clear statement about what they see as theory building and conceptual frameworks. They write that:

> Theory building relies on a few general constructs that subsume a mountain of particulars. Terms such as 'stress' or 'role conflict' are typically labels we put on bins containing a lot of discrete events and behaviours. When we assign a label to a bin, we may or may not know how all the contents of the bin fit together, or how this bin relates to another. But any researcher, no matter how inductive in approach, knows which bins to start with and what their general contents are likely to be. Bins come from theory and experience and (often) from the general objectives of the study envisioned. Laying out those bins, giving each a descriptive or inferential name, and getting some clarity about their interrelationships is what a conceptual framework is all about.
>
> (Miles and Huberman 1994: 18)

The label is not important, but the process of establishing a map or framework of how the research will be conducted and analysed is. As Polit and Hungler point out:

Frameworks are efficient mechanisms for drawing together and summarizing accumulated facts ... The linkage of findings into a coherent structure makes the body of accumulated knowledge more accessible and, thus, more useful both to practitioners who seek to implement findings and to researchers who seek to extend the knowledge base.

(Polit and Hungler 1995: 101)

So, a theoretical framework is an explanatory device 'which explains either graphically or in narrative form, the main things to be studied – the key factors, constructs or variables – and the presumed relationships among them' (Miles and Huberman 1994: 18). It is 'an efficient mechanism for drawing together and summarizing accumulated facts ... which makes the body of accumulated knowledge more accessible and, thus, more useful both to practitioners who seek to implement findings and to researchers who seek to extend the knowledge base' (Polit and Hungler 1995: 101).

I find that 'theory' and 'theoretical frameworks' can on some occasions be used in variable ways, depending on the interpretation and understanding of individual researchers. I do sometimes become concerned at the view that research cannot proceed unless it has a sound 'theoretical base', mainly because I am not always sure what that means in the context of some of the research being considered. These issues need to be discussed or else, 'what might become an opportunity for an informed dialogue about theory, and a concomitant review of the roles it can play, is represented instead as an obstacle' (Wolcott 2001: 80). I hope you will always able to engage in 'informed dialogue' with your supervisor and to ask for clarification if terminology, principles, meaning and ideas are new to you.

The 'critical review' in practice

All the work you have already done in identifying keywords, major issues and categories will now help in establishing a framework for your analysis and review of the literature. Even where all the necessary groundwork has been done, difficulties can still remain, not least because any research involving human beings has to take account of the inevitably large number of variables involved which make it difficult to establish any common patterns of behaviour or experience. And then there is the difficulty of researchers starting from different bases so that comparing like with like becomes problematic. However, in spite of the difficulties inherent in the production of any review of the literature, let's look now at short extracts from three successful reviews. The first two were produced by first-time researchers. The third was produced by two very experienced academics and researchers.

The Clara Nai review

The first extract comes from a literature review produced by Clara Nai. She was investigating barriers to what she described as continuous learning amongst mature workers at Singapore airport. She discussed in some detail her own methodology, the methodology used by other researchers and the problems she faced in synthesizing the very large amount of information obtained about barriers to learning. She had read a great deal and faced the usual difficulties in grouping what she felt to be significant research findings. She writes:

> Having read so much, it took me a while to reconcile what I can present in a condensed review. It seems so unfair that only a fraction of the months of painstaking reading could appear in print. Putting sentiments aside, I have decided . . . to classify the factors affecting participation under some major headings for ease of consolidation.
>
> (Nai 1996: 33)

I imagine a good many new and experienced researchers will sympathize with Clara's exasperation. Identifying categories early in reading helps, even if some have to be rejected and others added but if no attempt has been made, then deciding on categories becomes very difficult *and* extremely time-consuming. Clara sensibly examined the way other researchers had categorized their findings and decided to use the broad grouping into situational, institutional and dispositional barriers to learning adopted by Cross (1981). There is no reason why researchers should not adopt a methodology devised by someone else, *as long as the source is acknowledged.*

The choice of headings worked well. There is insufficient space here to reproduce the full review, but I hope the following extract from Clara's 'institutional barriers' section gives an idea of the way she approached the task.

Institutional barriers rank second in importance after situational barriers, accounting for between 10 and 25% of potential learners among respondents in most surveys (Cross 1981). They are policies and procedures usually unintentionally put up by policymakers, human resource personnel or educational providers.

Cross has grouped institutional barriers under 'scheduling problems', 'location/transportation problems', 'lack of interesting, practical or relevant courses', 'procedural registration problems', 'strict admission criteria' and 'lack of information'. Of these, up to a quarter cited inconvenient locations, inconvenient scheduling and the lack of interesting or relevant courses as the greatest barriers to participation.

(Nai 1996: 35–6)

Finally, she concluded that reports of research into initiatives relating to the removal of various institutional barriers for adult learners in the UK and the USA were not encouraging. Numerous obstacles were identified confronting adults who wished to continue their education. Even though some higher education institutions were beginning to reschedule class times, to waive tuition or to reduce fees for economically disadvantaged students, the findings were that many adults still faced difficulties in returning to study.

Brief though this extract is, does it begin to provide you with at least some background to the problem of institutional barriers and also to the way Clara grouped her findings?

The Gilbert Fan review

Time to move on to the second review, which was carried out by Gilbert Fan. At the time he carried out his research, he was a member of staff in a School of Health Sciences in Singapore and was involved in his institution's Diploma in Nursing programme. He knew that certain concerns were being expressed nationally and internationally about nurse education, including a decline in student enrolment in nursing programmes, the apparent low status of nursing, which was believed to have contributed to poor recruitment, and high attrition rates leading to a shortage of nurses. He decided that a study of students' perceptions of their Diploma programme in particular and of the nursing profession in general would be useful to him and would contribute to the School's understanding of the programme *from a student perspective*.

He had read widely and his literature review was extensive. He knew he could not include all his sources and so he had to decide on specific topics which were of particular interest to him and under which he could group his findings. Though there were relatively few Singaporean studies on which to draw, he found there was plenty to choose from other countries, mainly the USA, the UK and Australia. He grouped his findings under the headings of:

- the decline in student enrolment in nursing education;
- curricula, types of nursing education and nursing competencies;
- teaching and clinical supervision in nursing education programmes;
- the relationship between nursing education and the profession; and
- nursing as a career choice.

Each of the above topics was thoroughly explored and documented and the review ran to 32 pages – more than was required for a Master's thesis, but Gilbert was nothing if not thorough. This small extract, which covered only half a page, is part of the section on the decline in student enrolment but I hope it gives you an idea of how he approached his task.

Pillitteri (1994: 132) sees the decline in student enrolment in nursing education programmes to be a serious concern for the profession and Naylor (1990: 123) projected that the total number of new graduands from all the nursing programmes in the USA would drop from 82,700 in 1985 to 68,700 in 1995. Among the reasons for such a decline was that students did not find nursing attractive as a lifelong career. Such perceptions were perpetuated by unrealistic portrayal of nursing in the mass media and the alternative careers that women could enter today (Brooks 1989: 121; Fagin et al. 1988: 367; Kelsey 1990 cited in Pillitteri 1994: 132).

(Fan 1998: 31)

Subsequent paragraphs deal further with research findings from all four countries (the USA, the UK, Australia and Singapore) which, in spite of the fact that each country has a different system of nurse education, identified similar reasons for the decline in student recruitment and high turnover, namely the traditional structure of nurse education, poor career advancement, job dissatisfaction, inflexible work schedules, staff shortage, low pay, family commitments, relocation of family, unsupportive supervisors and lack of opportunities for career advancement. He supports each of the items with the name, date and page number of the sources and of course, the full details of each are provided in the full list of references at the end of the thesis.

Gilbert made a good job of categorizing his findings under the five main headings, each of which had sub-headings. Even with the ongoing work of recording, categorizing and re-categorizing, the production of this review must have been complex. However, he succeeded and not only produced a good review, but also a good thesis.

The Richardson and Woodley review

On to the third example which is a small extract taken from a journal article produced by John Richardson and Alan Woodley and entitled 'Another look at the role of age, gender and subject as predictors of academic attainment in higher education'

(Richardson and Woodley 2003). Both are experienced researchers, and over the years produced a number of research papers concerned with this topic (Woodley 1981, 1984, 1985, 1998; Woodley and McIntosh 1980 and Richardson and King 1998).

In 2003, they published the results of their updated and extended investigation into the academic attainment of mature students in higher education. Consider the first paragraph of the Introduction to this study which makes clear what they intend to do. They write:

> In this article, we examine the role of a student's age, gender and subject of study as predictors of their academic attainment in higher education, and in particular as predictors of the classes of first degrees awarded by institutions of higher education in the UK. There has been a good deal of interest in this topic over the last 30 years, and our analysis builds on the findings of several previous investigations that examined the performance of graduates in the UK.
>
> (Richardson and Woodley 2003: 475)

Readers are then referred to a table listing previous analyses of predictors of academic in UK higher education from 1964 to 2001.

They continue by analysing their own findings under the headings of: age and academic attainment; gender and academic attainment; subject of study and academic attainment. These are followed by variations and groupings relating to age, gender and subject of study. The following extract is taken from their section on age and academic attainment:

> Interest in the role of age as a predictor of academic attainment is often motivated by a stereotype of older people as being deficient in intellectual skills (Richardson and King 1998). Cross-sectional studies comparing groups of different ages have indicated that there is a slight decline in intellectual function between the ages of 18 and 60, with a more pronounced decline thereafter (e.g. Nyberg *et al.* 1996; Verhaeghen and Salthouse (1997). Such results are, however, contaminated by cohort differences in life experience, and

longitudinal studies comparing the *same* groups at different ages often find no statistically significant decline before the age of 60 (Schaie 1996: 107–36). When any age-related changes in performance are observed, they typically amount to a reduction in information processing, whereas access to stored information is usually unaffected (Klatzky 1988; Nyberg *et al.* 1996). There is thus no reason to expect a reduction in attainment with advancing age in situations that demand the retrieval of knowledge (Baltes *et al.* 1984), except when they involve time pressure (Verhaeghen and Salthouse 1997). Of course, one situation that fits the latter description is the traditional unseen examination.

(Richardson and Woodley 2003: 477–8)

Read this again, but perhaps more slowly this time. Take note of the language Richardson and Woodley use, the care they take in drawing conclusions from the research findings and the way some of the findings are qualified. If you have time, consult the full article and examine the ways in which findings are categorized.

Reviewing the reviews

Look back at all three extracts in this chapter. Richardson and Woodley already had extensive knowledge of their topic before they undertook the work involved in their 2003 article and they were able to produce an exhaustive review of previous studies relating to the influence of age, gender and subject of study on academic attainment. Clara Nai and Gilbert Fan were first-time researchers and though they knew a great deal about issues relating to their work and had identified a topic of interest very early in their studies, they did not have the advantage of a firm knowledge base about previous research. They were not required to produce an exhaustive review of the research findings relating to their topic: it was sufficient for them to produce a relatively brief account of the selected literature and to draw some conclusions where possible, bearing in mind the care needed in making claims. Their early ideas about likely headings, groups and categories were based mainly on their personal and professional experience and were gradually added to, adapted or completely changed during the course of their reading.

Remember!

We can all learn a great deal by reading what other researchers have done. Look critically at all reviews which come your way. Ask yourself whether they are furniture sale catalogues or well-organized accounts which are relevant to the topic. Research findings can be dangerous if they are used in an undisciplined way and I feel a certain anxiety when I am told that 'research proves x or y' when I see no corroborating evidence to warrant such an assertion. Watch your language! Inferences may possibly be drawn, results 'might indicate', but remember that in any dealings with human beings, 'proof' is hard to come by.

◉ The review of the literature checklist

1 Evidence of reading will always be required in any research.

Though in a small study, it may not be necessary to produce a full literature review.

2 Researchers collect many facts but then must select, organize and classify findings into a coherent pattern.

The aim is to produce a critical review, not a list of everything you have read.

3 Your framework will not only provide a map of how the research will be conducted and analysed but it will also give you ideas about a structure for your review.

It will help you to draw together and summarize facts and findings.

4 Literature reviews should be succinct and, as far as is possible in a small study, should give a picture of the state of knowledge and of major questions in your topic area.

If you have been able to classify your reading into groups, categories or under headings, writing your review will be relatively straightforward.

5 Ensure that all references are complete. Note the page numbers of any quotations and paraphrases of good ideas. You cannot use them without acknowledging the source. If you do, you may become involved in a plagiarism challenge.	It should be possible for any readers to locate your sources.
6 Watch your language. Perhaps inferences may be drawn, but 'proof' is hard to come by when dealing with human beings.	Make no claims which cannot be justified from the evidence you have presented. Consider again the wording Richardson and Woodley use in the extract from their article.
7 Examine your sources critically before you decide to use them.	Any sign of bias, inappropriate language, or false claims? Are you able to trust the authors' judgements?
8 Remember that unless you are comparing like with like, you can make no claims for comparability.	Researchers often start their research from different bases and make use of different methods of data collecting. You may still wish to use their findings, but be careful about how you discuss them.
9 Do not be tempted to leave out any reports of research merely because they differ from your own findings.	It can be helpful to include differing results. Discuss whether they undermine your own case – or not.
10 Start the first draft of your review early in your reading. Many more drafts will be required before you have a coherent and 'critical' account but better to start small and then build on your first attempt than to have to make sense of everything you have read at one attempt.	As you continue, entries will be deleted and others added, but you will have made a start. Better to be faced with a badly-written, inadequate review than a blank page.

Further reading

Baker, S. and Carty, J. (1994) 'Literature searching: finding, organizing and recording information', in N. Bennett, R. Glatter and R. Levačić (eds) *Improving Educational Management Through Research and Consultancy*. London: Paul Chapman Publishing.

Blaxter, L., Hughes, C. and Tight, M. (2001) *How to Research*, 2nd edn. Buckingham: Open University Press. Pages 110–25 give really useful guidance about reading for research, sources of information in the library and on the Internet, literature searches and critical reading.

Gash, S. (1989) *Effective Literature Searching for Students*. Aldershot: Gower.

Hart, C. (1998) *Doing a Literature Review: Releasing the Social Science Research Imagination*. London: Sage, in association with The Open University (Open University reader for course D820 'The Challenge of the Social Sciences'). Chapter 7, 'Writing the Review', is helpful, though its 30+ pages are rather detailed for researchers who are not required to produce a full literature review. However, even if no full review is required, the appendices on 'the proposal', 'how to cite references', 'presentation of a dissertation', 'managing information and keeping records' and 'a checklist of dos and don'ts for reviewing' will still be useful.

Laws, S. with Harper, C. and Marcus, R. (2003) *Research for Development: A Practical Guide*. London: Sage. Chapter 12, pages 213–32 provides excellent checklists about planning, carrying out and writing up the literature, together with guidance about using a library and how to use the Internet for research.

Murray, R. (2002) *How to Write a Thesis*. Maidenhead: Open University Press. Pages 101–16 discuss definitions and purposes of literature reviews, justification for the inclusion and omission of literature and plagiarism.

Richardson, J.T.E. and Woodley, A. (2003) 'Another look at the role of age, gender and subject as predictors of academic attainment in higher education', *Studies in Higher Education* 28 (4): 476–93.

Talbot, C. J. (2003) *Studying at a Distance: A Guide for Students*. Maidenhead: Open University Press. Pages 119–24 deal with literature searching and reviewing, using the World Wide Web for research, search strategies, information about bibliographic databases on the web and off-campus access to electronic resources. Brief but helpful.

 **Part II**

SELECTING METHODS OF DATA COLLECTION

INTRODUCTION

When you have decided on a topic, refined it and specified objectives, you will be in a position to consider how to collect the evidence you require. The initial question is not 'Which methodology?' but 'What do I need to know and why?' Only then do you ask 'What is the best way to collect information?' and 'When I have this information, what shall I do with it?'

No approach depends solely on one method any more than it would exclude a method merely because it is labelled 'quantitative', 'qualitative', 'case study', 'action research', or whatever. As I indicated in Chapter 1 some approaches depend heavily on one type of data-collecting method – but not exclusively. You may consider that a study making use of a questionnaire will inevitably be quantitative, but it may also have qualitative features. Case studies, which are generally considered to be qualitative studies, can combine a wide range of methods, including quantitative techniques. Methods are selected because they will provide the data you require to produce a complete piece of research. Decisions have to be made about which methods are best for particular purposes and then data-collecting instruments must be designed to do the job.

Constraints

The extent of your data collecting will be influenced by the amount of time you have. This may seem a rather negative approach, but there is no point in producing a grandiose scheme that requires a year and a team of researchers if you are on your own, have no funds and in any case have to hand in the project report in three months. Even so, if possible, efforts should be made to cross-check findings, and in a more extensive study, to use more than one method of data collecting. This multi-method approach is known as *triangulation*.

Laws points out that 'the key to triangulation is to see the same thing from different perspectives and thus to be able to confirm or challenge the findings of one method with those of another'. She warns that

> Accounts collected from different perspectives may not match tidily at all. There may be mismatch and even conflict between them. A mismatch does not necessarily mean that the data collection process is flawed – it could be that people just have very different accounts of similar phenomena. You need to critically examine the meaning of any mismatches to make sense of them.
>
> (Laws 2003: 281)

One problem for short-term researchers is that examining the meaning and making sense of any mismatches takes time and so most 100-hour projects are likely to be limited to single-method studies. You just do the best you can in the available time. There are likely to be other constraints. For example, if you wish to observe meetings, you will be limited by the number and timing of meetings that are scheduled to take place in the period of your study. The willingness of people to be interviewed, or observed, to complete the questionnaire or diaries will inevitably affect your decisions as to which instruments to use. You may feel that a postal questionnaire would be the most suitable method of obtaining certain information, but postal questionnaires can cost quite a lot of money, so you will have to consider whether funds can be found, and whether this expenditure would be worthwhile.

Reliability and validity

Whatever procedure for collecting data is selected, it should always be examined critically to assess to what extent it is likely to be reliable and valid. *Reliability* is the extent to which a test or procedure produces similar results under constant conditions on all occasions. A clock which runs ten minutes slow some days and fast on other days is unreliable. A factual question which may produce one type of answer on one occasion but a different answer on another is equally unreliable. Questions which ask for opinions may produce different answers for a whole range of reasons. The respondent may just have seen a television programme which affected opinions or may have had some experience which angered or pleased and so affected the response. Wragg (1980: 17), writing about interviews asks: 'Would two interviewers using the same schedule or procedure get a similar result? Would an interviewer obtain a similar picture using the procedures on different occasions?' These are reasonable questions to put to yourself when you check items on a questionnaire or interview schedule.

There are a number of devices for checking reliability in scales and tests, such as 'test–retest' (administering the same test some time after the first), the 'alternate forms method' (where equivalent versions of the same items are given and results correlated) or the 'split-half method' (where the items in the test are split into two matched halves and scores then correlated). These methods are not always feasible or necessary, and there are disadvantages and problems associated with all three. Generally, unless your supervisor advises otherwise, such checking mechanisms will not be necessary unless you are attempting to produce a test or scale. The check for reliability will come at the stage of question wording and piloting of the instrument.

Validity is an altogether more complex concept. Usual definitions of validity are that it tells us whether an item or instrument measures or describes what it is supposed to measure or describe, but this is rather vague and leaves many questions unanswered. Sapsford and Jupp (1996) offer a more precise definition. They take 'validity' to mean 'the design of research to provide credible conclusions; whether the evidence which the research offers can bear the weight of the interpretation that is put on it' (p. 1). They argue that what has to be established is whether data:

> *Do* measure or characterize what the authors claim, and that the interpretations *do* follow from them. The structure of a piece of research determines the conclusions that can be drawn from it and, most importantly, the conclusions that *should not* be drawn from it.
>
> (Sapsford and Jupp 1996: 1)

If an item is unreliable, then it must also lack validity, but a reliable item is not necessarily also valid. It could produce the same or similar responses on all occasions, but not be measuring what it is supposed to measure. Measuring the extent of validity can become extremely involved, and there are many variations and subdivisions. For the purpose of 100-hour projects that are not concerned with complex testing and measurement, it is rarely necessary to delve deeply into the measurement of validity, though efforts should be made to examine items critically.

Ask yourself whether another researcher using your research instrument and asking factual questions would be likely to get the same or similar responses. Tell other people (colleagues, pilot respondents, fellow students) what you are trying to find out or to measure and ask them whether the questions or items you have devised are likely to do the job. This rough-and-ready method will at least remind you of the need to achieve some degree of reliability and validity in question wording even though it is unlikely to satisfy researchers involved with administering scales and tests with large numbers of subjects. If you are involved in the validity of scaled measures, you might wish to consult the items included in the Further Reading at the end of this section.

Thinking about computer data analysis?   ◉

If you think you might wish to make use of computer software to analyse your returns, take care over the design of all your data-collecting instruments because the way you word questions may result in responses that are difficult to analyse. Ask what courses and advice are available about using computer packages for analysing quantitative *and* qualitative data. These days, simple data analysis is made fairly easy. There is no longer any necessity or requirement to learn and remember complex formulae. The computer does it for you. Magic? Well, a help but not magic. It's easy to become seduced by yards and yards of computer printouts, but they have to be filtered to get to the *meaning* of all those figures and sheets, to understand what can be claimed from them and what can't.

Using computer packages for data analysis requires preparation. For a start, make sure you are familiar with what your own or your department's computers will do. Obvious? Well, of course, but many new research students have optimistically bought a new, or even their first computer in the hope that it will simplify the whole business of research. It might, but not until you have mastered the techniques involved.

Find out what computer use and computer data analysis courses are available, if possible *before* your research proper begins. Ask for advice about who in your organization is available to give advice. These days, many departments have a research and data analysis adviser, so make sure you know who that is. The way you word your questions may influence the type of analysis you are able to carry out, so always make sure the wording is checked by your supervisor/research adviser/data analysis adviser before you finalize all data-collecting instruments and regardless of whether your research will be mainly quantitative or qualitative.

Not thinking about computer data analysis?

No problem with that and particularly in small or relatively small, time-limited studies, it may be better to keep to manual methods of data analysis and interpretation of the results. Research is not about computers, though there is little doubt that they have eased our burdens in many ways. As I've said throughout this book, it is about careful selection of a topic, being sure about the purpose of your study, negotiating access to institutions, materials and people, devising suitable methods of data collection, observing the ethics of research, collecting, analysing and interpreting results and producing a well-written report ON TIME. So, time to read on.

A reminder

It is often worrying for first-time researchers to know how many questionnaires should be distributed or interviews given. There are no set rules, and you should ask for guidance from your supervisor before you commit yourself to a grand plan that will be far in excess of what is required. Your aim is to obtain as representative a range of responses as possible to enable you to fulfil the objectives of your study and to provide answers to key questions.

Research instruments are selected and devised to enable you to obtain these answers. The instrument is merely the tool to enable you to gather data, and it is important to select the best tool for the job. The following chapters take you through the processes involved in the analysis of documentary evidence, designing and administering questionnaires, planning and conducting interviews, diaries and observation studies. Little attention is given to the analysis of data in this part, but all data have to be analysed and interpreted to be of any use, and so Chapters 12 and 13 in Part III should be studied in association with the chapters in Part II.

Further reading

Hayes, N. (2000) *Doing Psychological Research*. Buckingham: Open University Press. Pages 209–12 consider reliability in discourse analysis; pages 98–101 in psychometric tests and page 169 in qualitative research. Validity is examined throughout the book, so consult the index.

Oppenheim, A.N. (1992) *Questionnaire Design, Interviewing and Attitude Measurement*, new edition. London: Cassell. Oppenheim discusses the reliability of attitude questions, pages 147–8; of attitude scales, pages 163–6; of coding, pages 266–8; of questions, pages 144–8; and of scaled measures, pages 159–60, pages 162, 188 and 283. Validity is dealt with in even more detail, from pages 147–63. However, there is more, so once again, best to consult the index.

Punch, K.F. (1998) *Introduction to Social Research: Quantitative and Qualitative Approaches*. London: Sage. In four pages (99–102), Punch provides a brief but very sound introduction to reliability and validity. Well worth reading.

Sapsford, R. and Jupp, V. (1996) *Data Collection and Analysis*. London: Sage.

Scaife, J. (2004) 'Reliability, validity and credibility', Chapter 4 in C. Opie (ed.) *Doing Educational Research: A Guide to First-time Researchers*. London: Sage.

7

THE ANALYSIS OF DOCUMENTARY EVIDENCE

Brendan Duffy

Most projects will require the analysis of documentary evidence. This chapter aims to explain how to locate, categorize, select and analyse documents. Its approach is derived from historical methods which are essentially concerned with the problems of selection and evaluation of evidence. Such methods were first developed by von Ranke and have influenced the form of all academic report writing (Evans 2000: 18; Barzun and Graff 1992: 5). In some projects documentary analysis will be used to supplement information obtained by other methods, as for instance when the reliability of evidence gathered from interviews or questionnaires is checked. In others, it will be the central or even exclusive method of research. It will be particularly useful when access to the subjects of research is difficult or impossible, as in the case where a longitudinal study is undertaken and staff members no longer belong to the organization being investigated. The lack of access to research subjects may be frustrating, but documentary analysis of files and records can prove to be an extremely valuable alternative source of data (Johnson 1984: 23).

Approaches to documents

When embarking on a study using documents it is possible to have two different approaches. One has been called the 'source-oriented' approach in which you let the nature of the sources determine your project and help you generate questions for your research. The feasibility of the project would be determined by the nature of extant sources so that a particularly full collection of material, for example, on the restructuring of a college, would lead to an investigation of that area. You would not bring predetermined questions to the sources but would be led by the material they contain. The second and much more common way of proceeding would be to employ the 'problem-oriented approach' which involves formulating questions by using other research methods and then by reading secondary sources. This method investigates what has already been discovered about the subject before establishing the focus of the study and then researching the relevant primary sources (these terms are defined below). As your research progresses, a much clearer idea of which sources are relevant will emerge and more questions will occur to you as your knowledge of the subject deepens (Tosh 2002: Ch. 4).

The location of documents

Document searches need to be carried out in exactly the same way as literature searches in order to assess whether your proposed project is feasible and to inform yourself about the background to, and the nature of, the subject. The document search may have to cover both national and local sources of evidence.

At the local level, the nature of the project will lead you to particular sources. A project on the relationship between a college and its funding body would require a document search of the records of both institutions and account would have to be taken of their special characteristics. If the college had an academic board or equivalent, its minutes would be one source; if the funding authority's departments dealt with different aspects of the college's administration, their records would be significant. It is important to inquire what archives or collections of records exist in an organization. In schools, which records are preserved by the office, the governing body, the bursar or financial officer or the library and which records are stored by individuals or departments in the institution? Does the local education authority hold records for particular schools? How long do organizations hold on to records before they dispose of them? Schools have a legal duty to preserve attendance registers for the current year and the next two years. Informed advice, however, suggests that admission registers should be stored indefinitely. It has also been suggested by a headteachers professional association that pupils' records be kept for at least ten years and the results of public examinations kept indefinitely (Croner 2002: 1–360).

Local education authorities issue guidance on the preservation of records of different types including financial documents, documents related to supplies, employee-related documents and general documents. It can be helpful to be aware of these requirements and the arrangements for storing and gaining access to local documents by authorities. The safeguarding of 'school annals' to record events deserving of permanent record in the history of a school is at the discretion of the school. Researchers can be frustrated by the official and unofficial weeding policy of institutions and of government departments which may have resulted in the destruction of sources later discovered to be significant (Duffy 1998: 29–30).

National records have proliferated since the advent of a national education system and it is important to decide which official sources are needed for a particular local project. Such sources can be published *and* unpublished. A project may require a trawl of government green papers, white papers, guidance papers, government statistics, inspection reports, statutes, policy papers, as well as the scrutiny of the local sources. The Internet is an invaluable aid to locating official documents but as a researcher you must also be prepared to hunt down other sources of information particularly in the local context (McCulloch and Richardson 2000: 86). It can never be assumed, of course, that just because documents exist, they will be available for research. Some sources may be regarded as too confidential to be released, so enquiries would have to be made about access and availability.

The nature of documentary evidence

During the document search it is helpful to clarify exactly what kinds of documents exist. 'Document' is a general term for an impression left on a physical object by a human being. Research can involve the analysis of photographs, films, videos, slides and other non-written sources, all of which can be classed as documents, but the most common kinds of documents in educational research are written as printed or manuscript sources, so this chapter concentrates on these. Sources can also be quantitative or statistical in nature but it would be mistaken, of course, to regard these so-called 'hard' sources of evidence as being more reliable than other kinds of material. It is vitally important to employ the recommended critical method of analysis to check how the figures have been produced. What has been counted? How correctly? By whom? When? Where? And why? (Stanford 1994).

Primary and secondary sources

Documents can be divided into primary and secondary sources. **Primary sources** are those which came into existence in the period under research (e.g. the minutes of a school's governors' meetings). **Secondary sources** are interpretations of events of that period based on primary sources (e.g. a history of that school which obtained evidence from the governors' minutes). The distinction is complicated by the fact that some documents are primary from one point of view and secondary from another. If the author of the school history were the subject of research, for example, her book would become a primary source for the researcher. The term 'secondary analysis' used in a narrow sense by some social scientists to mean the re-analysis of data such as survey material or primary documents gathered by other researchers in collections is not to be confused with the use of secondary sources (Hakim 2000). Such 'secondary analysis' is, of course, primary research as defined here.

Deliberate and inadvertent sources

Primary sources can in turn be divided into:

1 **Deliberate sources**, which are produced for the attention of future researchers. These would include autobiographies, memoirs of politicians or educationalists, diaries or letters intended for later publication, and documents of self-justification (Elton 2002). They involve a deliberate attempt to preserve evidence for the future, possibly for purposes of self-vindication or reputation enhancement (Lehmann and Mehrens 1971).
2 **Inadvertent sources**, which are used by the researcher for some purpose other than that for which they were originally intended. They are produced by the processes of local and central government and from the everyday working of the education system.

Examples of such primary documents are:

- the records of legislative bodies, government departments, and local education authorities;
- evidence from national databases including performance data on individual schools;
- inspection reports;
- national surveys;
- the publications of professional associations, subject teaching associations and trades unions;
- the minutes of academic boards, senior management groups, middle management meetings, subject departments, working groups, staff meetings and parents' associations;
- letters and correspondence of educational institutions;
- annual governors' reports;
- handbooks and prospectuses;
- examination papers;
- attendance registers;
- personal files;
- staffing returns;
- option-choice documents;

- bulletins;
- newspapers and journals;
- budget statements;
- school or college web sites and other Internet material.

Such inadvertent documents are the more common and usually the more valuable kind of primary sources. They were produced for a contemporary practical purpose and would therefore seem to be more straightforward than deliberate sources. This may be the case but great care still needs to be taken with them because it cannot be discounted that inadvertent documents were intended to deceive someone other than the researcher, or that what first appear to be inadvertent sources (some government records, for example) are actually attempts to justify actions to future generations (Elton 2002: 71). Some of the documents generated by a school for an inspection may have the aim of giving the best possible impression to the inspectors; without the imminent inspection, the school might not be so prolific in its production of policy statements and schemes of work or so up-to-date in its staff handbook.

Witting and unwitting evidence

A final point about the nature of documents concerns their 'witting' and 'unwitting' evidence. Witting evidence is the information which the original author of the document wanted to impart. Unwitting evidence is everything else that can be learned from the document (Marwick 2001: 172–9). If, for example, a government minister made a speech announcing a proposed educational reform, the witting evidence would be everything that was stated in the speech about the proposed change. The unwitting evidence, on the other hand, might come from any underlying assumptions unintentionally revealed by the minister in the language he or she used, and from the fact that a particular method had been chosen by the government to announce the reform. If a junior minister is given the job of announcing a reduction in educational expenditure it may well indicate the expectation on the part of more senior colleagues that the government will be criticized. All documents provide unwitting evidence, but it is the task of the researcher to try to assess its precise significance.

The selection of documents

The quantity of documentary material that you can study will inevitably be influenced by the amount of time that is available for this stage of your research. It is not usually possible to analyse everything and so you must decide what to select. Familiarity with the different categories of evidence will help you to make decisions about what is fundamental to the project, and 'controlled selection' is then needed to ensure that no significant category is left out (Elton 2002). Try not to include too many deliberate sources and take care not to select documents merely on the basis of how well they support your own views or hypotheses. Your aim is to make as balanced a selection as possible, bearing in mind the constraints of time. Periodically, check with your schedule, and if you find that you are encroaching on time allocated for the next stage of your research, take steps to reduce your selection. Your perception of what is valuable will grow as the project develops.

Content analysis

The proper selection of documents is particularly important in what is termed 'content analysis' which has been defined as 'a research technique for making replicable and valid inferences from data to their context' (Krippendorff 1980: 21). Content analysis has been used to analyse bias in news reporting, the content of newspapers, the extent of sexual or racial stereotypes in textbooks, the differences in black and white popular song lyrics and the nationalist bias in history textbooks (Weber 1990: 10). It usually involves counting the number of times particular terms or 'recording units' occur in a sample of sources but it could also involve such methods as counting the number of column inches devoted to a subject in a newspaper or the number of photographs in a publication. It might be possible to study all the documents in a particular category such as school newsletters or prospectuses but in other cases a sampling technique is needed. Such an example would be if a daily newspaper is selected in a research project investigating tabloid newspapers' attitudes to a particular institution or organization. You could examine all the editions of a newspaper over a three-month period or you could take the first week in each month over a one-year period. The nature of the sample must be able to be defended and it must be sufficiently large to allow valid conclusions. If the researcher was interested in the media presentation of teachers' associations, the sampling of newspapers from the first week of each month would be very inappropriate because significant references to specific associations are unlikely to be confined to the first week of each month. Having established the frequency of your chosen terms, you must then be able to place them in context before interpreting and explaining them. In order to do that successfully it is necessary to apply the critical method advocated below. Content analysis of documents can be very arid in its approach if the nature of the documents is not analysed in the way suggested here and it may not be appropriate for many small-scale studies.

The critical analysis of documents

External criticism

The analysis of documents can be divided into **external** and **internal criticism**, even though these may overlap to a large extent. External criticism aims to discover whether a document is both genuine (i.e. not forged) and authentic (i.e. it is what it purports to be and truthfully reports on its subject) (Barzun and Graff 1992: 99n). For example, an observer could write a report of a meeting he had never attended or a play he had never seen. His report would be genuine, because he actually wrote it, but it would not be authentic because he was not present at the meeting or the play.

In external criticism it is necessary to know for certain that the author produced the document, so certain questions need to be asked. In the case of a letter, they would include the following:

- Was the author of a letter known to be in the place from which it came at the time it was written?
- Do other sources corroborate that the person wrote the letter? Is the letter consistent with all other facts known about the author?
- Does it use the same arrangements and have the same form as similar documents?
- Is it typical of other letters or documents written by the author?

It is unlikely you will need or be able to verify any forgeries or hoaxes but an attempt should be made to decide whether a person did actually compose the speech delivered or write the letter with her signature on it.

Internal criticism

The analytical method more likely to be used in small-scale educational research is internal criticism, in which the contents of a document are subjected to rigorous analysis which first seeks answers to the following questions:

- What kind of document is it? A government circular? A statute? A policy paper? A set of minutes? A letter from a long correspondence? How many copies are there?
- What does it actually say? Are the terms used employed in the same way as you would use them? Documents such as statutes or legal papers may employ a specialized language which must be mastered, and private correspondence may use terms in an idiosyncratic way that also needs to be understood. A curious example comes from the language used in government school inspections. Judgements that classified teaching as 'satisfactory' could, in fact, still lead to a school being judged a failure because of the supposed rising social expectations about school standards and the fact that inspectors take into account other factors such as the quality of pupils' work (Ofsted 2003). In this case, therefore, 'satisfactory' would mean 'unsatisfactory' (*Times Educational Supplement* 2003).
- Who produced it? What is known about the author?

- What was its purpose? Did the author aim to inform, command, remind (as in a memorandum) or want to have some other effect on the reader? A document is always written for a particular readership and shaped according to the writer's expectations of how intended readers will interpret it. In the same way, the reader is always conscious of the purposes and intentions of the writer during the act of reading.
- When and in what circumstances was it produced? How did it come into existence?
- Is it typical or exceptional of its type?
- Is it complete? Has it been altered or edited? It may be that there is more chance of completeness if it is published a long time after the events it describes.

You will also need to assess the assiduousness of the producers of documents. Staff will complete documents very carefully if they are to be used in appeals procedures or public meetings. For example, teachers' approach to reporting on a pupil will be different if they know the pupil's parents and others will see the document rather than just their colleagues.

After asking these basic questions, you will need to ask further questions about the author:

- What is known about the author's social background, political views, aims and past experience?
- Did the author experience or observe what is being described? If so, was he or she an expert on what was being witnessed and a trained observer of the events described?
- Did the author habitually tell the truth or exaggerate, distort or omit?
- How long after the event did the author produce the document? Is it possible that memory played tricks?

All these questions may not be relevant to all documents, but in aiming at critical analysis it is important not to accept sources at face value. Examine them carefully. Gaps in the evidence can sometimes be very significant as it may indicate a prejudice or a determination to ignore a proposed change. Decide whether a particular political affiliation might possibly influence the tone or emphasis of a paper and try to come to a conclusion based on all the available evidence. An assessment of the document's reliability must involve the question of : 'Reliable for what?' Is it a reliable explanation of the author's views on an issue, in other words, is it representative of those views? It might not be truthful in a more general sense in a way that, for instance the supporter of streaming in schools may not necessarily convey the truth about the effects of using this method of organizing classes in a school but it would be a truthful and therefore reliable expression of this individual's views on the subject. Alternatively the source might be a reliable example of its type, as in the case of a document from a long series.

Fact or bias?

One important aim of critical scholarship is to assess whether fact or bias is the main characteristic of a document (Barzun and Graff 1992: 189). Writers will rarely declare their assumptions so it is the task of the researcher to expose them if possible. Watch particularly for any terms that suggest partisanship. Ask yourself whether the evidence supplied in the document convincingly supports the author's arguments. Was the author a supporter of a particular course of action in which he had a stake? If the document goes against the author's own interest, it may increase the likelihood that it tells the truth. Was the author affected by pressure, fear or even vanity when writing the document (Best 1970: 105)? Look for clues.

If you detect bias, that does not necessarily mean that the document should be dismissed as worthless. In some cases the most useful evidence can be derived from biased sources which accurately reveal the true views of an individual or group. Inferences can still be drawn from the 'unwitting' testimony, even if the 'witting' evidence is thought to be unsound. A prejudiced account of curriculum development, for example, could provide valuable insights into the political processes involved in innovation. The biased document will certainly need to be analysed cautiously and compared with evidence from other sources, but it can still be valuable.

Try to stand in the position of the author of the document and to see through his or her eyes. Instead of jumping to early conclusions, deliberately seek contrary evidence to test the truthfulness of a document as rigorously as possible – and watch out for your own bias. It may be easier to recognize bias in others than in ourselves, and it is tempting to reject evidence that does not support our case, but try to resist the temptation. Sources can be interpreted in different ways (even though some sources can reasonably be understood in only one way) but the postmodernist view that documents can be subjected to an infinity of meaning has been brilliantly demolished by Evans (2000). The guiding principle in document analysis is nevertheless that everything should be questioned. Qualities of scepticism as well as empathy need to be developed.

It could be argued that the techniques of document analysis suggested here are merely the application of common sense (Tosh 2002: 105). This is partly true but as you study the sources, you will gradually gain insights and detailed knowledge which will give you a 'higher common sense' which will in turn permit a fuller appreciation of the worth of the evidence (Barzun and Graff 1992: 159–60). Eventually, the critical method becomes a habit which will allow you, in Marwick's phrase, to 'squeeze the last drop' from each document (Marwick 2001 [1989]: 233).

◉   **The analysis of documentary evidence checklist**

1 Decide how you want to use documentary evidence.	Will it be used to supplement other sources of evidence or will you use it as the exclusive method of gathering data?
2 Decide on your approach to the documents.	You can let the source material determine your research or, more commonly, you will formulate your research questions after reading the literature on the subject and then take these questions to the sources.

3 Undertake a document search to ascertain the existence of different sources of information.	These may be found in different places in an organization so it is important to be persistent. Always negotiate access to the documents and do not assume that you can consult them; some information may be confidential.
4 Analyse the nature of the sources used.	Some sources will be deliberately produced for the attention of future researchers but, more usually, sources will be inadvertently produced by the everyday working of the system/organization you are researching.
5 If the documents are bulky, it may be necessary to decide on a sampling strategy.	Try to read a balanced selection of documents in the time you have available. The strategy must be appropriate to the purposes of your research and be capable of being justified in the report.
6 Be aware that there may be different kinds of evidence in each document.	Look for 'witting' and 'unwitting' evidence.
7 Subject each document to the critical method and ask a range of questions.	What does it say? Who wrote it? Why? How did it come into existence? Is it typical of its kind? Is it complete?
8 Compare the document with other sources to see if it is accurate or representative.	
9 Then ask further questions about the authors of the document.	What is their background? And what are their social and political views? Did they experience or observe what they were writing about? Did they usually tell the truth?

10	Look for signs of bias in the document.	Remember that biased evidence can be very valuable.
11	Decide whether the document is reliable for a particular purpose.	Check it against other sources to ascertain its truthfulness but remember that although it may not be an accurate account of an event or development, it may be a reliable expression of the author's views.
12	Strive to gain a full appreciation of the value of a source.	Use your accumulating knowledge to gain insights and try to make the critical method a habit in your research methods.

8

DESIGNING AND
ADMINISTERING
QUESTIONNAIRES

You will only reach the stage of designing a questionnaire after you have done all the preliminary work on planning, consulting and deciding exactly what you need to find out. Only then will you know whether a questionnaire is suitable for the purpose and is likely to be a better way of collecting information than interviews or observation, for example. If it is, then you will need to ensure you produce a well-designed questionnaire that will you give you the information you need, that will be acceptable to your subjects and that will give you no problems at the analysis and interpretation stage.

It is harder to produce a really good questionnaire than might be imagined. They are fiendishly difficult to design and should never be considered by anyone who believes that 'anyone who can write plain English and has a modicum of common sense can produce a good questionnaire' (Oppenheim 1992: 1). Of course, as Oppenheim says, common sense and the ability to write plain English are always a help in any walk of life, but designing a questionnaire requires rather more. It requires discipline in the selection of questions, in question writing, in the design, piloting, distribution and return of the questionnaires. What is more, thought has to be given to how responses will be analysed *at the design stage*, not after questionnaires have been returned. If you send out questionnaires and just hope for the best, you may find the returns are impossible to deal with.

Exactly what do you need to find out?

Your preliminary reading and your research plan will have identified important areas for investigation. Go back to your hypothesis or to the objectives and decide which questions you need to ask to achieve these objectives. Then write out possible questions on cards or on separate pieces of paper, to aid ordering at a later stage. You will need several attempts at wording in order to remove ambiguity, to achieve the degree of precision necessary to ensure that subjects understand exactly what you are asking, to check that your language is jargon free, to decide which question types to use and to ensure that you will be able to classify and analyse responses. Guidance on analysis is provided in Chapter 12, and before you complete your questionnaire design, you should read this chapter carefully. Time spent on preparation will save many hours of work later on.

Question type

The more structured a question, the easier it will be to analyse. Youngman (1982) lists seven question types as follows:

Verbal or Open
The expected response is a word, a phrase or an extended comment. Responses to verbal questions can produce useful information but analysis can present problems. Some form of content analysis may be required for verbal material unless the information obtained is to be used for special purposes (see pages 128–9 in Chapter 7). For example, you might feel it necessary to give respondents the opportunity to give their own views on the topic being researched – or to raise a grievance. You might wish to use questions as an introduction to a follow-up interview, or in pilot interviews where it is important to know which aspects of the topic are of particular importance to the respondents.

Well-structured questions will not present so many problems at the analysis stage.

List	A list of items is offered, any of which may be selected. For example, a question may ask about qualifications and the respondent may have several of the qualifications listed.
Category	The response is one only of a given set of categories. For example, if age categories are provided (20–29, 30–39, etc.), the respondent can only fit into one category.
Ranking	In ranking questions, the respondent is asked to place something in rank order. For example, the respondent might be asked to place qualities or characteristics in order.
Quantity	The response is a number (exact or approximate), giving the amount of some characteristics.
Grid	A table or grid is provided to record answers to two or more questions at the same time.
Scale	There are various stages of scaling devices which may be used in questionnaires, but they require careful handling (more about scales in Chapter 12).

Students have discovered that once they have tried out and become familiar with different ways of analysing and presenting questionnaire responses to list, category, ranking, scale, quantity or grid questions, they are able to select the most appropriate format when they come to the stage of designing and analysing data in their project.

Question wording

Ambiguity and imprecision

Words which have a common meaning to you may mean something different to other people, so you need to consider what your questions might mean to different respondents. For example, suppose you wanted to find out how much time mature students spend studying. You ask:

How much time, on average, do you spend studying?

You invite your respondent to tick the box for 'a great deal', 'a certain amount', or 'not much'. What will you do with the responses? What will they mean? 'A great deal' may mean something different to student A than to student B. In any case, students may spend 20 hours a week at some times of the year but probably not more than four at other times. What is 'average'? If you really wish to know how much time students spend studying, you will need to find different ways of putting the question. When you think about this topic you may decide you have to ask students to keep a diary for a specific period of time. You may need to specify the time spent studying different subjects. It will all depend on exactly what it is you need to know. Once you are clear about that, you will be able to word your questions sufficiently precisely to ensure that they mean the same to all respondents.

Precision in wording is important. Remember that concepts such as 'satisfaction' and 'class' can't actually be observed. There are many 'satisfaction questions' in the questionnaires which regularly come through my door, from banks, credit card companies, hotels, shops, hospitals, financial advisers – and many others. 'How satisfied are you with . . .?', or even 'Are you satisfied with . . .', with an instruction to tick the Yes/No box. Satisfaction is a concept and as we can't actually observe concepts, we have to find different ways in which they might be observable, and therefore measurable. Rose and Sullivan provide a useful example of ways in which the concept of 'class' might be measurable. They write that:

> If we wish to understand something about class (a concept and therefore . . . not observable), what can we observe in the world which manifests class? That is, what indicators can be used for class so that we can obtain data about class? This is the essence of the measurement problem and when we link an unobservable concept with an observable indicator we are producing **operationalizations**.
>
> (Rose and Sullivan 1996: 12–13)

They explain that 'operationalizable' refers to 'the rules we use to link the language of theory (concepts) to the language of research (indicators)'. So, what indicators of 'class' or 'satisfaction' might there be? Think about it. Ask friends, colleagues, family members for measurable alternatives, and as always, go back to the beginning and ask yourself, *what do you really need to know?*

Assumptions

If respondents are confused, irritated or even offended, they may leave the item blank or even abandon the questionnaire. You want answers to all questions if at all possible, so try to avoid confusion and watch out for assumptions. Consider the question 'Which type of school does your child attend?' The respondent is asked to tick in the appropriate box from a long list of types of school. The researcher has assumed the respondent has one child, but what if she has no children? Does she ignore this question? What if she has more than one child – one in an infant school, one in a high school, and so on – what does she do then? Does she put the number of children in the appropriate box? Are you prepared for a category response, or had you intended this to be a list? It may not matter, but if your analysis is planned on the basis of a category response, you will give yourself extra trouble when list responses are given. Incidentally, your respondents might well ask why you want this information. Do you? Is the information essential for your study? If not, leave it out.

Memory

Memory plays tricks. If you were asked to say which television programmes you saw last week, could you remember everything? Could you be sure that one particular programme was last week – or was it the week before? Consider the following question, which appeared in a questionnaire concerned with parents' education.

What subjects did you study at school?

If respondents left school recently, they may be able to remember quite clearly, but if they left school 20 or more years ago, they may find it difficult to remember. If they do not include English in the list of subjects, would that mean that no English was studied or did they just forget to include it? Consider what information you really need. If you want to know which of a list of subjects that respondent studied, you might decide it would be better to provide a list of subjects which can be ticked. That way, you would ensure that main subjects were covered – but the type of question will depend on the type of information needed.

Knowledge

Take care over questions which ask for information that the students may not know or may not have readily to hand. For example, it may seem reasonable to ask mature students what the criteria are for allocating students to tutorial groups. But the likelihood is that they will not know: and if respondents have to search for information, they may put questionnaire to one side until they have time – and forget all about it.

Double questions

It may seem obvious to remind you that double questions should never be asked, but it's easy to overlook the following type of question:

Do you attend research methods and statistics courses?

Would the answer 'Yes' mean that you attend both, or one? If you need to know, the question should be divided into:

Do you attend research methods courses?
and
Do you attend statistics courses?

It's common to come across questionnaires with double questions, particularly in hotel feedback forms such as:

The management is always looking for ways of improving the service to guests. We should be grateful if you would circle the appropriate number below and return the completed form to reception.

How would you rate the service and cleanliness of the hotel?

Excellent	Very good	Good	Satisfactory	Less than satisfactory
5	4	3	2	1

I found this in the bedroom of a large chain hotel and all the following questions followed a similar format. Assuming any of the guests bothered to complete the questionnaire, I can imagine that responses to 2–5 would be grouped together and would therefore provide 'evidence' that 95 per cent of guests were very satisfied with the service and cleanliness of the hotel. The double question is obvious but there are other issues in this item. Perhaps you considered the service was good in parts. Helpful, pleasant and efficient receptionists; chamber maid who did a remarkably good job, *but* the porter was surly and the restaurant service appalling. As far as cleanliness was concerned . . . well, I won't go on.

Likert scales (originally devised by R. Likert in 1932) of the kind used in this hotel questionnaire are devices to discover strength of feeling or attitude towards a given statement or series of statements and the implication here is that the higher the category chosen, the greater the strength of agreement, but care has to be taken not to read too much in these ranked scales. They are usually, though not always, on a three, five or seven-point range and ask respondents to indicate rank order of agreement or disagreement by circling the appropriate number. They certainly arrange individuals or objects from the highest to the lowest, but the intervals between each may not be the same. We cannot say that the highest rating (5 in the hotel example) is five times higher than the lowest (which is 1). All that can be said is that they indicate order. In spite of these limitations, Likert scales can be useful, as long as the wording is clear, there are no double questions, and no unjustified claims are made about the findings.

Leading questions

It's not always easy to spot a leading question, but the use of emotive language or the way a question is put can lead respondents to answer questions in one way. For example:

Do you not agree that mature students should have the right to express their views in tutorials?

Well, it might be difficult for students to answer 'No' in response to that question.

Presuming questions

Presuming questions are often a source of error in questionnaires. When they are included it is often because the researcher holds strong views about a subject and overlooks the fact that everyone may not feel the same way. For example:

Does the university/college/hospital make adequate provision for counselling?

Is that for students, patients, staff – who else? You may think all institutions should provide a counselling service. But what if your respondents do not? What if they do not really know what a counselling service does? In its present form, 'adequate' is meaningless. There is a presumption in the question that a counselling service is necessary, and that makes the question invalid.

Hypothetical questions

Watch for questions that will provide only useless responses. Most hypothetical questions come into this category. For example:

If you had no family responsibilities and plenty of money, would you travel around the world and live in 5* hotels?

But, a respondent might answer, 'I do have family responsibilities. I have no money and never shall have as far as I can see, so what's the point of thinking about it?'

Offensive questions and questions covering sensitive issues

It goes without saying that questions that may cause offence should be removed. If you really need information on what might be regarded by some respondents as sensitive issues, you will need to take extra care in the wording and positioning of questions. Some researchers think it is better to place such questions towards the end of the questionnaire, the theory being that if respondents abandon the questionnaire at that point, you at least have answers to all the earlier questions.

Age is often considered to be in the sensitive category and rather than asking respondents to give their exact age, it may be better to ask them to tick in boxes to indicate age category (perhaps 21 or younger; 22–25; 26–30 etc. Be careful not to have overlapping categories. It's quite common to see age categories listed as 21 or less, 21–25, 25–30, etc.

Appearance and layout

An excellently prepared questionnaire will lose much of its impact if it looks untidy. Look at some of the published surveys which used a questionnaire as one method of data collection and they will give you ideas about layout. Recipients need to be encouraged to read and to answer the questions and they may be put off by a scruffy document that has been hastily prepared. There are no hard-and-fast rules about layout, but there are a few common-sense guidelines that will help appearance.

1 Questionnaires should be typed, word-processed (or printed if you are conducting a very large survey).
2 Instructions should be clear (in capitals, or in a different font).

3 Spacing between questions will help the reader and will also help you when you analyse responses.

4 If you want to keep the questionnaire to a limited number of sheets, it may be better to photo-reduce copy.

5 Keep any response boxes in line towards the right of the sheet. This will make it easy for respondents and will help you to record responses.

6 If you intend to use a computer program, allow space on the right of the sheet for coding, if necessary. Find more about coding in Chapter 12.

7 Look critically at your questionnaire and ask yourself what impression it would give if you were the recipient.

8 Take care over the order of the questions. Leave sensitive issues to later in the questionnaire. Start with straightforward, easy-to-complete questions and move on to the more complex topics (writing questions on cards or separate pieces of paper will make it easy to sort and re-sort questions).

9 Remember your promises of anonymity and confidentiality. Refer back to Chapter 3 if you've forgotten. Keep names off questionnaires if at all possible.

Drawing a sample

The number of subjects in your investigation will necessarily depend on the amount of time you have. If you are working on a 100-hour project, you will not be able to include all mature students in the country. If you have decided to restrict your research to one institution, then you will need to find out how many mature students there are. If there are 100, it will be unlikely that you will have the time or the means to include them all. You will need to select a sample.

In very large surveys, like the census, sampling techniques will be employed in order to produce a sample which is, as far as possible, representative of the population as a whole. Generalizations can then be made from the findings. In small studies, we have to do the best we can.

All researchers are dependent on the goodwill and availability of respondents, and it will probably be difficult for an individual researcher working on a small-scale project to achieve a true random sample. If that proves to be the case, you may be forced to interview anyone from the total population who is available and willing at the time. Opportunity samples of this kind are generally acceptable as long as the make-up of the sample is clearly stated and the limitations of the data are realized. However, even in a small study, efforts should be made to select as representative a sample as possible. Say you decide to include 50 per cent of your population. A random sample will give each of the individuals concerned an equal chance of being selected. You may decide to select alternate names on an alphabetical list, the first person being selected by sticking a pin in the paper. Everyone selected may not be willing to participate, and so it is wise to have reserve names available. For example, if the twentieth person refused or was not available, you might have decided *beforehand*, and as part of your research design, to approach the twenty-first.

There may be occasions when you wish to include representative sub-groups. You perhaps wish to select the appropriate proportion of men and women, of individuals in different age categories or some other sub-group of the target population. If so, you might have the following type of stratification.

Total target population: 100
Number of men: 60. Number of women: 40.

Instead of selecting alternative names, the sample population could be selected on the basis of every second man and every second woman, and so 30 men and 20 women would be selected.

If you wanted to find out how many men and women had German measles before the age of 10, you could take the process one step further, as follows:

	Men	Women	Total
Had German measles before age of 10	10	6	16
Did not have German measles before age of 10	20	14	34
Total	30	20	50

If sex and German measles were particularly important, then the sub-groups would be specified as part of the research design, and the sample would be drawn in the appropriate proportion from each sub-group or cell. This is a rather crude example, but, for a small-scale exercise it will generally be an acceptable way of selecting a sample. If a more scientific approach is required for your project, you will need to read further and to acquire a certain amount of statistical expertise.

Further reading on sampling is indicated at the end of the chapter.

Piloting the questionnaire

All data-gathering instruments should be piloted to test how long it takes recipients to complete them, to check that all questions and instructions are clear and to enable you to remove any items which do not yield usable data. There is a temptation in a small study to go straight to the distribution stage, but however pressed for time you are, do your best to give the questionnaire a trial run, even if you have to press-gang members of your family or friends. Ideally, it should be tried out on a group similar to the one that will form the population of your study, but if that is not possible, make do with whoever you can get. Respondents will tell you how long it took to complete the questionnaire, and if they leave any questions unanswered, you will be able to find out why. The purpose of a pilot exercise is to get the bugs out of the instrument so that respondents in your main study will experience no difficulties in completing it. It also enables you to carry out a preliminary analysis to see whether the wording and format of questions will present any difficulties when the main data are analysed.

Ask your volunteers the following questions:

1 How long did it take you to complete?
2 Were the instructions clear?
3 Were any of the questions unclear or ambiguous? If so, will you say which and why?
4 Did you object to answering any of the questions?

5 In your opinion, has any major topic been omitted?
6 Was the layout of the questionnaire clear/attractive?
7 Any comments?

Their responses will enable you to review the questionnaire ready for the main distribution. It will take you some time to achieve a good standard of design and presentation, but if the preparation is sound, it will save you hours and even weeks of work at the analysis stage.

Distribution and return of questionnaires

REMEMBER that under no circumstances can you distribute your questionnaires until you have obtained clearance to proceed from your supervisor, your institution's research committee, ethics committee and any other committee which has responsibility for scrutinizing students' topics, project plans and proposed methods of collecting data. In my view, written committee approval should always be obtained, so never assume it will be 'all right' and that verbal agreement given over a cup of coffee will suffice. It might, but it might not. You need to be sure of your own position. Once you have the necessary approval, you will need to decide how to distribute your questionnaire and what to do about non-response.

There are distinct advantages in being able to give questionnaires to respondents personally. You can explain the purpose of the study, and in some cases questionnaires can be completed on the spot. You are likely to get better cooperation if you can establish personal contact, but if that is impossible, you will need to investigate other ways of distribution. Permission can sometimes be obtained to distribute through internal mailing systems. Colleagues and friends may be persuaded to lend a hand. If all else fails, you may have to mail copies, but postal surveys are expensive and response rates are generally low, so you would only wish to resort to distribution by post if you found it impossible to contact subjects by any other means.

As I mentioned in Chapter 3, even if you will be meeting respondents face to face, it's my view that they should be provided with a written statement about *their* rights and *your* responsibilities and the purpose of the research. Make it clear that official approval has been given and say what will be done with the completed questionnaires. Who will see them? Will they be shredded when you have finished with them or when your report has been examined? Or will they be kept in your filing cabinet for years in case they come in handy? If confidentiality and anonymity are guaranteed, make it clear what you mean by both. Look back at Chapter 3 if you have doubts. Promise what you know you can honour and nothing more.

If you are not able to distribute your questionnaires face to face, a letter will be required, in addition to your statement. Take care with the wording of your letter. A letter that is too brusque or too ingratiating can have an adverse effect on response, so show your draft letter to a few friends and ask their opinion. Remember to give the return date, either in the letter or in a prominent position on the questionnaire. Experience has shown that it is unwise to allow too long. If no date is specified or if too long is given, it becomes too easy for subjects to put the questionnaire to one side, which often means that it will never be seen again. Two weeks is a reasonable time for completion. Give the precise day and date rather than relying on a polite request for the questionnaire to be returned in two weeks' time. For some reason, it seems to help to jog memories if the day as well as the date is stated.

Include a self-addressed envelope (stamped, if respondents have to return the questionnaire by post).

Non-response

Keep a record of the date questionnaires are distributed and the date they are returned. Generally, there is a good response at first and then returns slow down. Inevitably, they all will not be returned by the specified date but if you do not include any method of identification on the questionnaires, you will have no way of knowing who has replied and who has not and so there can be no follow-up. Non-response is a problem 'because of the likelihood – repeatedly confirmed in practice – that people who do not return questionnaires differ from those who do' (Moser and Kalton 1971: 267–8). So, if at all possible some effort should be made to encourage more people to return completed questionnaires.

Opinions vary as to the best time to send out follow-up requests, assuming your guarantees of anonymity and confidentiality will allow follow ups, but in a limited-time project you will need to write about a week after the original date if you are to complete data collection in the time allocated. In some large projects a third and even a fourth reminder will be sent, but the number of returns obtained by this process is unlikely to warrant the time and trouble it will involve.

Analysis of data

In an ideal world it would be best to wait for all questionnaires to be returned and to glance through all responses before beginning to code and record. In a limited-time project it may be necessary to begin recording responses as soon as the first questionnaires are returned. The procedures for analysing and presenting results described in Chapter 12, may influence the way you structure the questionnaire and word the questions, so before you decide finally on content and format, read this chapter carefully and make sure you read the checklist to this chapter to be sure you have covered all essential tasks.

⦿ Designing and administering questionnaires checklist

1 Make sure you have approval to proceed before you move too far on with your preparation. Never assume it will be 'all right'.

Check the requirements of your ethics, research and any other committees which have responsibility for approving research in your institution. Remember that approval may take some time so if you possibly can, submit your research proposals in good time.

2 Decide what you need to know and list all items about which information is required. Ask yourself why you need this information.

Don't clog up your questionnaire with irrelevant items in case they might come in handy. They won't.

3 Is a questionnaire the best way of obtaining the information?

Consider what information you need. If another method of data collecting is likely to be better, consider the alternatives.

4 If you decide a questionnaire will be best, begin to word questions. Write them on separate cards or pieces of paper, to help ordering later on.

Remember that concepts can't be measured, so if you really do need to know about respondents' satisfaction with x or y, think of indicators of satisfaction.

5 Check the wording of each question. Is there any ambiguity, imprecision or assumption? Are you asking respondents to remember things? Will they be able to? Are you asking for knowledge respondents may not have? Any double, leading, presuming, hypothetical or offensive questions?

Keep language simple. Don't use words respondents may not understand (that includes technical language), unless you are dealing with a professional group, all of whom understand your linguistic short cuts.

6 Decide on question type.

Verbal, list, category, ranking, scale, quantity or grid. Each type requires a different analysis (see Chapter 12 for further information about analysis).

7 When you are satisfied that all questions are well worded and of the right type, sort them into order.

It is often better to leave sensitive questions to the end.

8 Write out instructions to be included on the questionnaire.

Respondents must be quite clear about how they are to answer questions (ticks in boxes, circling items, Yes/No?).

9 Consider layout and appearance. Instructions must be clearly presented (perhaps a different font and displayed in a prominent position?). Decide whether you need a right-hand margin for coding.

Consult Chapter 12 about coding and possible ways of analysing responses before you finally decide on the wording, content and structure of your questionnaire.

10 Word-process your questionnaire. A scrappy appearance will not encourage respondents to take it seriously.

If you are fortunate enough to have a skilled typist who will do your word-processing for you, be thankful BUT it is your job to give precise instructions about layout.

11 Decide on your sample.

Try to select a sample which is as close to your final population as possible. If you have to make do with an opportunity sample, say why in your report.

12 Always pilot your questionnaire, no matter how pushed for time you are.

Ideally, it should be sent to people who are similar to your selected sample. However, if that is not possible, ask friends, family or colleagues to help.

13 Try out your methods of analysis. Again, *read Chapter 12 before you decide finally on format.*

Even with five or six completed pilot questionnaires, you will be able to see whether any problems are likely to arise when you analyse the main returns.

14 Make any adjustments to the questionnaire in the light of pilot respondents' comments and your preliminary analysis.

Consider timing. If it took your volunteers too long to complete, decide whether any items might be removed or reworded. Eliminate any items which are not directly related to your topic. Check again that nothing is included merely because it might come in handy at some future stage.

15 Decide how the questionnaire is to be distributed but before you distribute, check that you know what you mean by anonymity and confidentiality – AND that you make your definitions clear to respondents.	By post? Internal mail? By you personally distributing questionnaires face to face with respondents? If you decide on a postal survey, include a stamped addressed envelope. If respondents complete and return the questionnaire, they are doing you a favour so don't ask them to pay for the privilege. Also include a letter and a statement of conditions and guarantees explaining respondents' rights and your responsibilities.
16 Don't forget to say when you would like questionnaires to be returned, if possible. Give the preferred day and date.	Keep a record of when questionnaires were distributed and when returned.
17 Decide what you are going to do about non-respondents before you distribute the questionnaires.	Remember that you will not be able to send out reminders if all responses are guaranteed to be anonymous.
18 Begin to record responses as soon as completed questionnaires are received.	You have no time to wait for stragglers.
19 Do not get involved with complicated statistics unless you know what you are doing.	It is perfectly possible to produce a good report without extensive statistical knowledge, as long as the structure of the questionnaire is well thought out.

Further reading   ◉

Most books dealing with research methods will have a chapter on the design of questionnaires and so the only items listed here are standard texts, most of which should be available in libraries. All provide good advice and will provide a sound foundation if you plan to design a questionnaire as part of your investigation.

Bell, J. (2002) 'Questionnaires', Chapter 10 in M. Coleman and A.R.J. Briggs (eds) *Research Methods in Educational Leadership and Management*. London: Paul Chapman Publishing.

Bell, J. and Opie, C. (2002) *Learning from Research: Getting More from your Data*. Maidenhead: Open University Press. Chapters 5.2, 5.3 and 5.4 discuss the planning and preparation involved in the production of the questionnaire carried out by Chan (2000) in his doctoral study of student evaluation of teaching effectiveness. Part 2, incorporating Chapters 2.1–2.6 consider the preparation carried out by Fan (1998) as part of his Master's study of nursing students' perceptions of their nursing education. Both are well worth consulting as examples of the way two very different students approached the task of planning and designing questionnaires.

Blaxter, L., Hughes, C. and Tight, M. (2001) *How to Research*, 2nd edn. Buckingham: Open University Press. Pages 161–6 give useful advice about sampling.

Bowling, A. (2002) *Research Methods in Health: Investigating Health and Health Services*, 2nd edn. Maidenhead: Open University Press. Chapter 7 concentrates on methods of sampling. Chapters 11 and 12 consider aspects of questionnaire design such as planning, piloting, question-naire layout, the covering letter, order of wording and checking the accuracy of responses. Chapter 14 introduces issues relating to the preparation of quantitative data for coding and analysis, all of which is useful.

Cohen, L., Manion, L. and Morrison, K. (2000) *Research Methods in Education*, 5th edn. London and New York: Routledge Falmer. Chapter 4 (Sampling) and Chapter 5 (Validity and reliability) are well worth consulting.

Laws, S. with Harper, C. and Marcus, R. (2003) *Research for Development: A Practical Guide*. London: Sage. This book deals with sampling (pages 356–75) and questionnaires (pages 306–10).

Moser, C.A. and Kalton, G. (1971) *Survey Methods in Social Investigation*, 2nd edn. London: Heinemann. In particular, see Chapter 4 (Basic ideas of sampling), Chapter 11 (Mail questionnaires) and Chapter 13 (Questionnaires), which deals with general principles of design, question content, question wording, open and pre-coded questions and question order. This book is now more than 30 years old, but it is still one of the best of its kind I have seen. If your library still has a copy, make a point of consulting it.

Oppenheim, A.N. (1992) *Questionnaire Design, Interviewing and Attitude Measurement* (new edition). London: Cassell. Chapters 1, 2 and 3 provide guidance about survey design and Chapters 7, 8 and 9 cover questionnaire planning, question wording, basic measurement theory – and much more. An excellent book to keep for reference.

Rose, D. and Sullivan, O. (1996) *Introducing Data Analysis for Social Scientists*, 2nd edn. Buckingham: Open University Press. Chapter 3 (Preparing the data) considers operationalization, data preparation, coding for analysis, using 'open' and 'closed' questions and the principles of entering numeric data into a computer. Another very useful book to keep on hand for reference.

Youngman, M.B. (1994) 'Designing and using questionnaires', in N. Bennett, R. Glatter and R. Levačić (eds) (1994) *Improving Educational Management through Research and Consultancy*. London: Paul Chapman Publishing, in association with The Open University. This is a revised version of M.B. Youngman (1982) *Analysing Questionnaires*, Rediguide 12, Guides in Educational Research, University of Nottingham, Rediguides. The author covers the importance of planning, question specification, questionnaire design, distribution and return. This is an excellent chapter and worth keeping as a permanent record and checklist. During his career at the University of Nottingham, Michael Youngman gave generous support to struggling research students, of which I was one. I believe few of us would have survived without him.

PLANNING AND CONDUCTING INTERVIEWS

The ethics of conducting interviews ◉

In Chapter 3, I spoke about codes of practice, contracts and protocols which require researchers to ensure that participants are fully
aware of the purpose of the research and that they understand
their rights. It will be helpful if you refer to the 'ethical guidelines
and protocols' section in this chapter before you get too far in
planning your interviews, because you should not proceed without respondents' consent to participate. If you are researching in
a hospital or in fact in any health-related area, I should be very
surprised if you were not required to produce a written protocol.
Conditions vary and so it's essential that you find out what the
requirements are at an early stage.

Obtaining 'informed consent' may not be as easy as it sounds
and if you are working on a 100-hour project, you will have
little time to prepare and trial the sort of protocol required in a
major study (see Cohen et al. 2000: 50–6). However, in any size
of project, you will still have a responsibility to explain to
respondents as fully as possible what the research is about, why
you wish to interview them, what will be involved and what
you will do with the information you obtain. I personally feel
that this should not be presented verbally at the start of an
interview, but sent beforehand so that respondents have an

opportunity to query the meaning and implications of any statements – and even to withdraw at that stage. Better for participants to withdraw at the start rather than halfway through or after the interview.

In case you are coming to the conclusion that this is just one more bureaucratic and unnecessary procedure, I would ask you to remember that it's not only ensuring that your respondents know about their rights and your responsibilities but it is also protecting your own position.

Advantages and disadvantages of the interview

One major advantage of the interview is its adaptability. A skilful interviewer can follow up ideas, probe responses and investigate motives and feelings, which the questionnaire can never do. The way in which a response is made (the tone of voice, facial expression, hesitation, etc.) can provide information that a written response would conceal. Questionnaire responses have to be taken at face value, but a response in an interview can be developed and clarified.

There are problems, of course. Interviews are time-consuming, and so in a 100-hour project you will be able to interview only a relatively small number of people. It is a highly subjective technique and therefore there is always the danger of bias. Analysing responses can present problems, and wording the questions is almost as demanding for interviews as it is for questionnaires. Even so, the interview can yield rich material and can often put flesh on the bones of questionnaire responses.

Moser and Kalton (1971: 271) describe the survey interview as 'a conversation between interviewer and respondent with the purpose of eliciting certain information from the respondent'. This, they continue, might appear a straightforward matter, but the attainment of a successful interview is much more complex than this statement might suggest.

Wiseman and Aron (1972) liken interviewing to a fishing expedition and, pursuing this analogy, Cohen (1976: 82) adds that 'like fishing, interviewing is an activity requiring careful preparation, much patience, and considerable practice if the eventual reward is to be a worthwhile catch'.

Preparation for interviews follows much the same procedures as for questionnaires. Topics need to be selected, questions devised, methods of analysis considered and a schedule prepared and piloted.

Question wording

Though question wording is important, it may not be quite as important to be precise about the use of certain terms as for questionnaires, though of course the language you use must be understandable to the respondents. In the chapter on questionnaire design, I gave the example of students having been asked how much time they spent studying and suggested that 'a great deal', 'a certain amount' and 'not much', would mean different things to different people. In an interview, it would be possible to ask 'How much time do you spend studying?' and then to follow with a prompt on the lines of 'For example . . .'

Follow the rules laid down for questionnaire design (no leading, presumptive or offensive questions, etc.). Prepare topics and then questions on cards or on separate pieces of paper, so that you can decide the order of questioning when all topics have been covered. Consider which is likely to be the best order in which to ask questions. The order may be important in establishing an easy relationship with the interviewee. The manner in which you ask questions most certainly will be. Practise interviewing and managing your schedule to make sure your form of questioning is clear, does not antagonize the respondent and allows you to record responses in a way that you can understand when the interview is over.

The interview schedule

Structured and semi-structured interviews

If you are using a structured or semi-structured format which enables you to tick or circle responses on your previously prepared schedule, you should be able to leave the interview with a set of responses that can be fairly easily recorded, summarized and analysed. It's not quite so easy if you have decided on an unstructured format but you will still need to prepare a list of items you wish to discuss and a few prompts or probes to remind you about the particular issues you wish to cover. Let's say you are carrying out a survey of staff participation in a company's in-house French language programme. Company headquarters are in Paris and it was felt that the language programme would be a good idea. However, take-up was disappointing, possibly because though half an hour of work time was allowed, participants had to give a further half hour in their own time. You think it might be useful to know whether there was any difference between men and women participants; the length of time staff had worked for the company; whether they had spent any time at the Paris headquarters; their seniority in the firm and (an issue which had unexpectedly cropped up during the pilot interviews); whether attendance brought any increase in salary or even promotion and, of course the extent of employees' participation in the French language programme.

It's fairly easy to circle numbers on your checklist, but not so easy to write down what people say. The last thing you want to do is to write furiously throughout the interview, so the more items you can surreptitiously circle, the better. You need to record whether your respondent is male or female but you don't need to ask. You can see, so circle the M or F at the start of your schedule.

You might prepare the draft schedule on the following lines. Try it out with your pilot study volunteers and if it does not work, then redraft until you are satisfied it serves your purpose.

**Title: Survey of staff participation in the French
language programme**

Date of interview: Venue:

Name/number of interviewee: M or F

Q 1: To what extent have you participated in the French language
programme?

Prompt:	6-week basic programme	1	2	3
	12-week improvers' programme	1	2	3
	1-year advanced programme	1	2	3
	2-year bilingual oral programme	1	2	3

1 = not at all (any particular reasons?)
2 = to a certain extent (ask for examples)
3 = a great deal (ask for examples)

You might then wish to probe further.

After the interview, all the circled numbers can be entered into your summary sheet and the process of analysing responses has begun. Some people add a summary column on the right-hand side of the schedule; others prefer to work on a separate sheet.

Questions and coding can be developed during the course of pilot interviews. There may be changes as you go on. What seemed to be a good idea at the start may not be appropriate as you proceed. There is no reason why code numbers should be indicated on the schedule at all. Unless you plan to key in your numbers direct to a computer, there is no reason really why you should work with numbers. You could have letters which will immediately give you the key to the question item. If the majority of your data collecting is through interviews, you are unlikely to accumulate very large numbers and if you are coding by hand, the letters have considerable advantages over numbers. So, on your summary sheet, you would have headings of M and F and the numbers of participants who were male or female would be listed under the appropriate heading. Easy.

Unstructured interviews

Unstructured interviews centred round a topic may, and in skilled hands do, produce a wealth of valuable data but such interviews require a great deal of expertise to control and a great deal of time to analyse. Conversation about a topic may be interesting and may produce useful insights into a problem, but it has to be remembered that an interview is more than just an interesting conversation. You need certain information and methods have to be devised to obtain that information, if at all possible.

Preliminary interviews can probably be placed at the 'completely unstructured' end of the continuum of formality. This is the stage when you are trying to find out which areas or topics are important and when people directly concerned with the topic are encouraged to talk about what is of central significance to them. You are looking for clues as to which areas should be explored and which left out. Interviews of this kind require only the minimum of note-taking, and as long as your notes are clear enough to enable you to extract points of interest, and topics for inclusion in the study, they will suffice.

Most interviews carried out in the main data-collecting stage of the research will come somewhere between the completely structured and the completely unstructured point on the continuum. Freedom to allow the respondents to talk about what is of central significance to them rather than to the interviewer is clearly important, but some loose structure to ensure all topics which are considered crucial to the study are covered does eliminate some of the problems of entirely unstructured interviews. The **guided** or **focussed interview** fulfils these requirements. No questionnaire or checklist is used, but a framework is established by selecting topics on which the interview is guided. The respondent is allowed a considerable degree of latitude within the framework. Certain questions are asked, but respondents are given freedom to talk about the topic and give their views in their own time. The interviewer needs to have the skill to ask questions and, if necessary, to probe at the right time, but if the interviewee moves freely from one topic to another, the conversation can flow without interruption.

The advantage of a focussed interview is that a framework is established beforehand and so recording and analysis are greatly simplified. This is important for any research, but particularly so for limited-time studies.

Group interviews and focus groups

One-to-one interviewing is not the only way of meeting respondents and in some cases you might feel it would be more useful to consider group interviewing. There is nothing new about group interviewing, though focus groups in particular have recently become much more popular, especially in social science and health research. As their name indicates, the purpose of focus groups is to focus discussion on a particular issue. They can be structured, where there are pre-prepared questions and checklists, or completely unstructured, where the intervention of the researcher is minimal. It all depends on the purpose of the interview. Sometimes, they are informal gatherings of a varied group of people who may not know each other, but who might be thought to have an interest or concern in issues like community policing or council taxes. The intention (and the hope) are that participants will interact with each other, will be willing to listen to all views, perhaps to reach consensus about some aspects of the topic or to disagree about others and to give a good airing to the issues which seem to be interesting or important to them. The researcher becomes less of an interviewer, more of a moderator or facilitator.

In my experience, which may be very different from yours, focus groups are more likely to include members who either have similar characteristics or experience (for example, they may all have had the same type of illness) or are known to have a professional concern about and knowledge of the issues involved.

Focus groups are undoubtedly valuable when in-depth information is needed 'about how people *think* about an issue – their reasoning about *why* things are as they are, *why* they hold the views they do' (Laws 2003: 299). However, there can sometimes be problems.

Hayes warns us that:

Groups have to be carefully balanced in relation to the age, sex and ethnic status of respondents: for example, if young people, women, or people in ethnic minority groups are in disproportionately fewer numbers in the group they may feel socially constrained and not contribute freely to the discussion. It may sometimes be necessary to have single sex groups in similar age ranges in order for the atmosphere to be permissive and relaxed.

(Hayes 2000: 395)

A couple of strong personalities can also influence and in some cases actually take over a group and make it difficult for the less assertive members to speak. Denscombe (1998: 115) warns that 'it is men who tend to hog the centre stage in group discussions', leaving the women (or at least some of them) silent – though that may not be your experience! He draws our attention to another issue, which is that if 'group members regard their opinions as contrary to prevailing opinion within the group, they might be inclined to keep quiet, or moderate their views somewhat' (p. 115). He adds that 'the privacy of the one-to-one interview does not pose this difficulty'. Of course he is right, though one-to-one interviews can present their own set of difficulties.

With experience, researchers will devise their own techniques of keeping the strong personalities in line and of drawing the silent members into the group. Laws (2003: 300) suggests that one way might be to make a periodic check in order to discover whether all group members are in agreement with statements being made, on the lines of 'Is that what everyone thinks?' or 'Does everyone agree with xyz?' – and that seems to be a reasonable approach.

There appear to be many views about the 'right' and the 'wrong' way to manage group and particularly focus group interviews. Some people consider a checklist, topic guide and prepared questions are essential: others disagree and feel that such a structure would be too directive to achieve the required exploration of respondents' beliefs, interpretations and understanding of issues. All I can say, as I always do, is that we all have our own ways of doing things, so suit yourself, select the approach which is right for your purpose and call it what you will. As long as you remember that the ethics of research always have to be honoured, that consent has to be given, full information provided about the purpose of the research and guarantees given about your definition of anonymity and confidentiality, all will be well.

Tape-recording interviews

It's always difficult to decipher who said what in group interviews, but in one-to-one interviews, tape-recording can be useful to check the wording of any statement you might wish to quote, to allow you keep eye contact with your interviewee, to help you look interested – and to make sure that what you write is accurate. It can be particularly helpful if you are attempting any form of content analysis and need to be able to listen several times in order to identify categories but perhaps it can be most useful because it allows you to code, summarize and to note particular comments which are of particular interest without having to try to write them down during the course of the interview (see Chapter 7 for Brendan Duffy's discussion of content analysis).

However, you cannot assume that all your respondents will be willing for their comments to be recorded and the knowledge that the tape is running can sometimes inhibit honest responses. Interviewees will, rightly, wish to know what you propose to do with the tape, who is to have access to it and how long it will be kept. You need to be prepared for a refusal. Even if respondents had agreed to a tape recording earlier, they may still refuse when the time comes and so you have to do all the necessary preliminary preparation of questions, prompts and probes in order to ensure, or try to ensure that all the main issues you wish to explore have been covered – and you will also need a checklist or schedule *and* a summary sheet.

Your difficulties are not at an end even if respondents do agree to be recorded. Many experienced researchers and supervisors feel strongly (and in fact state categorically) that all tapes must be transcribed. They make the point that if no transcription is done and made available for scrutiny if required, then interviewers can say what they like. Perish the thought, but they might even make up 'quotations' that suit their purpose. However, if you have to do the typing yourself, you can count on at least four hours work for every hour of interview, even if you are a skilful and quick typist, but significantly more if you are not. If voice transcription software becomes more sophisticated, and cheaper, then it might be possible for interview recordings to be transferred direct to a word program which would save all those hours of transcribing and could also be a great help in content analysis. However, for the time being, you are likely to depend on typing or word-processing from your own audio recording. In a short project, it is questionable whether you have the time for transcription, but in case anybody wishes to check any particular point, make sure you keep the tape until after the report has been examined – and until you are sure that no corrections or rewriting are required.

If respondents do not agree for the interview to be recorded, all is certainly not lost. We all learn to devise our own shorthand system but as soon as the interview is over, do your utmost to write up as much as you can remember. If your interview guide or schedule has been well planned *and piloted*, your questions, items and headings will help you not only to record responses but to remind you of what was said under each heading. Prompts listed on the schedule may never need to be used as prompts, but they will still serve as sub-headings and will provide the beginnings of a structure for your report. Whenever possible, statements that will be quoted in the report should be verified with the respondent. The last thing you want is for a statement to be challenged at the report stage.

One other thing. Sometimes, and particularly if respondents have enjoyed the interview, they may ask if you will let them know how the research goes. There can be time and money costs here, so take care not to promise too much. (Remember the problems Stephen Waters faced in Chapter 3?) However, your interviewees will have given you their time free, so if you can possibly manage it, it would be a courtesy to agree to let them have a very brief summary of findings – as long as such findings are not confidential. Once the summary is produced, it can be presented, if required, at meetings of research committees, ethics committees, departmental meetings, governing bodies, and to those who were involved in piloting your data-collecting instruments.

Bias – the old enemy

There is always the danger of bias creeping into interviews, largely because, as Selltiz et al. (1962: 583) point out, 'interviewers are human beings and not machines, and their manner may have an effect on respondents'. Where a team of interviewers is employed, serious bias may show up in data analysis, but if one researcher conducts a set of interviews, the bias maybe consistent and therefore go unnoticed. Dictionary definitions of 'bias' generally centre on the notion of distortion of judgement, prejudiced outlook, unfair influence. That sounds obvious enough but there can be problems over interpretation because one person's 'fair and unbiased point of view' may well be judged to be 'prejudice' by another (Bell and Opie 2002: 233).

Many factors can result in bias and there are always dangers in research carried out by individual researchers, particularly those who have strong views about the topic they are researching. It can occur in many ways, deliberately or unwittingly. It is very easy to fall into the bias trap, for example by selecting only those items in the literature review which support your point of view; using inappropriate language which might indicate strength of feeling in one direction and permitting value judgements to influence the way research findings are interpreted. Gray (2000) in her doctoral study of truancy in Western Australian schools, was very conscious of the fact that she was researching a topic in which she had a keen interest and about which she held strong views. She recalls that it was her constant questioning of practice and her critical attitude towards the interpretation of data which helped her to recognize signs of bias – and it is this kind of discipline which is required.

Miles and Huberman warn that:

> We have moments of illumination. Things 'come together'. The problem is that we could be wrong. A near-library of research evidence shows that people (researchers included) habitually tend to *overweight* facts they believe in or depend on, to *ignore or forget confirming instances* far more easily than disconfirming instances (Nisbet and Ross 1980). We do this by differentially weighting information, and by looking at part of the data, not all of them.
>
> (Miles and Huberman 1994: 253–4)

Jan Gray called her 'moments of illumination' when things 'came together' as 'the process of enlightenment'. She still had to ask herself whether she had 'overweighted' any facts because of her personal beliefs. Perhaps one her main strengths was that she knew what the dangers were. She was constantly on the lookout for signs of bias and she placed great emphasis on reflection on practice and on triangulation. (See Bell and Opie 2002: 129–70 for a discussion of Jan's research.)

So, we must be wise and vigilant, critical of our interpretation of the data, regularly question our practice and wherever possible triangulate. A supervisor who is familiar with the literature relating to your subject will quickly remind you if you have placed too much emphasis on x or y or have ignored a or b, and it's always wise to listen to what supervisors have to say. If you don't agree, that's up to you and as long as you make your own strong case, based on the available evidence and not merely on your opinions, you will be safe.

Remember!

People who agree to be interviewed deserve some consideration and so you will need to fit in with their plans, however inconvenient they may be for you. Try to fix a venue at a time when you will not be disturbed. Trying to interview when a telephone is constantly ringing and people are knocking at the door will destroy any chance of continuity.

Before you make the appointment, make sure official channels, if any, have been cleared. A letter from your supervisor, head of department, principal or research officer, saying what you are doing and why will always help. Of course, your statement about guarantees, anonymity and confidentiality issues should have been sent before the interview takes place.

It is difficult to lay down rules for the conduct of an interview. Common sense and normal good manners will, as always, take you a long way. You should always introduce yourself and ask if the respondent has any queries. When you make the appointment, say how long you anticipate the interview will take. Ask if that is acceptable and if the respondent says that is too long, you just have to do the best you can to discuss your main issues early. You're not in charge: the respondents are and you need them more than they need you. Interviews are very time-consuming. If you allow one hour maximum for the actual interview, there is also travelling time and time lost through any one of numerous mishaps (respondent late home, sudden crisis with children which causes delay, unexpected visitor who interrupts the interview, etc.). Then there is the time needed to consider what has been said during the interview, to go through notes and to extend and clarify points that may have been hastily noted. If you are working full-time, you are unlikely to be able to carry out more than one interview in an evening, and even if you are able to devote yourself full time to the task, it is difficult to cope with more than three or four interviews during the course of a day. Your original project plan should take account of the time required for planning and conducting interviews, for coping with cancelled arrangements, second visits and finding replacements for people who drop out.

Interviewing is not easy and many researchers have found it difficult to strike the balance between complete objectivity and trying to put the interviewee at ease. It is difficult to know how these difficulties can be overcome, though honesty about the purpose of the research and integrity in the conduct of the interview will all help. Daphne Johnson, a very experienced researcher and skilful supervisor, makes the point that it is the responsibility of the interviewer, not the interviewee to end an interview. She writes:

> It may have been difficult to negotiate access and to get in in the first place, but the interviewer who, once in, stays until he is thrown out, is working in the style of investigative journalism rather than social research . . . If an interview takes two or three times as long as the interviewer said it would, the respondent, whose other work or social activities have been accordingly delayed, will be irritated in retrospect, however enjoyable the experience may have been at the time. This sort of practice breaks one of the ethics of professional social research, which is that the field should not be left more difficult for subsequent investigators to explore by disenchanting respondents with the whole notion of research participation.
> (Johnson 1984: 14–15)

◉ Planning and conducting interviews checklist

1 Decide what you need to know.

List all the items about which information is required.

2 Ask yourself why you need this information.

Examine your list and remove any item that is not directly associated with the task.

3 Is an interview the best way of obtaining the information?

Consider alternatives.

4 If so, begin to devise questions in outline.

The final form of questions will depend on the type of interview.

5 Decide on the type of interview.

A structured interview will produce structured responses. Is this what you want, or is a more open approach required?

6 Refine the questions.

Write questions on cards. Check wording (see questionnaire checklist).

7 Consider how questions will be analysed.

Consult Chapter 12 before deciding finally about question type and question wording.

8 Prepare an interview schedule or guide and draft a summary sheet.

Consider the order of questions. Prepare prompts in case the respondent does not provide essential information freely.

9 Pilot your schedule and summary sheet.

Both need to be tested, and you need practice in asking questions and recording responses.

10 Revise the schedule, if necessary.

Take account of pilot respondents' comments.

11 WATCH FOR BIAS

If you have strong views about some aspect of the topic, be particularly vigilant. If someone else asked the same question, would they get the same answer?

12 Select who to interview.	Interviews take time. Try to select a representative sample. Decide what to do if selected people are not willing or able to give an interview. Be realistic about the number of interviews that can be conducted in the time available.
13 Try to fix a time and place where you will not be disturbed.	
14 Make sure official channels have been cleared, and let interviewees see any protocol documents beforehand.	A letter from your supervisor, head or principal, explaining the purpose of the research may be helpful.
15 Introduce yourself and give interviewees the opportunity to ask for any necessary clarification. You will, of course, have already sent a letter and a statement outlining the purpose of the research.	Say what will happen to the information provided by the interviewee. Clarify the meaning of anonymity in the context of the study.
16 Agree with the interviewee how long the interview will last.	Do your utmost not to exceed the time limit.
17 Try to check the accuracy of your notes with interviewees, particularly if some items might be quoted in the report.	But don't promise to check with respondents after the interview if this is likely to prove difficult.
18 If you wish to tape-record the interview, you must obtain permission from the interviewee.	Remember that it takes a long time to transcribe a tape-recorded interview, if this is what you intend to do. Write up as you go along. Don't wait until all interviews are completed.
19 Honesty and integrity are important.	Make no promises that cannot be fulfilled. Respect respondents' views about anonymity. If you know a respondent has been indiscreet in revealing confidential information, *never* take advantage.

20 Common sense and good manners will take you a long way.	People who agree to be interviewed are doing you a favour. They deserve consideration.
21 Don't queer the pitch for other researchers by disenchanting respondents with the whole notion of research participation.	There are many ways in which participants can become disenchanted. Appointments not kept or the interviewer arriving late; taking longer than promised; promising to check for accuracy; promising a summary of findings but not delivering; conducting the interview in a hostile manner – and failing to thank the interviewee.

Further reading

Bowling, A. (2002) *Research Methods in Health: Investigating Health and Health Services*, 2nd edn. Maidenhead: Open University Press. Chapters 11 and 13 in Section IV discuss interviews and their response rates in quantitative research, including techniques of survey interviewing. Chapter 16 in Section V deals with unstructured interviews and focus groups in qualitative research.

Darlington, Y. and Scott, D. (2002) *Qualitative Research in Practice: Stories from the Field*. Buckingham: Open University Press (originally published by Allen and Unwin Australia, 2002). Chapter 3 considers the various stages of in-depth interviewing. It is perhaps unlikely you will have the time to become involved in such interviews but time is not the only pre-condition. As Darlington and Scott make clear, considerable skill, experience *and* training are required. If you have these attributes and feel you would be interested in considering this approach, it would be advisable to consult your supervisor and to read this chapter before making up your mind.

Denscombe, M. (1998) *The Good Research Guide for Small-scale Social Research Projects*. Buckingham: Open University Press. Chapter 7 'Interviews' is an excellent chapter, including when it is appropriate to use interviews for research, types of research interview, group and focus interviews, interviewer effect, planning and recording the interview – and much more. Helpful checklists are provided. If you have very limited time, this is the chapter I would suggest you might wish to consult.

Hayes, N. (2000) *Doing Psychological Research: Gathering and Analysing Data*. Maidenhead: Open University Press. Chapter 7 deals with interviewer effects, conducting interviews, stages of interview research and ethical issues in interview research.

Keats, D.M. (2000) *Interviewing: A Practical Guide for Students and Professionals*. Buckingham: Open University Press. Keats considers the use of interviews in research, and in particular issues involved in interviewing young children, the elderly and people from ethnic communities.

Kitzinger, J. and Barbour, R.S. (1999) 'Introduction to the challenge and promise of focus groups', in R.S. Barbour and J. Kitzinger (eds) *Developing Focus Group Research: Politics, Theory and Practice*. London: Sage.

May, T. (2001) *Social Research: Issues, Methods and Process*, 3rd edn. Buckingham: Open University Press. This book is particularly useful in a number of ways, particularly Chapter 6 'Interviewing: methods and process' which provides a review of different types of interview in social research, issues in interviewing and the analysis of interviews. The section on group and focus interviews is also helpful.

Oliver, P. (2003) *The Student's Guide to Research Ethics*. Maidenhead: Open University Press. Pages 12–16 discuss informed consent and situations where engaging in research may be ethically undesirable. Chapter 3 'Research and the respondent: ethical issues during the research' considers the ethics of tape-recording interviews and the right of respondents to end involvement in the research. These few extracts (and much more) are well worth consulting.

Wellington, J.J. (1996) *Methods and Issues in Educational Research*. University of Sheffield Division of Education: USDE papers in Education. Pages 59–63 deal with focus groups, consider what makes them rather different from group interviews and gives three short examples of various uses of focus groups.

10

DIARIES, LOGS AND CRITICAL INCIDENTS

On the face of it, diaries are an attractive way of gathering information about the way individuals spend their time. In research, diaries are not personal records of engagements or journals of thoughts and activities, but records or logs of professional activities. They can provide valuable information about work patterns and activities, provided diary keepers are clear about what they are being asked to do, and why.

They almost always cover an agreed time span – a day, a week, a month, or occasionally much longer – depending on what information is required. At certain specified times, 'on the spot' or retrospectively, respondents are asked to say what they did and in some cases, why. Instructions need to be explicit. Do you really want to know that someone had a cup of tea, paid the milkman or had a bath, or are you interested only in specifically job-related activities?

Completing diary forms can be time-consuming and irritating for a busy person who has to keep stopping work to make an entry and if respondents are not fully in sympathy with the task, or have been press-ganged into filling in diary forms, they will probably not complete them thoroughly, if at all.

As in all research activities, it is essential to contact and preferably to meet the people who will be giving up their time, so that you can explain the purpose of the exercise fully, discuss any possible difficulties and, if possible, resolve them. Reluctant diarists will rarely provide usable data, so preliminary consultation is of the utmost importance. As with any other form of data collecting, some form of check with diary keepers is often desirable and sometimes essential if interest is to be maintained.

In any diary exercise there can be problems over representativeness. Was this day of the week typical of others or is Monday always the crisis day? Is this week exceptional? Oppenheim draws attention to this problem and reminds us that:

> The respondents' interest in writing up the diary will cause them to modify the very behaviour we wish them to record. If, for instance, they are completing a week's diary of their television viewing behaviour, this may cause them to engage in 'duty viewing' in order to 'have something to record', or they may view 'better' types of programmes in order to create a more favourable impression.
>
> (Oppenheim 1992: 252)

This may well be true, but many other methods of data collection can also have an effect on normal behaviour, as many researchers have discovered during the course of their investigations.

The diary-interview method

There are many different ways in which diaries are used. They can be standalone methods of data collection or be part of a larger study incorporating interviews, questionnaires and observation. In 1977, Zimmerman and Wieder used diaries in their ethnographic study of the counter-culture in the USA as a *preliminary* to interviewing in cases where it was not at first clear what were the right questions to ask. In an article on their **diary-interview method**, they discussed the role of diaries as 'an observational log maintained by subjects which can then be used as a basis for intensive interviewing' (Zimmerman and Wieder 1977: 481).

The potential for diaries as question-generating devices is clear, but Zimmerman and Wieder took this process a step further. They viewed the use of a diary, in conjunction with the diary interview, as an approximation to the method of participant observation, including: the length of time involved; the fact that any observer, even a participant, may have an effect on normal behaviour; and, in some studies, moral, legal or ethical constraints. They proposed the use of the diary interview method 'for those situations where the problems of direct observation resist solution, or where further or more extended observation strains available resources' (p. 481).

They asked their respondents to record in chronological order the activities in which they engaged over a seven-day period, following the formula what/when/where/how? The 'what?' involved a description of the activity or discussion recorded in the diarists' own categories. 'When?' involved reference to the time and timing of the activity, with special attention to recording the actual sequence of events. 'Where?' involved a designation of the location of the activity, suitably coded to prevent identification of individuals or places. The 'how?' involved a description of whatever logistics were entailed by the activity (p. 486).

Clearly, diarists must be of a certain educational level to understand the instructions, let alone complete the diary. They must also have time. If you are asking colleagues to cooperate by completing diaries, be very sure that the diary is the best way of obtaining the information you need and that you can convince your diarists that what they are doing is likely to be of practical use.

Variations in diary use and design

There are many variations in the way diaries are structured, the time over which they are conducted and the detail required, as will be seen in the following accounts of the primary pupils' food diary, the supply teachers' diary and time log, the general practitioners' time logs, the asthma treatment diary and the heads of department critical incidents diary.

The primary pupils' food diary

Burgess incorporated diaries as a method of data collecting in many of the research projects he conducted over the years. In his chapter 'On diaries and diary keeping' in Bennett, Glatter and Levačič (1994), he discusses two very different diary studies. The first (Morrison and Burgess 1993 and Burgess and Morrison 1993) related to a primary pupils' food diary study. The Zimmerman and Wieder what? when? where? how? approach was again adopted. The pupils were asked:

What did you eat and drink today?
When did you eat and drink today?
Where did you eat and drink today? (at school, home, somewhere else?)

(Burgess and Morrison 1993: Appendix)

Other items were added, namely whether they had enjoyed a celebration, like a birthday, on any day and whether they liked what they had eaten or drunk. As the diary was to be completed by children, a specific approach needed to be devised.

First, it was important to talk with pupils to explain what it is that had to be done. Secondly, the time period over which a diary would be kept was limited to one week including a weekend ... Inside the diary there were a series of instructions which were included in a covering letter addressed to each pupil.

(Burgess 1994: 304)

The supply teachers' diary and time log

In the second study, Burgess worked on a very different and far more detailed diary study concerning the experience of and relationship amongst teachers, substitute teachers and pupils when regular teachers were unable to take a timetabled class. Sheila Galloway and Marlene Morrison also worked on the project and conducted the fieldwork (Morrison and Galloway 1993). A three-column grid was devised, the 'time' in the first column, the 'main activities' in the second and 'other' in the third. The purpose of this **time grid** or **time log** was to provide a framework within which supply teachers could record what happened and when, but which also gave them freedom to develop their ideas. The researchers felt that this format allowed the diary writers to 'place limits on the extent to which they give access to their world and their work' (Burgess 1994: 308).

The general practitioners' time log

Sutherland and Cooper also used a time log as part of their investigation into ill health and job dissatisfaction among general practitioners (GPs) working in the UK. GPs were asked to complete what amounted to a detailed record of how they spent their day, in order to identify the amount of time spent on various activities, the necessity (or otherwise) and purpose of those activities. The log consisted of six columns, with the headings of start time, duration, activity, time problem (who/what/why?), outcome, feelings/reaction/further action (Sutherland and Cooper 2003: 184). After three or four days of entries, or when the log was completed, the doctors were asked to rank the importance of the activities, which could well have been the most difficult part of the log exercise for professionals who might have found everything they did important.

Busy doctors were being asked to complete full-day records of their activities, to include reasons for any time problems, what happened as a result of time delays, how they felt about the delays (angry/frustrated/pleased?) and what action was taken. It had to be a log which could be 'easily completed with minimum effort' (p. 66) and no doubt the diarists had to be convinced there was some purpose to the exercise. In fact, the diary exercise was designed to: 'highlight interruptions, failure to delegate, and the ways in which other people disrupted your schedule. Ultimately, it should be possible to use your time log to identify the source of disruptions and enable you to prioritize key activities' (Sutherland and Cooper 2003: 67). It was anticipated that identification of problem areas would enable doctors to produce an action plan to improve their time management behaviour and to learn how to 'Work smarter not harder' (p. 69). I think many stressed GPs would feel that the possibility of an improved, less stressful professional life would be worth the effort of completing the log.

The asthma treatment diary

Bowling (2002: 426) reports on two interesting but very different diary studies carried out by Hyland and Crocker (1995) and by Hyland (1996) who carried out diary-with-questionnaire studies into the impact of asthma treatment on patients. Patients were asked to complete 'quality of life' diaries over a six-month period but in short time slots. The first asked patients to complete daily diaries over a two-week period. This was followed by a request for them to produce a diary for the first week of every month for six months and finally, the researchers sent out questionnaires three and six months after treatment. They concluded that 'the diaries proved to be better longitudinal correlations with the physiology of the respondents in comparison with the questionnaires, while the questionnaires had better cross-correlations with physiology' (Bowling 2002: 426).

So, as always, the selection of the data-collecting instruments depends on the purpose of the study, the type of information needed, *and* the willingness of respondents to spend the necessary time completing diaries, questionnaires or being interviewed.

The heads of department critical incidents and problem-portfolio logs

In many ways, the **critical incidents technique** adopts the same, or similar processes adopted by Burgess in his supply teachers' study and by Sutherland and Cooper in their GP time log. Both attempted to identify essential and important aspects of work behaviour and both were concerned with which tasks were 'critical' and which were 'non-critical'. Oxtoby also used a job diary/log in his study of how heads of department (HoDs) in further education colleges in England and Wales spent their time and at first considered the possibility of asking diarists to identify 'critical incidents' in their working day. He defined a critical incident as being a task or an incident which makes the difference between success and failure in carrying out important parts of the job (Oxtoby 1979: 239). He writes that:

> The idea is to collect reports as to what people do that is particularly effective in contributing to good performance and then to scale the incidents in order of difficulty, frequency and importance to the job as a whole. The technique scores over the use of diaries in that it is centred on specific happenings and on what is judged to be effective behaviour. But it is still laborious and does not lend itself to objective quantification.
>
> (Oxtoby 1979: 239–40)

The use of job diaries/logs is perhaps the most simple and widely accepted way of finding out how time is spent in any group or institution, but as Oxtoby discovered:

> Self-recording can be inaccurate – many of the shorter episodes tend to get omitted – and compiling a detailed diary is usually a tiresome and onerous business. Although it is undoubtedly valuable in terms of enabling people to make more effective use of their time, a diary does not provide much reliable information about the skills or qualities developed. Moreover, the prospect of using diaries to compare differences between large numbers of staff and their jobs is extremely daunting, if only because of the difficulties in handling the data. There are snags, therefore, in employing job diaries to analyse the diversity of HoD activities.
>
> (Oxtoby 1979: 240)

Eventually, he decided on a 'problem portfolio' approach originally advocated by Marples (1967) in which respondents were asked to record information about how each problem arose, methods used to solve it, difficulties encountered, and so on.

As will be apparent from the above, there can be problems in the use of diaries as a method of gathering evidence, not least the time respondents need to complete the forms. However, diaries can produce a wealth of interesting data and are relatively simple to administer – at least if there are only a few diarists. Analysis of completed forms is not so simple, however, so, as always, you will need to consider how responses will be analysed *before* you put your subjects to the trouble of filling in the diaries. If you are considering using diaries as part of your project, you may wish to consult the checklist at the end of this chapter before you distribute them.

Personal research diaries

Personal research diaries or logs come into a different category from the above. These are for you and can be invaluable in tracking the progress of your research, recording names, addresses, notes of telephone calls, good ideas you had in the middle of the night – anything that happens (or might happen). From the start of any research or any major writing job, I always carry a notebook around, small enough to fit into a pocket. Everyone has different ideas about what should go in and what should be left out. I have no difficulty in deciding because I include everything. Rough notes, target dates (and targets achieved or not achieved), dates of interviews, dates questionnaires were distributed (and returned). Names and telephone numbers of people I have spoken to or met. Difficulties experienced, advice to myself not to do something in this or that way again! Reminder about what I must ask the librarian. A note about how I might resolve the problem of . . . something or other, which occurred to me when I was sitting on a bus. If I hadn't written it down at that time, I should in all probably have forgotten it the next day. I might have remembered that I had a good idea while sitting on a bus but . . . what on earth was it? A reference (new to me) that someone told me about when I was having a sandwich in the cafeteria. Times I left home to see someone and time returned, if I remember. Every entry with a date. Do this tomorrow . . . Write this up immediately! Transfer this reference to the main list of references. I recall that one student considered my way of jotting down everything was disorganized. I suppose it is, but I do star and highlight items that need to be given further thought and as I've said numerous times in this book, we all have our own ways of working so adopt ways of doing things that seem to work for you. As far as I am concerned, the only rule is that *you start your diary, log (call it what you will) as soon as you start your research and keep it going.*

The ethics of diary use

Burgess (1994: 308) expresses concern about the extent of intrusion into diary writers' lives and urges researchers to be aware of this possibility. For example, in the food diary, he asks researchers to consider the extent to which the exercise constitutes intrusion into the lives of the children and their families before selecting the diary approach. He draws our attention to the fact that if the purpose of the supply teacher diary is 'to gain access to material that would otherwise be hidden from the researchers' view . . . to what extent is such a device intrusive on the lives and work of teachers?' (p. 308). I suppose it can equally be said that interviews, questionnaires and observations can also intrude. Researchers frequently use diaries as one of several methods of data collecting in their investigations. All I can say is that the impact of our research on the respondents must always be considered before decisions are made about which approach to adopt and that the same ethical considerations should apply to diary studies as for any other method or technique.

⊙ Diaries, logs and critical incidents checklist

1 Decide what you need to know.

List all the items about which information is required.

2 Ask yourself why you need this information.

You may decide you don't need it after all.

3 Is a diary or critical-incidents checklist the best way of obtaining the information?

Would another approach be better?

4 Diary completion is not generally a suitable tool for use with people of limited educational background.

Make sure your respondents will be able to understand what is required and to fulfil your requirements.

5 Instructions must be precise.

Diarists must be quite clear about what you want them to do.

6 Make sure respondents know *why* they are being asked to carry out this chore and what you plan to do with the information.

Allow time at the planning stage to discuss with your respondents what is involved.

7 Always pilot your diary before you distribute it to your respondents.

No matter how busy you are, this must be done.

8 Decide how you propose to deal with responses *before* you ask for diaries to be completed.

9 Try to find time to check progress with the diarists.

If you are asking people to carry out this task for more than one day, evidence seems to indicate that a solicitous inquiry about how things are going may help them to keep on with the task.

10 Remember to get permission to approach your diarists.

11 Write up your findings as soon as you can.

Your pilot exercise will give you some ideas about likely main headings and analysis.

12 Completing a diary is a chore. Don't forget to thank your respondents.

Give them feedback if you can, but don't promise anything if you are unlikely to have to time to do it.

Further reading

Bowling, A. (2002) *Research Methods in Health: Investigating Health and Health Services*, 2nd edn. Maidenhead: Open University Press. Ann Bowling, writing about the use of diaries with patients, refers to two major diary exercises relating to a trial of asthma treatments. See Hyland, M.E. and Crocker, G.R. (1995) 'Validation of an asthma quality of life diary in a clinical trial'. *Thorax*, 50: 724–30. Also, Hyland, M.E. (1996) 'Diary assessments of quality of life', *Quality of Life Newsletter*, 16: 8–9.

Burgess, R.G. (1994) Chapter 21, 'On diaries and diary keeping', in N. Bennett, R. Glatter and R. Levačić (eds) *Improving Educational Management through Research and Consultancy*. London: Paul Chapman Publishing, in association with The Open University. In this chapter, Burgess discusses the use of logs, diaries and journals, and includes examples of the supply teacher project considered in this chapter and also of an interactive video use diary. He includes ethical questions relating to intrusion into the lives of respondents.

Hart, E. and Bond, M. (1995) *Action Research for Health and Social Care: A Guide to Practice*. Buckingham: Open University Press. Pages 201–4 give two extracts from diary studies, one relating to outpatients' clinic experiences; the second an extract from a log.

Hayes, N. (2000) *Doing Psychological Research: Gathering and Analysing Data*. Buckingham: Open University Press. Chapter 9, 'Analysing documents' (pp. 147–55), gives useful guidance about the advantages, disadvantages, design and analysis of diary studies. Worth consulting.

Morrison, M. (2002) Chapter 13, 'Using diaries in research', in M. Coleman and A.R.J. Briggs (eds) *Research Methods in Educational Leadership and Management*. London: Paul Chapman Publishing. This chapter provides examples of extracts from several diaries and includes sections on researchers' and research informants' diaries, the design and analysis of diaries and combining diaries with interviews.

Sutherland, V. and Cooper, C.L. (2003) *De-stressing Doctors: A Self-management Guide*. London: Butterworth Heinemann.

● 11

OBSERVATION STUDIES

No doubt it will seem unnecessary to remind you, once again, that before you begin to consider observation as one of your data-collecting techniques, you need first to decide *what* you wish to observe, *what* your main areas of interest are and *why* you think observation will produce the information you need. Is it to be one of several data-collecting methods or the only one? Are you considering observation as a form of validating other evidence? Do you really need evidence from observation, because it requires considerable skill, 'a capacity for original thinking and the ability to spot significant events. It is certainly not an easy option' (Nisbet 1977: 15). Careful planning and piloting are essential, and it takes practice to get the most out of this technique. However, once mastered, it can reveal characteristics of groups or individuals which would have been impossible to discover by other means. Interviews, as Nisbet and Watt (1980: 13) point out, provide important data, but they reveal only how people *perceive* what happens, not necessarily what actually happens. Observation can be useful in discovering whether people do what they say they do, or behave in the way they claim to behave. However, observation also depends on the way people perceive what is being said or done.

On occasions, I have been to meetings and after discussing what happened with colleagues, I have begun to wonder whether I was at the same meeting. We had very different recollections of who said what and what decisions were made. If three or four people stand at a window overlooking a busy street, observing what is going on for five minutes or so, and then write up what they have seen, the accounts are likely to vary. The observers will have their own focus and will interpret significant events in their own way. As observers, we 'filter' the material we obtain from observation and that can lead us to impose our own interpretations on what is observed and so fail to understand 'what an activity means for those who are involved in it' (Darlington and Scott 2002: 75–6).

The fact that we are all fallible does not mean there is little point in including observation as one of our data-collecting techniques but it does mean that we have to be particularly aware of the dangers, do our best to eliminate preconceived ideas and prejudices and constantly look out for possible signs of bias.

Solo observers are always in danger of accusations of bias or misinterpretation and particularly if you are researching in your own professional area, try to persuade, or even blackmail a friend or fellow student to join you for as many observation sessions as can be managed.

Observation can be structured or unstructured, participant or non-participant. Each approach has some advantages but also disadvantages. All require a degree of expertise, some more than others; but if you have, after careful thought, decided to include observation as one of your data-collecting instruments, then you will need to decide which approach to adopt, and why.

Unstructured observation

Researchers who decide to adopt an unstructured approach to observation generally do so because though they may have a clear idea of the purpose of the observation, they may not be so clear about the detail. They are prepared to spend sufficient time on fieldwork, familiarization and accumulation of data, from which they anticipate that focus and structure will emerge (Punch 1998: 186). In other words, as in grounded theory, the researcher will 'Postpone definitions and structures until a pattern has been observed . . . The researcher develops the conceptual categories *from* the data and then continues with the fieldwork in order to elaborate these while the data are still available for access' (Bowling 2002: 367).

Unstructured observation can be useful to generate hypotheses, but it is not easy to manage. If the nature of your research points you in the direction of unstructured observation, read as widely as you can, ask colleagues and friends if they know of anyone who successfully adopted this approach and consult your supervisor before you commit yourself to this – or for that matter any other approach.

Participant observation

Some of the disadvantages of unstructured observation may also apply to participant observation, which involves the researcher participating in the daily life of an individual, group or community and listening, observing, questioning and understanding (or trying to understand) the life of the individuals concerned. In some cases, researchers may have been involved for months or even years in a community in order to become generally accepted as one of the group. In others, researchers remained clearly outside the group, as was Lacey (1976: 65) who wrote about his experiences at 'Hightown Grammar' where, for three years, he taught, observed classes and talked to teachers and pupils.

Cohen, Manion and Morrison draw attention to some of the criticisms levelled at participant observation.

> The accounts that typically emerge from participant observations echo the criticisms of qualitative data ... being described as subjective, biased, impressionistic, idiosyncratic and lacking in the precise quantifiable measures that are the hallmark of survey research and experimentation. While it is probably true that nothing can give better insight into the life of a gang of juvenile delinquents than going to live with them for an extended period of time, critics of participant observation will point to the dangers of 'going native' as a result of playing a role within such a group.
>
> (Cohen et al. 2000: 313–14)

Experienced participant observers are well aware of the dangers of bias but it is difficult to stand back and adopt the role of objective observer when all the members of the group or organization are known to you. If you are researching in your own organization, you will be familiar with the personalities, strengths and weaknesses of colleagues, and this familiarity may cause you to overlook aspects of behaviour which would be immediately apparent to a non-participant observer seeing the situation for the first time.

In spite of the criticisms, participant observation can yield valuable data. Researchers are able to observe changes over time. Rather than having to depend on one-off observations or at best observations carried out over a limited period of time, the participant observer is able to share in the lives and activities of other people; to learn their language and interpret their meanings; to remember actions and speech; and to interact with people in their own environment (Burgess 1982: 45). By listening and experiencing, 'impressions are formed and theories considered, reflected upon, developed and modified' (May 2001: 174).

May acknowledges that:

> participant observation is not an easy method to perform, or to analyse, but despite the arguments of its critics, it is a systematic and disciplined study which, if performed well, greatly assists in understanding human actions and brings with it new ways of viewing the social world.
>
> (p. 174)

I agree, but in 100-hour projects, it might be unwise to undertake participant *or* unstructured observation unless you are already experienced, have the time and are very familiar with the techniques involved. In order to derive worthwhile information from the data, you will probably need to adopt a more structured approach and to devise some form of recording in order to identify aspects of behaviour which you have identified beforehand as being of likely relevance to the research.

Structured observation and keeping records

The structured approach can also be criticized as being subjective and biased. You have decided on the focus rather than allowing the focus to emerge. However, you will already have formulated a hypothesis or identified the objectives of your study and the importance of observing some aspect of behaviour will have become apparent.

Whether your observation is structured or unstructured and whether you are observing as a participant or a non-participant, your role is to observe and record in as objective a way as possible.

The fact that different observers can, and do produce different accounts of situations is worrying for all researchers who hope to include observation as one of their methods of collecting data. In Denscombe's opinion:

> It is precisely this problem which is addressed by systematic observation and its use of an *observation schedule*. The whole purpose of the schedule is to minimize, possibly eliminate, the variations that will arise from data based on individual perceptions of events and situations. Its aim is to provide a framework for observation which *all* observers will use.
>
> (Denscombe 2003: 194–5)

Observation schedules can take the form of a checklist, a diary, chart, time or critical incidents log – or whichever approach suits your purpose. Spradley (1980), Williams (1994), Denscombe (2003) and Bowling (2002) all give examples of charts, grids, categories and other methods of recording which will give you a range of useful ideas for devising schemes of your own. The sad fact is that in spite of all the tried-and-tested methods that have been employed by researchers over the years, there never seems to be an example that is quite right for a particular task. Inevitably, you will find you have to adapt or devise a completely new approach, and all new systems need careful piloting and refining in the light of experience. If you have access to only one group or one meeting, you must be quite sure that your selected method of recording is going to work. You will probably need to devise your own system of shorthand symbols and these will have to be memorized because you can't always be consulting your notes during the course of a meeting or observation of a group. You will need to decide beforehand how often to record what is happening (all the time? every three seconds? every five minutes? every twenty minutes?) and with whom (all the group? individuals?).

Preparation is all-important. Charts and seating plans have to be prepared. You will need to discuss with whoever is in charge where it would be best to sit. Opinions vary. In a lecture room, there is some merit in sitting where the students can see you. At least that way they are not always turning round to see what you are doing, but if participants have other views, listen – and conform. An observer can never pass entirely unnoticed, but the aim is to be as unobtrusive as possible so that observed behaviour is as close to normal as possible.

It's impossible to record everything, so you need to be clear whether you are interested in the *content* or *process* of a group or meeting, in *interaction* between individuals, in the *nature of contributions* or in *some specific aspect* such as the effectiveness of questioning techniques. Once you have decided what you wish to find out and have satisfied yourself that you need this information to further your research, then you will be in a position to consider what methods of recording will best suit your purposes.

Recording behaviour

One of the commonly used methods of recording behaviour is based on a system of interaction-process analysis originally devised by R.F. Bales in 1950. He devised a method of classifying or coding under one of 12 headings which enabled the observer to make a record of the behaviour of individuals in groups. Examples of his categories of behaviour are 'shows tension release' and he then identifies indicators of tension release (jokes, laughs, shows satisfaction) and 'shows antagonism' (deflates others' status, defends or asserts self). Since 1950 many different types of approach have been devised, some relatively simple and others extremely complicated. The Flanders system, which was derived from the Bales method of classifying behaviour, is one of the best known. Flanders (1970) devised ten categories of teacher/student behaviour (the Flanders interaction analysis categories), which the observer used as a basis for categorizing and recording what took place in the classroom. Observers were required to record what was happening every three seconds and to enter the appropriate category number on a prepared chart. The problem with Flanders-type systems is that the categories are quite complex, have numbers of sub-sections and inevitably involve the observer making some value judgements as to which category is closest to the particular types of behaviour.

The requirement to record every three seconds means that the observer has to be fully conversant with categories and criteria and to recall instantly the number assigned to particular aspects of behaviour. This takes a considerable amount of practice. The more complicated (and so more thorough) the system of categories, the harder it is to manage.

I have to confess that the one time I tried to use the 'every three seconds' approach was a failure. Trying to keep track of the time and at the same time observing and classifying activities under Flanders-type headings became impossible and so a simpler system had to be devised. I had go back to basics and to ask myself again why I was observing the meeting. What exactly did I want to find out? What was feasible to record? And only then was I able to eliminate any irrelevances and begin to simplify the categories.

Most researchers I know have devised their own system of categories, and limited them to about three or four. Are you interested in who is aggressive, time-wasting, positive in moving forward the business of the meeting, disagreeing about much (or all) that is being proposed – or none of those things? Ask yourself whether you are more interested in the *behaviour* of individuals or the *content* of what is being said. Or perhaps you might be interested only in how long each individual speaks and who is silent throughout. If one of your categories happened to be 'disagreement', participants may not need to speak. A lot can be deduced from facial expressions, nods, scowls or signs of dissent from the 'silent' individuals. It's up to you to decide on your categories and, once having decided, to devise ways of recording.

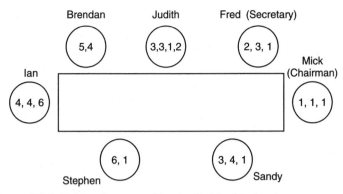

Figure 11.1 Table plan recording individual behaviour according to categories.

The way in which observations are recorded is a matter of personal preference. If you are observing a meeting, it's helpful to have a table plan before the meeting starts as in Figure 11.1. Each of the categories is given a number and obviously you will know which number applies to which category. In Figure 11.1, if category number 1 deals with aggressive behaviour, you would put '1' underneath or at the side of each participant for each indication of such behaviour. Or you could record behaviour in a chart as in Figure 11.2.

Contributions might also be plotted on a graph or presented in whichever way clearly illustrates the nature of the contributions made. And always bear in mind that it will not be enough merely to present the information as observed. Commentary on the significance (or lack of significance) will also be necessary.

Content

The analysis of the content of a meeting or group discussion is rather more straightforward. If the main interest is in who makes most contributions and spends most time speaking (not necessarily the same thing), then a simple chart on the lines

Participants	Categories						
	1	2	3	4	5	6	Totals
Chairman (Mick)	✓✓✓						③
Secretary (Fred)	✓	✓	✓				③
Judith	✓	✓	✓✓				④
Brendan				✓	✓		②
Ian				✓✓		✓	③
Stephen	✓					✓	②
Sandy	✓		✓	✓			③
Totals	⑦	②	④	④	①	②	

Figure 11.2 Chart recording total number of entries for each behaviour category.

shown in Figure 11.3 might be devised. In this case, a vertical line would indicate that the named person spoke for a set time (say, half a minute or less). A following horizontal line would indicate that the same person continued to speak for the same set period.

The previous examples appear to be fairly simple to manage and should produce useful, though limited, information. If all you need to know is who spoke most or which topics took up most time, then they will suffice and adaptations to these charts have been used to good effect in many different situations. However, if you wish to find out who says most about what, then a more complex system is needed, and it may be best to make fuller notes during the course of the observation and then transfer to a summary chart.

Do your best to get some observation practice to try out your recording skills. If you have the opportunity (and obtain permission) to attend a formal meeting as an observer, ask if you might see an agenda beforehand. Sometimes this will be granted;

Participants	
Mick	$/// =$
Fred	
Judith	$/ \equiv //$
Brendan	$//$
Ian	$//// = / \equiv$
Stephen	$//$
Sandy	$/ = //$
Multiple speaking	$///$

Figure 11.3 Example of a chart recording speaking contributions by individuals.

sometimes not. It's a great help if you are able to see what items are to be considered, so it's worth asking.

If you are unable to attend any meetings, group sessions or classes, try out your recording skills on a television programme. Political discussions are good, because they often degenerate into arguments, with everyone speaking at the same time. Select no more than three categories, such as 'dissent', 'aggression', 'agreement', but make sure you are clear about how you define each of these categories. What are the indicators of 'aggression' (shouting, pointing of a finger, sneering, what else?) Devise your own chart and see if you can record the contributions. Ten minutes might be quite enough but that would give you ideas about the complexity of recording, even when your categories seem to be perfectly clear. You may discover that categories can sometimes overlap, contributions to the discussion can come thick and fast and you have to concentrate, to look at contributors' expressions, to listen for mixed messages *and* to put your number in the right place at the right time. Your first shot at a chart may not suit you and so you will need to devise one or two different designs to see which you find easiest for recording, analysis and interpretation after the event.

A few words of warning – again   ◉

At the beginning of this chapter, I said that observation can often reveal characteristics of groups or individuals that would have been impossible to discover by other means. This has been demonstrated in many research studies which made extensive use of observation techniques, but the greatest care has to be taken to ensure that you get the most out of your periods of observation. You are unlikely to have three years in which to begin an investigation with an entirely open mind and to evolve hypotheses and methods as you go along. It is likely you will only have one opportunity to observe a meeting, group or class and so you will need to be quite clear about the purpose of your observation and why you are observing that particular group or individual. You may discover that unforeseen and interesting information emerges during the course of your observation, but you will be mainly dependent on the decisions taken before you begin your period of observation for the type of data you eventually gather. If you make a decision before a meeting that your main interest is the content of the meeting, then charts, grids or checklists have to be devised with that aim in mind. It will be too late to record interactions. If your main interest is process, then other methods will have to be found to record how a class or a meeting is conducted. As you select and refine your methods, keep constantly in mind the same old questions: 'What do I need to know?' 'Why do I need to know it?' and 'What shall I do with this information when I have it?'

Pilot exercises and practice in recording will answer some of these questions and will point to weaknesses in technique. When you begin your one-off observation exercise, you need to be as sure as you can that you are prepared and ready.

After the event

The task is not complete when the observation has taken place and records have been made. If you were observing a meeting and felt at the end of it that it was rather ineffectual, you would need to analyse the reasons. Was the process altogether too formal? Did the chair (or someone else) speak for 80 per cent of the time? Were contributions from some people dismissed? Some forms of interaction analysis can help you to classify process and content, but whatever methods of recording you have selected, it is essential to consider the event as a whole, as soon after the event as you can. Review in your mind what took place and decide whether any conclusions can be drawn that might be of interest in your study.

Useful though grids, forms and checklists are, they are limited. They cannot take account of emotions, micropolitical processes behind some of the interactions, the influence of certain key members of the group, and the effect they can have on the way meetings and discussions are conducted and decisions reached.

The work which goes into recording and adding up the numbers of committee or group members who showed aggression, agreement, dissent or who spoke for a specified period of time is important, but it is even more important to place what you observe in its organizational and/or curricular context, to look beyond the event itself and, in Nisbet's words, 'to spot significant events' (1977: 15).

⦿ Observation studies checklist

1 Decide exactly what you need to know.

List all topics/aspects about which information is required.

2 Consider why you need this information.

Examine your list and remove any item that is not directly associated with the task.

3 Is observation the best way of obtaining the information you need?

Consider alternatives.

4 Decide which aspects you need to investigate.	Are you particularly interested in content, process, interaction, intervention – or something else?
5 Request permission to observe.	Clear official channels and also discuss what is involved with the individuals concerned.
6 Devise a suitable grid, checklist or chart.	Consult published examples and adapt where necessary. Decide on your categories.
7 Consider what you will do with the information.	Is it likely to produce anything of interest? Will the data be sufficiently complete to enable you to come to any conclusions?
8 Pilot your method and revise if necessary and invite someone to observe with you. Compare notes afterwards to see if you saw the same things.	Memorize categories. Devise your own system of shorthand (symbols, letters, etc.). Practise recording until you are confident you can cope.
9 Prepare carefully before the observation.	Draw a plan of the room, indicating seating arrangements and layout. Make sure you have enough copies of grids or checklists. Consult minutes of previous meetings, agendas, schemes of work, etc.
10 Discuss where you will sit with whoever is in charge and with people who will be observed.	You want to be as unobtrusive as possible. Exactly where you sit will depend on your own preferences and the views of participants.
11 Remember that no grid, no matter how sophisticated, will tell the full story.	Try to place the event in its organizational context. Obtain as much information about the organization/institution/committee or group before the observation.

12 Always write up field notes as you go along, add items to your summary sheet and write your thoughts about significant events.	If you wait until you have time, you will forget important items.
13 Analyse and interpret the data. Do your best to eliminate bias or misinterpretation.	Statements about what has been observed are only part of the task. Consider what the facts indicate or imply.
14 Don't forget to thank the people who have allowed you to observe.	You may need their help again!

Further reading

Bowling, A. (2002) *Research Methods in Health: Investigating Health and Health Services*, 2nd edn. Maidenhead: Open University Press. Chapter 25, 'Unstructured and structured observational studies', provides useful information about participant observation; gaining access; establishing validity and reliability (reducing observer bias); structured and unstructured observations; and analysis and categorization of data. Page 375 gives a useful summary of the main points covered in the chapter.

Darlington, Y. and Scott, D. (2002) *Qualitative Research in Practice: Stories from the Field*. Maidenhead: Open University Press. First published in 2002 by Allen and Unwin in Australia. Chapter 4, 'Observation', is helpful and well worth consulting. The authors provide guidance about the observation process, including useful reminders about the ethics of observation. This chapter also includes discussions with two researchers who used observation in conjunction with various other methods of data collection.

Denscombe, M. (2003) *The Good Research Guide*, 2nd edn. Maidenhead: Open University Press. Chapter 11, 'Observation', of the second edition of this excellent book is well worth consulting. Denscombe covers the advantages and disadvantages of systematic observation; observation schedules; types of events and behaviour to be recorded; suitability for observation; sampling; the advantages and disadvantages of participant observation; making field notes (and the dangers of field work) and ethics. Two useful checklists are provided, one concerned with observation schedules and the other a general checklist dealing with participant observation.

May, T. (2001) *Social Research: Issues, Methods and Process*, 3rd edn. Buckingham: Open University Press. Chapter 7, 'Participant observation: perspectives and practice', pages 146–74, deals with the practice of social research (the researcher's role, access, field notes); the analysis of observations; and issues in participant observation.

Moyles, J. (2002) 'Observation as a research tool', in M. Coleman and R.F. Briggs (eds) *Research Methods in Educational Leadership and Management*. London: Paul Chapman Publishing.

Punch, K.F. (1998) *Introduction to Social Research: Quantitative and Qualitative Approaches*. London: Sage Publishing. Pages 184–90 consider structured and unstructured observation, recording observational data, ethnographic observation and participant observation.

Williams, G.L. (1994) 'Observing and recording meetings', in N. Bennett, R. Glatter and R. Levačić (eds) *Improving Educational Management through Research and Consultancy*. London: Paul Chapman Publishing. Chapter 22 is thorough and helpful. Williams discusses content and process observations, decision-making processes and problem solving. He also includes several observation forms which may give you some ideas about how to design your own.

 **Part III**

INTERPRETING THE EVIDENCE
AND REPORTING THE FINDINGS

INTRODUCTION

Data collected by means of questionnaires, interviews, diaries or any other method mean very little until they are analysed and evaluated. Gathering large amounts of information in the hope that something will emerge is not to be recommended in any small or smallish investigation, but particularly not for new researchers. As I said in the introduction at the beginning of this book, those of you who have a limited statistical background cannot attempt highly complex surveys involving advanced statistical techniques, but that does not mean that a worthwhile study cannot be carried out. It is all a case of working within your level of expertise, selecting research methods which are suitable for the task and which can be readily analysed, interpreted and presented.

If at some stage you decide to carry out a large quantitative study, then you will undoubtedly need to get to grips with statistical procedures and with a range of computer skills and computer software such as the Statistical Package for the Social Sciences (SPSS). Every institution of higher education should have specialists who will advise. Make use of them. They will keep you on the straight and narrow and will ensure you do not waste valuable time following false trails.

In many projects and theses, it will be sufficient to understand simple arithmetical procedures such as averages and percentages.

If your data-collecting instruments are well devised and have been well piloted, you have already done the groundwork for the collection, analysis and presentation of information.

Before you begin your study of the next two chapters there are a number of issues which have been raised earlier but which need to be reiterated. In Chapter 1, I briefly discussed the question of generalization. Bassey (1981: 85–6) drew attention to the problems of generalizing from insufficient data, and made a strong case for individual researchers working to a limited time scale to produce research structured in response to an existing or potential problem so that the results might be of use to the institution. Such research, he felt, might go some way to solving a particular problem or lead to informed discussion of how a particular problem might be tackled. He commended the descriptive and evaluative study of single pedagogic events and (writing about education case-study methods), concluded that:

> An important criterion for judging the merit of a case study is the extent to which the details are sufficient and appropriate for a teacher working in a similar situation to relate his decision-making to that described in the case study. The relatability of a case study is more important than its generalizability.
>
> (Bassey 1981: 85)

I raise this issue again here because in the analysis, interpretation and presentation of data, care has to be taken not to claim more for results than is warranted, and equal care has to be taken not to attempt generalizations based on insufficient data. In relatively small projects, generalization may be unlikely, but relatability may be entirely possible. Well-prepared, small-scale studies may inform, illuminate and provide a basis for policy decisions within the institution. As such, they can be invaluable. There is no need to apologize about inability to generalize, but there would be every need to apologize if data were manipulated in an attempt to prove more than could reasonably be claimed.

INTERPRETING THE EVIDENCE
AND REPORTING THE FINDINGS

Raw data taken from questionnaires, interview schedules, check-lists, etc. need to be recorded, analysed and interpreted. A hundred separate pieces of interesting information will mean nothing to a researcher or to a reader unless they have been categorized and interpreted. We are constantly looking for similarities and differences, for groupings, patterns and items of particular significance.

You may have ideas about categories before the data are collected. Your informed hunch tells you that the likelihood is that responses will tend to fall into any one of six or seven main categories. There can be dangers in placing too much reliance on preconceived ideas, not least the possibility that your line of questioning may direct respondents to reply in certain ways. However, assuming you have been able to eliminate bias of this kind, your first-thoughts categories will give you a start in the process of collating the findings. Others will undoubtedly emerge as your research proceeds but start with broad categories, and only move to more detailed examples when it becomes apparent that they merit a label of their own.

In Chapter 8, Michael Youngman suggested that in question-naires, it is helpful to identify question types and to work out ways in which responses can be analysed and presented. You will recall that he listed seven question types (list, category, quantity, ranking, grid, scale and verbal). In this chapter, some of these question types will be used to illustrate ways in which responses might be interpreted and presented.

List questions

Let us say you wish to find out what qualifications your mature students had before they registered for the course. You produce a list question which invites subjects to tick appropriate boxes. They may well tick more than one box and so you will need to be ready to deal with multiple responses. In Question 1, categories have already been selected (None, professional qualification, successful completion of Access or Return to Study course, A level or equivalent and Other).

Question 1

What qualifications did you have before you started your degree course?

(Please tick the appropriate box or boxes)

None ☐   Professional qualification* ☐

Successful completion ☐   A level or equivalent* ☐
of Access or Return to
Study course

Other* ☐

Please specify*_____

_____

_____

A summary sheet needs to be prepared for all items before questionnaires are distributed, so that returns can be entered as they come in. We all have our own ways of recording returns, but if you decide to record question by question, the following is probably as simple a way as any.

Summary sheet for Question 1

Question 1 Qualifications before entry				
None	*Professional*	*Access/Return to Study*	*A level*	*Other*
~~HHH~~ 1	~~HHH~~ ~~HHH~~ ~~HHH~~ ~~HHH~~ ~~HHH~~ 111	~~HHH~~ ~~HHH~~ ~~HHH~~ ~~HHH~~ ~~HHH~~ ~~HHH~~ 11	~~HHH~~ ~~HHH~~ 11	~~HHH~~ ~~HHH~~ ~~HHH~~ 1
6	28	32	12	16

Once the summary sheet is complete, you will begin to have a picture of the types of qualifications the students had before beginning their degree course. The information can be presented in a variety of ways. A simple table, followed by commentary highlighting any items of interest is one option (see Table 12.1).

Table 12.1 Qualifications of mature students before entry to their degree course

None	*A level*	*Professional*	*Access/Return to Study*	*Other*
6	12	28	32	16

The full list of 'Other' qualifications will need to be recorded on a separate sheet and if sufficient recurring types of qualifications emerge, then reference can be made to them in the commentary.

A vertical bar chart would be another option (see Figure 12.1). The variable (qualification/s) would be on the horizontal axis and the frequency (number of students) on the vertical axis. (Note that 'n' = number.)

Which is clearer? The table or the bar chart? Any data which tell you nothing of significance may as well be abandoned, but there are interesting features here. Thirty-two of the 50 students in our sample (64 per cent) took Access/Return to Study courses, whereas only 12 (24 per cent) had A levels or equivalent. It might be interesting to discover which group performed better in examinations. Six students (12 per cent of the total of 50) had no qualifications at all on entry. How then had they prepared themselves for their undergraduate studies? Are they coping? It might be useful to follow up these and similar issues in interviews.

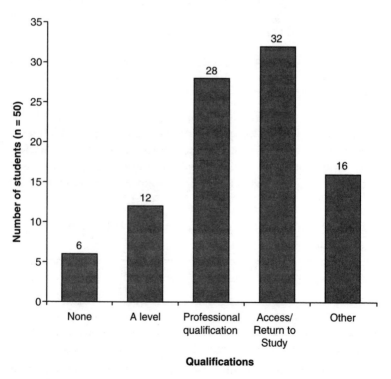

Figure 12.1 Qualifications of students before entry to their degree course.

Quantity and category questions

What Michael Youngman described as quantity and category questions are, at first sight, simpler to deal with. They require one answer only. The response to a quantity question is a number (exact or approximate), giving the amount of some characteristics. The response to a category question is one only of a given set of categories. For example, if age categories are provided (20–29, 30–39, etc.), the respondents can only fit into one category.

In the mature students' study, you will probably need to know students' ages. If you have spent time on question wording and have refined the focus of each question, you will have decided whether you want to know students' ages at the time they registered, at the time they completed the questionnaire, or at some other stage. You decide to ask a straight question.

Question 2

> **How old were you when you first registered for your degree course?**

What will you do with responses? *What exactly do you want to know?* The average age of students? If so, you will need to decide what sort of average (or measure of central tendency) will suit your purpose – *the arithmetic mean, the median,* or *the mode.*

Measures of central tendency

The **arithmetic mean** is simple. It is obtained by adding together each item (or value) and dividing by the total number of values. So, if we take 12 respondents (Group A) whose ages are 26, 26, 27, 28, 29, 30, 30, 31, 32, 33, 34, 34, and add those values together: that gives us 360. Divide 360 by 12. The mean is 30.

Another group of 12 (Group B) might have a different range of ages. For example, 21, 22, 24, 25, 25, 29, 31, 31, 32, 35, 40 and 45. The mean is also 30 but in these two cases, there is a clear difference in the dispersion of results.

The **median** allows us to find the middle value. This is particularly useful when there are extremes at both ends or at either end of the range which may affect the mean to a significant extent. To find the median, values must be listed in order – which in this case has already been done. If we had an odd number of values, the middle value would be the median. Where we have an even number, as in Group A, the average of the two middle values (30 + 30) is taken and so 30 is the median. The fact that in this case the mean and the median are the same is because there are no extreme values at either end. There is an age progression, but if the ages were 21, 22, 29, 29, 30, 30, 33, 33, 33, 36, 39, 84, then the differences would become apparent. The mean would be 34.9, whereas the median would be the average of the middle points, which would be 31.5. You would then need to decide whether the median gives a more realistic picture than the mean.

The **mode**, which is not often used in small studies, relates to the most frequently occurring value. In this last example, the modal score is 33.

Each of these measures of central tendency has different uses. As always, it all depends on what you need to know and why.

Look at the Group A and Group B examples again. The two groups have a very different spread of age. In Group A, the range is from 26 to 34 and so ages are close to the mean and the median. In Group B, they range from 21 to 45 and so are not clustered around the mean age. Is that worthy of comment? If so, ways have to be found of dealing with measures of spread, or dispersion. Commonly used measures are **range**, **interquartile range** and **standard deviation**.

Range is simply the difference between the highest and lowest values measured. For Group A, the range is 8 years, but for Group B it is 24 years. The range is not a particularly good measure of dispersion, as it can be influenced by one high and/or one low value and takes no account of the numbers of responses in the middle of the group.

The interquartile range gives a more accurate picture and reduces the importance of the extreme ends of the range. It is derived from the median. The highest and the lowest quarter of the measures are omitted and the interquartile range of the middle 50 per cent of the values is quoted.

For Group A, the top three values (34, 34 and 33 – one quarter of the twelve values) are omitted, as are the lowest three values (26, 26 and 27). This gives an interquartile range of 28–32, or four years.

For Group B, the values 45, 40 and 35 are omitted, as are 21, 22 and 24. That gives an interquartile range of 25–32, which is seven years. Is that worth commenting on? In some cases, it certainly will be. If the median has been selected as providing the best indication of the average of a set of data, then the interquartile range will indicate the extent to which data vary.

If the mean has been selected, then the standard deviation has to be used to summarize dispersion. It reflects the spread and the degree to which the values differ from the mean. It uses values for all the group rather than for a section, whereas other measures do not. Any book on statistics will give the mathematical expression for standard deviation and how it can be calculated. To carry out the calculations by hand can be tedious, particularly for a large group. However, many calculators can do this very quickly and the calculation is written into many computer programs so that the standard deviation is automatically produced in association with the mean. In fact, the standard deviation for Group A is 2.8 and for Group B it is 7.

In the case of these two groups, all the measures – the range, interquartile range and standard deviation – indicate that Group B has a wider spread than Group A. Used on their own, means and medians may not be sufficiently descriptive to provide a complete picture of the data. You will need to decide whether one of these measures of dispersion is also necessary when you analyse and interpret your data.

It was a straightforward matter to determine the mean and the median of data derived from Question 2. However, you might decide you do not wish to ask subjects to say how old they are. Perhaps you consider it would be more sensitive to ask them to tick a box or circle a number to indicate the age category into which they fit. Decide whether you wish to have categories (or class intervals) of five (20–24, 25–29) or ten (20–29, 30–39). How important is it to have the groups of five? If the answer is 'not very', then take the wider span. It will be easier to manage.

Make sure your instructions are clear. In the Alternative Question 2, respondents would be asked to circle the number (1–5) under the appropriate age category. A respondent of 32 would circle the number 2 underneath the 30–39 age category. Take particular care to ensure that the likely full age range of your respondents is provided.

Alternative Question 2

Age when you first registered for your degree				
20–29	30–39	40–49	50–59	60+
1	②	3	4	5

If you wished to find the arithmetic means of respondents' ages from the class intervals this is still straightforward. Take the mid-point of each class interval and multiply that age by the number in each class. That is, mid-point × frequency, as follows:

Table 12.2 Arithmetic mean of respondents' ages

Age	Frequency	Mid-point	Frequency × mid-point
20–29	34	25	850
30–39	10	35	350
40–49	4	45	180
50–59	1	55	55
60+	1	60	60
Total	50		1495

If 1495 is divided by the number of respondents (50) that gives a mean of 29.9. The first class interval (20–29) includes those who entered higher education on their twentieth birthday and also those who entered the day before their thirtieth birthday. The interval therefore covers almost 10 years, with the exception of the final class (60+). Usually, it is anticipated that only a small number of responses will fall into the final class. In the above example, the one respondent could be any age from 60 upwards and so it is necessary to assign an arbitrary mid-point. For the purpose of this exercise, the age 60 was selected.

You would then need to decide how to present the information in a way which best illustrates the age balance of the sample. You have several options. You could provide a simple chart derived straight from your summary sheet (Table 12.3).

Table 12.3 Age distribution of students at initial registration

Age	Number of students
20–29	34
30–39	10
40–49	4
50–59	1
60+	1
Total	50

The same data could be represented by a histogram. A histogram is the same as a bar chart, but the bars are touching, to reflect the continuous nature of the variable which in this case is 'age' (Figure 12.2).

Alternatively, you might decide a pie chart would represent a clearer (or different) picture. Pie charts can be awkward to draw unless you have access to a computer graphics program but easy if you have. They are useful, particularly if you wish to illustrate the **proportion** of students who fall into the different age groups. In this case, frequencies are changed to percentages. The 30–39 age range accounts for 20 per cent of the total sample. The circumference of a circle is 360° and so one per cent will be 3.6°. Multiply 20 by 3.6 which gives an angle of 72°. If you are producing the pie chart by hand, this simple calculation will allow you to draw in the segments using a protractor and a compass but it's tedious so if

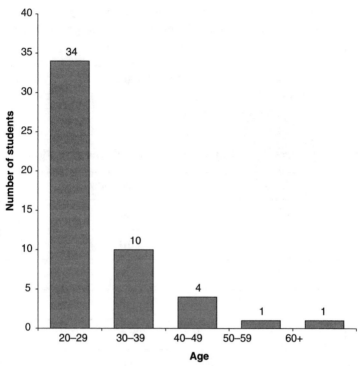

Figure 12.2 Age distribution of mature students at initial registration.

you possibly can, make use of a 'Tables and Figures' computer program. Once you know how, it's easy, but not until you learn 'how' – and that can take a little time. It becomes immediately apparent from Figure 12.3 that if numbers are small, percentages can be misleading so if at all possible, include numbers with the percentages.

Do the table, histogram or pie chart provide any interesting findings? You might comment on this skewed age distribution, to the effect that few students over the age of 39 had committed themselves to the three-year full-time undergraduate course. But why would that be interesting? Subsequent interviews might provide further information about motives. Would you have expected the age distribution to be weighted at the younger end? When you examine the university records for the full mature

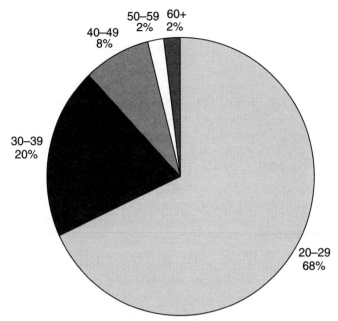

Figure 12.3 Age distribution of students at the start of their course.

student population (assuming you have permission to get access to the records), does your sample follow the same pattern, or is it different? If it is significantly different, then that might indicate that further study is needed to try to find out why. Do university records indicate a gradual (or sudden) change in the age profile of students? What about the balance of women to men?

Would it be helpful to know whether most of the younger students are women? If you have asked students to indicate whether they are male or female, you would be able to find that out, *but* if you have not, it will be too late once the questionnaires are returned. Your pilot and trial collation and presentation of data should give you clues as to which information is likely to be of interest and at that stage there is still time to make adjustments to your data-collecting instruments. The trials will also allow you to prepare the types of summary sheets which will suit your purpose – and for that, you may need to code your data.

Coding

Miles and Huberman, writing about qualitative data analysis explain that:

> *Codes* are tags or labels for assigning units of meaning to the descriptive or inferential information compiled during a study. Codes are usually attached to 'chunks' of varying size – words, phrases, sentences or whole paragraphs, connected or unconnected to a specific setting.
> (Miles and Huberman 1994: 56)

They take the view that it is not the words themselves that matter, but their *meaning*.

> Codes are used to retrieve and organize the chunks ... The organizing part will entail some system for categorizing the various chunks, so the researcher can quickly find, pull out, and cluster the segments relating to a particular research question, hypothesis, construct, or theme. Clustering, and ... display of condensed chunks then sets the stage for drawing conclusions.
> (Miles and Huberman 1994: 57)

So, coding allows you to 'cluster' key issues in your data and allows you to take steps towards 'drawing conclusions'. The data you have collected mean very little until you have identified your clusters and can begin to understand what they all mean.

If you plan to enter your data direct on to the computer, you will need to use the numerical labels, as in:

Question 1: Qualifications

None	1
Professional qualifications	2
Access/Return to Study	3
A level or equivalent	4
Other	5
No reply	9

You might decide to break down the 'Professional qualifications' returns, if you have sufficient items, and possibly to indicate 'degree in another subject', 'nursing qualification', 'engineering qualification' or 'forestry management qualification'.

In Alternative Question 2, codes for 'age' could be allocated in the same way:

20–29	1
30–39	2
40–49	3
50–59	4
60+	5
No response	9

These numbers are **nominal scales** which have no numerical significance and so any numbers could have been used. Remember that there must be no overlapping categories. It's obvious with the age example because a respondent could not be classified as being in the 20–29 and the 30–39 category, but particularly when you are dealing with open or verbal responses and invariably with qualitative rather than quantitative analysis, it can be really quite difficult to select guaranteed non-overlapping categories.

If you are involved in a very small project and only need basic information, such as additions or percentages, you may decide you don't need to go to the lengths of coping with computer statistical analysis, unless you are using the exercise as a trial for a larger investigation. However, you will still need to prepare a coding frame, which is your classification system and your key. In questionnaires, you will have a good idea of many, or even most of the categories and so will be able to plan your coding frame at the same time as you design your questionnaire. Even so, it's unlikely you will have covered all possibilities, so wait until you have returns from your pilot studies and again, after a number of returns from the main distribution before you begin to complete your coding frame. It's irritating if you find you were originally wrong because that means you have to adjust codes and to go through all the returns again.

Open questions may well produce unexpected items. Type out all the responses and then try to identify any recurring items. They will form the basis of your coding system, but remember that quite often only two or three identical, or similar responses may give you too many categories. Particularly in a small project, there is likely to be a limit to how many are reasonable. You will always need an 'odds and ends' category and remember to allow for a 'no response' category. The number '9' is often used for 'no response' and if this number suits you, keep it for all 'no response' items. If you don't need numerical codes, then use 'NR' because there is considerable merit in adopting letters, or even words, instead of numbers. Letters and words are easily identified, whereas numbers have to be checked against your coding frame.

If you have an **ordinal scale**, as in a Likert scale (Likert 1932), where numbers are rated or ranked, the numbers are already provided for you, so the coding frame would follow the same numerical approach, namely:

Strongly disagree	Disagree	Neutral	Agree	Strongly agree
1	2	3	4	5

Of course, if you are not concerned about computer recording and analysis, you could equally well decide to use the easily recognized letters SD, D, N, A and SA. At least with the letters you are not constantly referring back to the coding frame to make sure you have the right number.

There are no set ways of coding. It is a case of deciding on a system which will suit your data and your way of managing it. Try out different summary sheets and coding frames. Keep things as simple as possible. If you are concerned mainly with a quantitative study and wish to make use of computer software to analyse your returns, prepare as well as you can before you finalize your data-collecting instruments. As I've said before (but it's sufficiently important to repeat again here), find out if there is anyone in your department or institution whose job it is to help students to organize and code data and to select suitable computer packages which will not be beyond your level of computer expertise. Attend any courses which are offered by your computer centre, IT department or library. Try out imaginary returns from your questionnaire and see if your program can cope with them. Better to find out you asked the questions in the wrong way as soon as possible than when all returns are received.

Time to move on to grids, scales and verbal questions.

Grids

The simple response questions such as list, quantity and category are relatively easy to deal with. Grids require a little more care. A grid (or table) question will ask students to provide answers to two or more questions at the same time.

Go back to the question about students' qualifications before they started their degree course. Instead of merely asking whether they had 'no qualifications', a 'professional qualification', 'A level or equivalent', 'successful completion of an Access or Return to Study course' or 'other' qualification, you might decide it would be more useful to learn about study carried out after the age of 18. If so, a grid question could be devised.

Question 3

Since the age of 18, how many years have you spent on the following? Ignore periods of less than one academic year.				
	1–2 years	*3–4 years*	*5–6 years*	*More than 6 years*
Professional qualification				
GCE A level or equivalent				
Access/Return to Study course				
Other (please specify)				

Here there are two dimensions – years of study and type of study. Students might have spent one year on an Access course, two years on an A level course, four on a professional qualification, three on some other course. In that case, ticks would be placed in three of the boxes.

The returns could be presented in table form in much the same style as the original question, but it would also be possible to produce a compound bar chart which compares numbers of students by years of study spent on different courses (see Figure 12.4).

Scales

The examples so far ask respondents to give factual information. **Scales** are devices to discover strength of feeling or attitude. There are many different types of scale, some of which require quite complex construction and analysis. Thurstone (Thurstone and Chave 1929) and Guttman (1950) scales in particular require careful handling. The most straightforward and easiest to manage

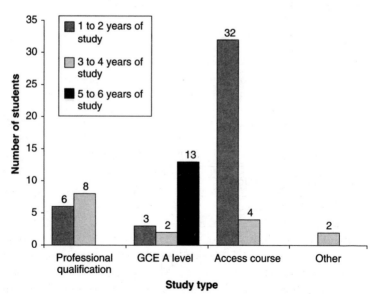

Figure 12.4 Years spent on study since the age of 18.

attitude scale is probably the Likert, devised by the man who invented them (Likert 1932). Likert scales ask respondents to indicate strength of agreement or disagreement with a given statement or series of statements, generally on a five- or seven-point range, by circling the appropriate number. Answers are then scored, generally from 1 (strongly disagree) to 5 (strongly agree) and a measure of respondents' feelings can be produced.

A simplified Likert scale might be used in the following case:

Question 4

I consider my chances of doing well in finals are good

Strongly disagree	*Disagree*	*Undecided*	*Agree*	*Strongly agree*
1	2	3	4	5

Responses could be presented as shown in Table 12.4. A bar chart would also illustrate the range of responses, as in Figure 12.5.

Table 12.4 Levels of agreement among mature students that chances of success in finals are good

Strongly disagree	*Disagree*	*Undecided*	*Agree*	*Strongly agree*	*Totals*
10	7	6	16	11	50
(20%)	(14%)	(12%)	(32%)	(22%)	(100%)

It is clear from Table 12.4 and from the bar chart (Figure 12.5) that more than half the students (54 per cent) are optimistic about their results, but what about the rest? Will these percentages be influenced by the faculty to which students belong? It would be interesting to find out.

Early findings from the pilot study may have alerted you to the likely importance of the faculty dimension. If so, you would have been able to ask students to complete a combined Likert scale/grid question, which might produce the results shown in Table 12.5.

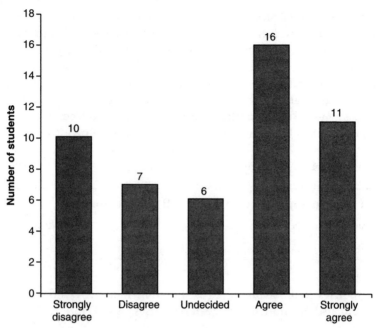

Figure 12.5 Levels of agreement among mature students (n = 50) that chances of success in finals are good.

Table 12.5 Levels of agreement among mature students that chances of success, by faculty, are good

Faculty	Strongly disagree	Disagree	Undecided	Agree	Strongly agree	Total
Maths	4	0	0	0	0	4
Science	6	6	2	0	0	14
Social Science	0	0	4	16	0	20
Humanities	0	1	0	0	11	12
Totals	10	7	6	16	11	50

Presenting these data in tabular form is perfectly acceptable, but ask yourself whether other methods of presentation would illustrate the position more clearly. In this case, numbers may not present the same picture as would percentages, though as

I've pointed out before, in small studies it is dangerous to use percentages without the associated numbers. They can be misleading and give the impression that the sample is bigger than it in fact is. However, if you decide it is likely to be important to discover the proportion of students who disagree or agree with the statement *by faculty*, then frequencies can be converted to percentages and a percentage component bar chart produced (Figure 12.6).

Does Figure 12.6 illustrate the position better? You will need to decide. What does emerge is that the table and the bar chart make it clear that there are major differences in the perceptions of Maths and Science students compared with Social Science and Humanities. The percentage component bar chart demonstrates the extent of the differences. So, what is happening in Maths and Science? Were the students inadequately prepared? Are there lessons to be learnt from these data? Or are the students

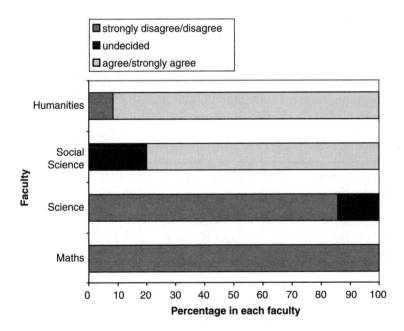

Figure 12.6 Percentage of students by faculty who feel their chances of doing well in finals are good.

unnecessarily pessimistic about their prospects? All these questions could be followed up in interviews with students and with tutors.

The table and bar chart illustrate the extent to which there is a relationship between faculty and students' perceptions of chances of success in finals. Data plotted on to a scattergram (or scattergraph) may also indicate a relationship between two variables. As part of your investigation, you may have hypothesized that first-year coursework scores will be the same as the first-year examination scores. Unlikely though that would be, let's say that the results support your hypothesis. You discover that first-year examination scores are indeed the same as coursework scores. If you produce the figures in a table they will be the same as in Table 12.6.

It's obvious that both scores match exactly, though I imagine a few questions might be asked at examination board meetings if such results were produced. However, never mind. These figures are merely being used to illustrate how a 'perfect' positive correlation, which is what we have here, might be presented. If these data were to be plotted on a graph, with the examination score as the horizontal axis and the coursework score on the vertical axis, then a perfect straight line would be produced, as in Figure 12.7.

Another sample might produce different data, as in Table 12.7.

Table 12.6 First-year examination and coursework scores (1)

Student number	Examination score	Coursework score
1	30	30
2	35	35
3	40	40
4	45	45
5	50	50
6	55	55
7	60	60
8	65	65
9	70	70

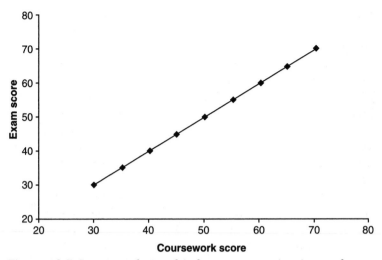

Figure 12.7 Positive relationship between examination and coursework scores.

Table 12.7 First-year examination and coursework scores (2)

Student number	Examination score	Coursework score
1	30	70
2	35	65
3	40	60
4	45	55
5	50	50
6	55	45
7	60	40
8	65	35
9	70	30

These data, transferred on to a graph (Figure 12.8), demonstrate that again, the correlation is 'perfect', but this time, as the examination score increases, the coursework decreases, and vice versa. There is therefore a negative relationship between the two variables. In reality, such relationships are rare. More realistic data might be in the third example (Table 12.8).

When the points are plotted on the graph, the resulting figure

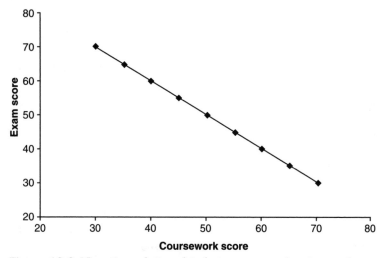

Figure 12.8 Negative relationship between examination and coursework scores.

Table 12.8 First-year examination and coursework scores (3)

Student number	Examination score	Coursework score
1	37	45
2	42	40
3	46	44
4	53	68
5	54	60
6	59	50
7	63	55
8	72	85
9	74	75

(Figure 12.9) shows whether there is a general trend in the results and indicates the scatter of results. In this case, since the general trend is for an increase in examination score associated with an increase in coursework score, a positive relationship exists, but it is not perfect. (The line drawn here is merely to illustrate the extent to which the scatter points relate to the perfect relationship.)

Some data, when plotted on a scattergram, may be completely

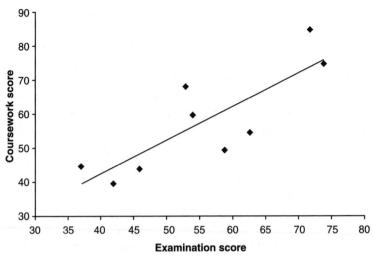

Figure 12.9 Positive (though not perfect) relationship between examination and coursework scores.

random, with no discernible pattern. In this case, it is reasonable to assume that there is little or no relationship between variables. In other cases, there may be clusters, or groups of points on the scattergram, suggesting that within the total sample, there are smaller groups within which the individuals have similar characteristics. Take care though. Unless calculations for correlation coefficients are carried out, only inferences can be drawn – not direct causal relationships. If you feel correlation coefficients are necessary, then you will have to become familiar with the necessary statistical techniques or to make use of a computer package such as the Statistical Package for the Social Sciences (SPSS) or whichever package your supervisor suggests.

Verbal questions

A study of responses to verbal (or open) questions will often provide useful pointers to the types of issues it may be worthwhile to follow up in interviews. These questions are often included on questionnaires to allow respondents to draw attention to anything about which they feel strongly. Referring to such responses is often a way of starting an interview.

The usual practice is to write or type out all the responses on separate sheets. This allows all items to be scanned in order to see whether there are any recurring themes. If you are interested in discovering whether students identify any barriers to learning, you will be looking particularly for statements which relate to problems with study, tutor support, etc. Some of the responses will probably provide useful quotations to illustrate certain points in the report – though the temptation to give greater emphasis to statements which happen to support your particular point of view has to be resisted.

Some form of content analysis may be necessary in order to deal with such material. If so, follow the same content analysis procedures as would be applied for the study of documents (see Chapter 7). As always, you will be looking for categories and for common criteria, if any.

Conclusions

Only the simplest methods of presentation have been considered in this chapter. They provide a starting point. The tables and charts are easy to manage, whether or not you have access to a computer graphics program. You may be able to devise different question types and different methods of analysis and presentation. The advantage of familiarizing yourself with a range of question types is that once you have experimented with different formats and know how to produce tables, charts or graphs, you will be able to draw on whichever format suits the data and the purpose. A diagram can often simplify quite complex data which could take a paragraph or more to explain.

When you move on to larger and more complex investigations, you will need to familiarize yourself with more complex methods of analysis and with the use of appropriate computer programs. These days you can generally access such programs from your own departmental, computer centre or library terminal – or from your home computer, always providing you have the appropriate password, user word and permission/s. Try out some of the programs, using data with which you are familiar, possibly data which have been collated, analysed and presented 'by hand' in connection with one of your 100-hour projects. This will allow you to understand the principles and get to grips with the practicalities of the system.

◉ **Interpreting the evidence and reporting the findings checklist**

1 All data must be recorded as soon as they are available.

Make sure you prepare and pilot summary sheets before the main data collection begins.

2 Look for similarities, groupings, clusters, categories and items of particular significance.

100 separate pieces of interesting information will mean nothing to a researcher or a reader until they are analysed and interpreted.

3 First-thoughts categories will be a start in the process of collating findings.

Though you may find you have to amend them after your pilot studies and when your data are assembled.

4 Prepare final summary sheets.

Your pilot studies will show you whether they are appropriate for your purposes.

5 Experiment with different ways of presenting findings. Tables, bar charts, histograms? Other diagrams or graphs?

If you plan to use computer statistical packages, find out what help is available *before* you begin your pilot studies and try out possible packages.

6 If you need to discover the average of certain values, decide whether the mean, median or mode is the most suitable.

Remember that each of these measures of central tendency has different uses.

7 Used on their own, means and medians may not be sufficiently descriptive to provide a complete picture of the data.

A measure of dispersion may be required – range, interquartile range or standard deviation.

8 Try out codes for your data. If you plan to use computer statistical packages, you will require numerical codes. If not, letters will suffice.	Do not attempt complex statistical techniques unless you have the expertise to cope. It is perfectly possible to produce a worthwhile investigation without an in-depth knowledge of statistics and without access to a computer. However, if you can familiarize yourself sufficiently well with computer techniques, it can save you many hours and produce good-looking charts, tables and figures – once you know how.
9 All data require interpretation.	It is not enough only to describe.
10 Don't claim more for your research than your evidence will support.	And watch out for possible bias.

Further reading

There are many good books on the market now which deal with basic statistical techniques. If you feel you need to learn more, ask your supervisor for suggestions, consult what is available at your library and see what is on the shelves of good bookshops. Consult the introduction, contents pages and indexes of books to see whether your understanding of 'basic' is the same as the author's. If any of the following are in your library catalogue, you might also wish to consult them.

Argyrous, G. (2002) *Statistics for Social and Health Research*. London: Sage publications. This book discusses various statistical concepts and an introduction to SPSS. Includes a CD-ROM with sample data sets.

Bryman, A. and Cramer, D. (1994) *Quantitative Data Analysis for Social Scientists*. London: Routledge. I still find this to be the most readable book on the topic. 'Rather old' in publishing terminology but still very good value.

Cramer, D. (2003) *Advanced Quantitative Data Analysis*. Buckingham: Open University Press. This book considers a variety of techniques used to analyse quantitative data. Useful examples are provided, together with a glossary of key concepts. Very sound, but some previous basic statistical knowledge will be a help.

Cramer, D. and Howitt, D. L. (2004) *The Sage Dictionary of Statistics*. London: Sage Publications. Very helpful reference work for use by anyone studying statistics in the social sciences and readable for first-time and for more experienced researchers.

Hardy, M. A. and Bryman, A. (eds) (2004) *Handbook of Data Analysis*. London: Sage Publications. This is a really good guide to basic issues in data analysis. Not a book to read from cover to cover but very good to keep on hand for reference.

Miles, M. B. and Huberman, A. M. (1994) *Qualitative Data Analysis* (2nd edn). Thousand Oaks, CA: Sage Publications. Everything in this excellent book is worth reading and noting. I particularly like Chapter 3, 'Focussing and bounding the collection of data', which includes 'Linking qualitative and quantitative data', 'Management issues bearing on analysis' and 'Data management', and Chapter 4, 'Early steps in analysis', which considers issues relating to codes and coding – and, of course, much more.

Opie, C. (ed.) (2004) *Doing Educational Research: A Guide to First-time Researchers*. London: Sage. Chapter 7 by Clive Opie considers the statistical analysis of quantitative and qualitative data. Chapter 8 by Ann-Marie Bathmaker outlines the use of the NUD-IST (Non-Numerical, Unstructured Data Indexing, Searching and Theorising) software for analysing qualitative data. She considers the practicalities of using NUD-IST, provides a critique of the software in the light of experience and concludes with recommendations for new users. Really helpful. Chapter 9 by Michael Pomerantz discusses the ATLAS.ti computer software application which allows the user to study and analyse interview transcripts. Clive Opie ends the book with a glossary of terms used in quantitative analysis.

Oppenheim, A. N. (1992) *Questionnaire Design, Interviewing and Attitude Measurement* (New Edition). London: Cassell. Chapter 9 discusses some basic measurement theory, including ordinal scales, nominal measures, the reliability and validity of scaled measures. Chapter 14 considers coding (code books, coding frames and problems of coder reliability). Very thorough and useful to keep on hand for reference.

Pallant, J. (2004) *SPSS Survival Manual: A Step By Step Guide to Data Analysis Using SPSS for Windows (Versions 10 and 11)*. Maidenhead: Open University Press. This new edition outlines basic techniques of data analysis and provides examples of how to present results in reports. It is thorough, as clear as this topic can be and offers useful research tips. A web site accompanies the book (www.openup.co.uk/spss) and to access the two data files from which the examples of research are taken, go to www.openup.co.uk/spss.data. Part one: Getting Started, includes designing a study, preparing a codebook and getting to know SPSS. Parts two to five discuss the preparation of data files and preliminary analysis and consider the use of a variety of statistical techniques. I found Part four: Statistical Techniques to Explore Relationships among Variables, to be particularly helpful. This book is not bedtime reading, but if you plan to use SPSS, it could be invaluable as a reference manual. However, it is detailed and you will need to allocate a significant amount of time to absorb the parts you need.

Punch, K. F. (1998) *Introduction to Social Research: Quantitative and Qualitative Approaches*. London: Sage Publications. Chapter 7 deals with the analysis of quantitative data and Chapter 10 discusses the analysis of qualitative, including a good section on coding. All well worth consulting and absorbing.

13

WRITING THE REPORT

Getting started

When all the hard work of gathering and analysing evidence is complete, you will need to write the final report. Bodgan and Biklen, writing about the problems of getting started, offer the following advice:

> Novice writers are big procrastinators. They find countless reasons not to get started. Even when they finally get themselves seated at their desks, they always seem to find diversions: make the coffee, sharpen the pencil, go to the bathroom, thumb through more literature, sometimes even get up and return to the field. Remember that you are never 'ready' to write; writing is something you must make a conscious decision to do and then discipline yourself to follow through.
>
> (Bogdan and Biklen 1982: 172)

All this is easier said than done, and it is not only novice writers who are procrastinators, but remember that a study is not finished until it is written up and, in your original planning, time has to be allowed for writing – and rewriting. That does not mean that you put off thoughts of writing until all the data have been collected.

If you have followed some of the earlier advice, you will already have produced an account of what you have read about the topic, so you will not have to waste time going back to books and articles read some time ago. You will have your bibliographical cards and/or computer records in good order, with notes and useful quotations to guide your writing, and you will not have started your project unless your objectives were clear, though you may have amended these as your investigation developed.

Report and thesis writing is not, or should not be, a frantic activity carried out at the end of the project. It is a process of varied stages all of which need to be recorded at the time they are completed. Your first drafts will need to be revised and in some cases completely rewritten, but the foundations for the report should have been established at the planning stage.

Writing requires discipline, and even the most experienced of researchers need to impose some sort of self-control to ensure that the task is completed in time. We all have different ways of working and what suits one person may not suit another. If you have adopted the principle of 'thinking on paper' (Wolcott 1990: 31), you will already have some drafts and even if they are rough, it's always better to face badly-written and incomplete drafts than a blank page.

You will, of course, have ensured that all references are complete and checked before you reach the final stages of your research but if, in spite of all your efforts, you do happen to come across an incomplete reference, make a note of it, but if you're in the middle of a good writing session, *don't stop*. Go back to it later.

There are no hard-and-fast rules about when and how to write. I accept that it would be sensible to write according to a strict schedule (always between 8–10 pm on weekdays; always between 6–8 am every day). I try to do that, but I just don't seem able to keep to such a regular pattern. Things and sometimes people get in my way. Ideally, I have to be quiet and alone to write, with all my source material around me. Other people say they can't write in silence. They need the accompaniment of the radio or a CD.

We're told it's a good idea to aim at so many words in every writing session and I did once know someone who could produce 1000 words of good quality writing most days, but only one. I've never managed to achieve that though I do make plans to complete particular sections or even paragraphs at one sitting. I work to an agenda and if I can achieve more than one item, I feel full of virtue and have even been known to declare a dividend and to give myself time off for such good behaviour. We all have to have our little treats in life.

If I can, I set aside writing days (whole days sometimes, which everyone I know says is thoroughly bad practice), when I know I can be more or less alone and free from distractions, but I only write for two hours at a time. I've learnt that if I press on for hour after hour, I begin to write rubbish. I don't know it's rubbish at the time but when I read it after it has 'gone cold' the next day or next week, then I most certainly do. After two hours or so, assuming I've reached a stage from which it will be easy to move on, I can have a cup of tea, wander around, go to the Post Office. Anything to give myself a break before I move on to the next stage.

I am regularly told by colleagues that I have bad writing habits and I suppose I do. However, I am quite disciplined in a number of ways. My index and reference systems are generally quite good, so I can find what I need most of the time. Bitter experience has taught me that keeping unindexed notes, transcriptions, references and rough drafts in what Miles and Huberman (1994: 56) describe as an 'alpine collection of information' is a thoroughly bad idea. Experience has also taught me to write on one side of the paper only, and to try to keep to one paragraph to a page. I know that my early drafts won't be good enough, so I need to be able to move paragraphs around. I can, and do, cut and paste on the computer of course, but I only move to a proper draft on the computer after early drafts are beginning to take shape. You may work differently and that's fine, *as long as you have some system and plan of your own which enables you to write to an agenda.* As Barzun and Graff (1977: 325) remind us, 'The writer's problem is the inverse of the reformed drunkard's. The latter must never touch a drop; the former must always do his stint.' The way in which we always do our stint is up to us, but we have less discretion in the way our report should be structured.

Structuring the report

Institutions generally provide guidelines about the way the final report should be provided and it goes without saying that these guidelines should be followed to the letter. If for any reason guidelines are not provided, something on the following lines will generally be acceptable.

1 Title page

Include the title of your study, your name and the date. The title should accurately reflect the nature of your study and should be brief and to the point. A subtitle may be provided if it clarifies the purpose of the study.

2 Acknowledgements

You may wish to acknowledge the help given to you in the preparation of your report. If so, acknowledgements and thanks generally come after the title page.

3 Contents

4 The abstract

In most cases, an abstract will be required, though practices vary, so consult the 'house' rules. It is quite difficult to say in a few words what your investigation set out to do, the methods employed and what conclusions were reached. The following example is one way in which the task might be approached.

This project attempts to identify effective teaching and learning strategies and any barriers to learning as perceived by mature students at Writingwell University. Data were gathered from questionnaires, interviews and observation of and participation in lectures, seminars and tutorials. The report concludes that there is scope for consideration of more varied approaches to the delivery of the curriculum and for consultations with mature students about ways in which changes might be introduced.

If you are allowed more space, you will be able to develop this abstract to provide the reader with more information, but for short reports, something on the above lines will generally suffice.

Get into the habit of looking at abstracts which are usually placed at the beginning of journal articles. Ask yourself whether they give a good idea of what the article is about, how data were collected, and what conclusions were reached.

5 Aims and purpose of the study

This should be a brief explanation of the purpose of the research. Explain the research problem in a few sentences. State aims/ objectives/hypotheses. Provide any background to the study which is necessary to place the study in its context.

Draw attention to any **limitations of the study** at this stage. An individual researcher with only 100 hours or so to complete a project can neither hope to become involved in complex sampling techniques nor to interview hundreds of people. You cannot do everything in a small study, and your supervisor will know that, but in this section you should make it clear that you know what the limitations of the study are. Be honest.

6 Review of the literature

Not all reports will require a review of previous research, though for Master's and doctoral studies a review will normally be expected. In a short project, and subject to your supervisor's agreement, you may have decided to use your reading mainly to support or to reject arguments throughout the report, but the value of a review to the reader is that it explains the context and background of the study. Remember Haywood and Wragg's warning that critical reviews can too often turn out to be uncritical reviews – 'the furniture sale catalogue, in which everything merits a one-paragraph entry no matter how skilfully it has been conducted' (Haywood and Wragg 1982: 2). A selection has to be made, and only books and articles which relate directly to the topic should be included.

The review, if required, can be written first and, if you have managed to discipline yourself sufficiently well to write up sections and sub-sections as you have completed them, much of the work of this section will be ready for revision before you begin to collect data. You may find that you need to adapt your original version, but you should not need to start from the beginning by reading through notes to decide what should be included and what left out.

In Chapter 6, I indicated that Clara Nai adopted this approach. She identified headings under which she could group her findings and in so doing, produced a framework which enabled her to highlight key issues and, at a later stage in her dissertation, to place her own research findings into the wider context.

7 Methods of data collection

An alternative heading might be 'Some considerations of method' – or any other title which in your view describes the content of the section well. This section explains how the problem was investigated and why particular methods and techniques were employed. Accounts of the procedure, size of sample, method of selection, choice of variables and controls, and tests of measurement and statistical analysis, if any, should be provided. Consult your supervisor about how much detail is required. Nisbet and Entwistle (1970: 169) point out that it is unnecessary to describe in detail any tests or procedures which are well known and frequently used, but if you have devised any of your own systems of measurement, it's likely that full information will be needed.

All important terms should be defined precisely and any deficiencies in the methods mentioned. It's important to bear in mind that in certain kinds of investigation, the research needs to be repeatable, and a fellow researcher should be able to obtain enough information from this section to make this possible.

8 Statement of results

This is the heart of the report and will consist of text and, if necessary, tables or figures, depending on the nature of the project. The way results are presented is important. Tables, charts, graphs and other figures should illustrate and illuminate the text. If they do not, then there is no point in taking up space. The text, which should be written after the results are prepared, should not duplicate information in the tables and figures but should highlight significant aspects of the findings so that all relevant facts are presented in a way which draws attention to what is most important. It is quite an art to achieve this balance, and you may find you need several drafts before you are satisfied with the result.

All tables and figures should be numbered, given a title and carefully checked before you submit your report. Tables are generally numerical presentations, in lists or columns, though there can be tables of names or other items. Figures are other types of presentation of data. It's customary to place the number and name of tables above the table, and figures below. It is quite a good idea to look at the way other students have presented them – and take care to follow any institutional guidelines.

9 Analysis and discussion

It is often best to start this section with a restatement of the problem before discussing how the results affect existing knowledge of the subject. If your research aimed to test certain hypotheses, then this section should demonstrate whether they were or were not supported by the evidence. Any deficiencies in the research design should be mentioned, with suggestions about different approaches which might have been more appropriate. Implications for improvement of practice, if any, should also be drawn out.

Most researchers find it best to write sections 6, 7 and 8 in sequence to ensure continuity and logical progression. It is quite feasible to write some sections as discrete units at different times, but these three sections need to be considered as a whole. If you have to take a break from writing, make sure you reread everything that has gone before to ensure a smooth continuation and to avoid repetition.

10 Summary and conclusions

The main conclusions of the report that have been discussed in section 8 should be summarized here briefly and simply. Only conclusions that can be justifiably drawn from the findings should be made. That sounds (and is) obvious, but there is often a great temptation to drop in an opinion for which no evidence is provided in the report. Take care or you may spoil a good report by including a throwaway remark.

Before you write this section, read through the whole report and make a note of key points. Readers who want a quick idea of what your research is about will look at the abstract, possibly the introduction and almost certainly at the summary and conclusions. This final section should be sufficiently succinct and clearly expressed to enable readers to understand quite clearly what research has been done and the conclusions that have been drawn *from the evidence*.

11 List of references

It is worthwhile at this stage in your writing to remind you about Blaxter, Hughes and Tight's guidance on the use and abuse of references. They write that references should not be included to 'impress your readers with the scope of your reading', nor to 'replace the need for you to express your own thoughts' but they should be used to:

- justify and support your arguments
- allow you to make comparisons with other research, . . .
- demonstrate your familiarity with your field of work.

(Blaxter, Hughes and Tight 2001: 127)

You are not in the business of producing the longest list of references ever known and it would be a pity to spoil a good report with irrelevant references, so check carefully that each one is there for a purpose.

Opinions vary as to whether a full bibliography or a list of references, or both, should be included. My view is that only items which have been cited in the report should be included. However, some institutions also wish to have a bibliography which includes all sources consulted during the preparation of the investigation. You will need to consult your supervisor about institutional practice.

If you adopt the Harvard method of referencing, which I have recommended in this book, then references will appear in alphabetical order, which simplifies the process and avoids overlap. The amount of time it takes you to produce a bibliography, list of references, or both, will depend on how meticulous you were when you first recorded your sources. This is the time when all your hard work and systematic recording will really pay off.

12 Appendices

Copies of any data-collecting instruments (questionnaires, interview schedules, etc.) that have been used should be included in an appendix, unless you have been instructed otherwise. Your tutor will not wish to receive all the completed questionnaires and would no doubt be dismayed if weighty parcels arrived on the doorstep, but one copy of any data-collecting instrument that has been used is generally required.

13 Length

Guidelines about length will be provided by your supervisor and many institutions will have rules about this. If you have not been told what length is expected, ask. If a maximum number of words is stipulated, try not to exceed that number. You may be penalized for exceeding the limit.

14 Quotations

All quotations must, of course, be acknowledged. Remember that your tutor has probably read the same books, so is likely to recognize the source. As I have said in Chapter 4, if you are quoting only a few words or one sentence, it will be sufficient to indicate this by using inverted commas in the main text, with the source in brackets. For example, as Laws (2003: 424) says, 'Your style should be determined by your own natural way of expressing yourself and the needs of your audience . . .'. If the quotation is longer, indent it and use single spacing unless institutional rules say otherwise:

> Your style should be determined by your own natural way of expressing yourself and the needs of your audience. However, bear in mind that while some audiences might be impressed by a complex way of writing, the main purpose of the exercise is to convey information. Clear and simple expression will help people to make sense of the material you present, and therefore act upon it.
>
> (Laws 2003: 424)

15 Presentation

These days, reports are generally typed or word-processed in double line spacing. Pages should be numbered. Type or write on one side of the page only, leaving a left-hand margin of one and a half inches. Incidentally, if you are hopeless at typing and can afford to pay for your copy to be produced by someone more skilled than you, make sure your writing is legible. It is not the typist's job to correct spelling, punctuation, headings, grammar or wording. Do not expect your abbreviations to be interpreted, nor your arithmetic to be checked. It is your job to hand in good, clear copy with very precise instructions about how things are to be done. If you make changes after the final copy is produced, you may have to pay more than you had bargained for, so take care.

The need for revision

I've never known anyone who has been able to produce a perfect first draft so don't delude yourself that you will be the exception. You won't be. You may find you need two, three or even more drafts before you are satisfied with the final result, so time must be set aside for this writing and refining process.

One problem about spending so much time on drafts is that parts of them may seem right simply because you have read them so often. Another is that you may be so familiar with the subject that you assume something is understandable to the reader when it is not. Time will give you a better perspective on your writing, so you should put the script aside, for several days if you can, so that you can return to it with a more critical eye. This will help you to identify repetitive passages, errors of expression and lack of clarity.

Work through your first draft section by section to ensure its sense, accuracy, logical sequencing and soundness of expression. If you wrote or typed only one paragraph on one side of each sheet, as suggested, this correcting and reordering stage will be relatively straightforward and the cut and paste facility on computers has greatly eased the burden of draft writers. Check spelling. Computer spell checks help, though remember that most computers will use American spelling, so always keep a dictionary to hand, to make sure you are right. Check quotations, punctuation, references, repetition, consistency of tenses and the overuse of certain terms. *Roget's Thesaurus of English Words and Phrases* may help you to find alternative forms of expression.

Remind yourself as you read that whatever structure has been selected, your readers will wish to be quite clear why you carried out the investigation, how you conducted it, what methods you used to gather your evidence and what you found out. It is not enough to describe: you will be expected to analyse, to evaluate and, if the evidence merits it, to make recommendations.

If research findings are to be put into practice, they have to be presented in a way in which practitioners and policy-makers can understand them. Please bear this in mind when you present your projects. There is no special academic language that should be used in academic papers. Good, clear English remains good, clear English, whatever the context. Technical language may well save time when you are talking to colleagues with a similar background to your own, but it rarely translates well on to paper, and your readers (and your examiner) may become irritated by too much jargon or obscure language.

The need for revision and rewriting was emphasized in a recent radio interview, when a world-famous economist who had many scholarly books to his credit, was complimented by the interviewer on his style of writing. 'It must be a great advantage', said the interviewer, 'to be able to write so freely and so easily. How do you do it?' The economist revealed his secret as follows:

> First, I produce a draft and then I leave it alone. I go back to it after a few days and decide it has been written by an ignoramus so I throw it away. Then I produce a second draft and leave it alone for a few days. I read it and decide there are the germs of a few good ideas there but it is badly written, so I put it to one side. After a few days, I write a third draft. When I read it again, I discover the ideas are developing, that there is some coherence to my arguments and that the grammar is not too bad. I correct this draft, change paragraphs around, insert new thoughts, remove overlapping passages and begin to feel progress is being made. After a few days, I read through this fourth draft, make final corrections and hand over the fifth draft to the typist. At this stage, I find I have usually achieved the degree of spontaneity for which I have been striving.

You may not need five drafts. Three may be enough if you write well, but rest assured that no one gets away with one or two – and most of us take four or five.

When you have completed the writing to the best of your ability, try to enlist the help of someone who will read the manuscript to look for any remaining errors. Failing that, you could read your report out loud, though make sure you are alone or your family may feel the strain has been too much for you! Reading aloud is particularly useful for detecting the need for better linking passages.

Any possibility of plagiarism?

In Chapter 4, I discussed the issue of plagiarism but this is sufficiently important to repeat here. You are plagiarizing if you copy someone else's words and claim them as your own and you cannot use other people's data or their ideas unless you provide adequate attribution. I am sure some students fall into the plagiarism trap because they genuinely did not know that 'it is not acceptable to put together unacknowledged passages from the same or from different sources, linking these together with a few words or sentences of your own and changing a few words from the original text' (University of Manchester 1997: 2). I'm confident your institution will have guidelines on plagiarism, so make sure you see them. Excuses that 'nobody ever told me I couldn't take assignments or answers to exam questions off the Internet without acknowledgement' or 'everybody does it, so why not me?' are not acceptable and if it is discovered that you have committed the sin of plagiarism, you could be suspended or even expelled from your programme. So, take great care to ensure that you have been meticulous in recording sources, making it clear in your notes which are direct quotations, your paraphrasing or merely your own thoughts.

There has been sufficient publicity recently to ensure that all researchers know, or should know what plagiarism means and what the penalties for infringements are. There have been some unfortunate, well-publicized cases recently which have brought discredit to the individuals and the institutions concerned, and this issue is not going to go away. Make sure you are absolutely clear about what is permissible and what is not.

Evaluating your own research

There are no universally accepted yardsticks for judging research reports but if you were asked to review a piece of research done by someone else, you would need to decide on the criteria by which you would judge it. Look at a journal article, or a novel, assuming you have had time to read a novel recently, and ask yourself, 'Is this a good report/novel?' If you consider it is good – or bad, try to decide how you came to this conclusion. Then, read your own draft. Do you think it is good? Are some parts better than others? Why? It's not easy to make such judgements about your own work, but there are some questions which should always be asked and better that you should identify areas of weakness, if any, while there is time to correct them rather than leaving it to the examiner. So, before you hand over what you hope will be your final draft, ask yourself:

1   Is the meaning clear? Are there any obscure passages?
2   Is the report well written? Check tenses, grammar, spelling, overlapping passages, punctuation, jargon.
3   Is the referencing well done? Are there any omissions?
4   Does the abstract give the reader a clear idea of what is in the report?
5   Does the title indicate the nature of the study?
6   Are the objectives of the study stated clearly?
7   Are the objectives of the study fulfilled?
8   If hypotheses were postulated, are they proved or not proved?
9   Has a sufficient amount of literature relating to the topic been studied?
10 Does the literature review, if any, provide an indication of the state of knowledge in the subject? Is your topic placed in the context of the area of study as a whole?
11 Are all terms clearly defined?
12 Are the selected methods of data collection accurately described? Are they suitable for the task? Why were they chosen?
13 Are any limitations of the study clearly presented?
14 Have any statistical techniques been used? If so, are they appropriate for the task?

15 Are the data analysed and interpreted or merely described?
16 Are the results clearly presented? Are tables, diagrams and figures well drawn?
17 Are conclusions based on evidence? Have any claims been made that cannot be substantiated?
18 Is there any evidence of bias? Any emotive terms or intemperate language?
19 Are the data likely to be reliable? Could another researcher repeat the methods used and have a reasonable chance of getting similar results?
20 Are recommendations, if any, feasible?
21 Are there any unnecessary items in the appendix?
22 Would you give the report a passing grade if you were the examiner? If not, perhaps an overhaul is necessary.

When you have provided yourself with honest replies to the above questions, try to persuade a friend to read your draft, to mark typographical or grammatical errors and to question awkward wording. You will have read the script many times but another pair of eyes will often spot errors you never noticed.

Once you have satisfied yourself that you have been able to answer all the above questions to your satisfaction, and have made any corrections identified by your reader, you will be ready to produce the final draft. Check the final, typed copy because even expert typists can make mistakes.

Finally, congratulate yourself on an excellent job completed on time. Hand in your report and give yourself an evening off!

◉ Writing the report checklist

1 Set deadlines.	Allocate provisional dates for sections, sub-sections and the whole report. You may need to make adjustments, but the handover date is fixed, so try to work round it. Keep an eye on your schedule.
2 Write regularly if you can.	

3 Create a rhythm of work, if at all possible.	Don't stop to check references, but tag or star any omissions or queries which must be checked later.
4 Write up a draft section as soon as it is ready.	Try to produce a draft of the literature review, no matter how rough, as soon as the bulk of the reading is completed.
5 Stop at a point from which it is easy to resume writing.	
6 Leave space for revisions.	Use one side of the paper only. Try to keep to one paragraph per page on your early drafts.
7 Publicize your plans.	You may need a little help from your friends to meet deadlines.
8 Check that all essential sections have been covered.	Abstract, outline of the research, review of previous work, statement of the scope and aims of the investigation, description of procedures, statement of results, discussion, summary and conclusions and references.
9 Check length is according to institutional requirements.	You don't want to be failed on a technicality.
10 Don't forget the title page.	
11 Any acknowledgements and thanks?	
12 Include headings where possible.	Anything to make it easier for readers to follow the structure will help. And it helps you to ensure you are following a logical pattern.
13 Number tables and figures and provide titles.	Put numbers and titles above tables, but below figures.
14 Make sure all quotations, paraphrases, good ideas of authors, etc. are acknowledged.	Check that quotations are presented in a consistent format and omissions indicated by . . .

15 Provide a list of references.	Unless instructed otherwise, include only items to which reference is made in the report. Check that a consistent system is used and that there are no incomplete references.
16 Appendices should only include items that are required for reference purposes. Do not clutter the report with irrelevant items.	Unless instructed otherwise, one copy of each data-collecting instrument should be included.
17 Remember to leave sufficient time for revision and rewriting.	Check that you have written in plain English. Check that your writing is legible.
18 Try to get someone to read the report.	Fresh eyes will often see errors you have overlooked.
19 Read the report aloud.	This will often identify any dubious punctuation and poor linkages.
20 Check through the 22 questions above for a last time. Are you sure you have dealt with each one honestly?	Make one final check of the typed final draft. Even expert typists can make mistakes.

Further reading

Creme, P. and Lea, M.R. (2003) *Writing at University: A Guide for Students*, 2nd edn. Maidenhead: Open University Press. This second edition has coverage of report and thesis writing, electronic writing, learning journals and the Internet. Useful.

Denscombe, M. (2003) *The Good Research Guide*, 2nd edn. Maidenhead: Open University Press. Chapter 15, 'Writing up the research', goes through the procedures involved, including what should be included, style and presentation. A helpful checklist is provided.

Hyatt, D. (2004) 'Writing research', in C. Opie (ed.) *Doing Educational Research: A Guide for First-time Researchers*. London: Sage. In this chapter, Hyatt discusses what is required for student academic writing, academic writing conventions, structuring a research-based assignment and 'Some advice I've been given (or wish I'd been given!)'. A useful chapter.

Laws, S. (2003) *Research for Development: A Practical Guide*. London: Sage. Chapter 21, 'How to write an effective research report', also includes guidance about what must be included in a research report (and what must be left out), and warnings about common pitfalls. Checklists provided.

Maimon, E. and Peritz, J. (2004) *A Writer's Resource: A Handbook for Writing and Research*. Maidenhead: Open University Press. This is an interesting book which addresses many of the problems facing researchers, particularly as they write assignments, research papers, theses – and reviewing and editing what has been written. The only slight problem is that it is written for an American student audience. Good writing is good writing wherever you are, but particularly when it comes to referencing and documentation style, there are certain marked differences between American and UK requirements. Even so, there is enough in this book to make it well worth keeping on hand.

Miles, M.B. and Huberman, A.M. (1994) *Qualitative Data Analysis*, 2nd edn. Thousand Oaks, CA: Sage Publications. Chapter 12, 'Producing reports', provides brief but good advice about structuring a report, under the headings of 'Voices, genres, and stances' (How do we speak to the reader?), 'Style', 'Formats' and 'Structures'.

Murray, R. (2002) *How to Write a Thesis*. Maidenhead: Open University Press. This book is written mainly with Master's and doctoral students in mind, though the advice given can equally be applied to writing up any research. Rowena Murray takes us through the various stages of planning, structure, the writing process, dealing with deadlines and revising. The sections on 'Starting to write' and 'Seeking structure' are particularly useful.

Wolcott, H.F. (2001) *Writing up Qualitative Research*. London: Sage Publications. In Chapter 2, I said that everything Wolcott has written is worth reading and this book in particular is excellent. I still go back to it, particularly if I am stuck and just can't get going. If you can get hold of a copy, read it all! His chapter headings are 'Getting going' ('Writers who indulge themselves by waiting until their thoughts are "clear" run the risk of never starting at all' (p. 22)), 'Keeping going', 'Tightening up' and 'Finishing up'. He advises us to 'think on paper' and that is some of the best advice any researcher can be given. As I also said in Chapter 2, he can be funny – and that helps.

Woods, P. (1999) *Successful Writing for Qualitative Researchers*. London: Routledge.

POSTSCRIPT

There may be occasions when, in spite of careful planning and preparation, a project does not go according to plan. For example, you may find that people who said they were willing to provide information by a certain date fail to do so, or that results are not forthcoming. If things do wrong, consult your tutor to discuss the best course of action. You may have learnt a great deal about conducting an investigation and the topic you were researching, even though the outcome may not be what you had hoped. If you are not able to produce a report on the lines you planned, you may be able to submit a report of what you have been able to do, together with an account of what went wrong and why and, if appropriate, how you would have planned and carried out the investigation if you were starting again. The important thing is to ask for help. Intelligent people who are first-time researchers sometimes feel they ought to be able to sort themselves out, and by not making use of supervisors, computer centre staff and librarians, may waste a great deal of time. I said in the Introduction to this book that we all learn how to do research by actually doing it. This is quite true, but anyone carrying out an investigation for the first time needs some assistance. Make sure you take advantage of any that is available.

Just one final word. People who agree to be interviewed or to complete questionnaires, diary forms or logs, groups who agree to your observing meetings and keepers of archives who allow you to consult documents, deserve consideration and thanks. Daphne Johnson sums up the position well:

> If files are left in disarray, papers borrowed and not returned, or respondents subjected to too lengthy or frequent interviews at inconvenient times, the researcher's welcome will be worn out. All social researchers are to some extent mendicants, since they are seeking a free gift of time or information from those who are the subject of study. But researchers who bear this fact in mind, and who, without becoming the captive of their respondents, can contrive to make the research experience a helpful and profitable one, will almost certainly be gratified by the generosity with which people will give their time and knowledge.
>
> (Johnson 1984: 11)

REFERENCES

Aldridge A. and Levine, K. (2001) *Surveying the Social World: Principles and Practice in Survey Research*. Buckingham: Open University Press.

Argyrous, G. (2002) *Statistics for Social and Health Research*. London: Sage.

Baker, S. (1999) 'Finding and searching for information sources', Chapter 5 in J. Bell, *Doing Your Research Project: A Guide for First-time Researchers*, 3rd edn. Buckingham: Open University Press.

Baker, S. and Carty, J. (1994) 'Literature searching: finding, organizing and recording information', in N. Bennett, R. Glatter and R. Levačić (eds) *Improving Educational Management through Research and Consultancy*. London: Paul Chapman Publishing, in association with The Open University.

Bales, R.F. (1950) *Interaction Process Analysis: A Method for the Study of Small Groups*. Cambridge, MA: Addison-Wesley.

Baltes, P.B., Dittmann-Kohli, F. and Dixon, R.A. (1984) 'New perspectives on the development of intelligence in adulthood', in P.B. Baltes and O.G. Brim Jr. (eds) *Life-span Development and Behavior*, 6: 33–76. Orlando, FL: Academic Press.

Barbour, R.S. and Kitzinger, J. (eds) (1999) *Developing Focus Group Research: Politics, Theory and Practice*. London: Sage.

Barzun, J. and Graff, H.F. (1977) *The Modern Researcher*, 3rd edn. New York: Harcourt Brace Jovanovich.

Barzun, J. and Graff, H.F. (1992) *The Modern Researcher*, 5th edn. London: Wadsworth.

Bassey, M. (1981) 'Pedagogic research; on the relative merits of the search for generalization and study of single events', *Oxford Review of Education*, 7(1): 73–93.

Bassey, M. (1999) *Case Study Research in Educational Settings*. Buckingham: Open University Press.

Bassey M. (2001) 'A solution to the problem of generalisation in educational research: fuzzy prediction', *Oxford Review of Education*, 27(1): 5–22.

Bassey, M. (2002) 'Case study research', Chapter 7 in M. Coleman and A.R.J. Briggs (eds) *Research Methods in Educational Leadership and Management*. London: Paul Chapman Publishing.

Bathmaker, A-M (2004) 'Using NUD-IST', in C. Opie (ed.) *Doing Educational Research: A Guide to First-time Researchers*. London: Sage.

Bell, J. (1996) 'An investigation into barriers to completion of post-graduate research degrees in three universities'. Unpublished report funded through the Leverhulme Emeritus research fund.

Bell, J. (2002) 'Questionnaires', in M. Coleman and A.R.J. Briggs (eds) *Research Methods in Educational Leadership and Management*. London: Paul Chapman Publishing.

Bell, J. and Opie, C. (2002) *Learning from Research: Getting More from your Data*. Buckingham: Open University Press.

Bennett, N., Glatter, R. and Levačić, R. (eds) (1994) *Improving Educational Management through Research and Consultancy*. London: Paul Chapman Publishing, in association with the The Open University.

Best, J.W. (1970) *Research in Education*, 2nd edn. Englewood Cliffs, NJ: Prentice-Hall.

Blaxter, L., Hughes, C. and Tight, M. (2001) *How to Research*, 2nd edn. Buckingham: Open University Press.

Bogdan, R.C. and Biklen, S.K. (1982) *Qualitative Research for Education: An Introduction to Theory and Methods*. Boston, MA: Alleyn & Bacon.

Bowling, A. (2002) *Research Methods in Health: Investigating Health and Health Services*, 2nd edn. Maidenhead: Open University Press.

Brewer, J.D. (2000) *Ethnography*. Buckingham: Open University Press.

Brown, S. and McIntyre, D. (1981) 'An action-research approach to innovation in centralised educational systems', *European Journal of Science Education*, 3(3): 243–58.

Bryman, A. and Cramer, D. (1994) *Quantitative Data Analysis for Social Scientists* (revised edition). London: Routledge.

Burgess, R.G. (ed.) (1982) *Field Research: A Sourcebook and Field Manual*. London: George Allen and Unwin.

Burgess, R.G. (1994) 'On diaries and diary keeping', in N. Bennett, R. Glatter, and R. Levačić (eds) *Improving Educational Management through Research and Consultancy*. London: Paul Chapman Publishing, in association with The Open University.

Burgess, R.G. and Morrison, M. (1993) 'Teaching and learning about food and nutrition in school', in *The Nation's Diet Programme: The Social Science of Food Choice*. Report to the ESRC.

Busher, H. (2002) 'Ethics of Research in Education', Chapter 5 in M. Coleman and A.R.J. Briggs (eds) *Research Methods in Educational Leadership and Management*. London: Paul Chapman Publishing.

The Caldicott Committee (1997) Report on the review of patient-identifiable information. London: Department of Health.

Casey, K. (1993) 'The new narrative research in education', *Review of Research in Education*, 21: 211–53.

Chan, T. (2000) 'Student evaluation of teaching effectiveness'. Unpublished PhD thesis, University of Nottingham.

Clough, P. (2002) *Narratives and Fictions in Educational Research*. Maidenhead: Open University Press.

Cohen, L. (1976) *Educational Research in Classrooms and Schools: A Manual of Materials and Methods*, 4th edn. London: Routledge.

Cohen, L. and Manion, L. (1994) *Research Methods in Education*, 4th edn. London: Routledge.

Cohen, L., Manion, L. and Morrison, K. (2000) *Research Methods in Education*, 5th edn. London and New York: Routledge Falmer.

Coleman, M. and Briggs, A.R.J. (eds) (2002) *Research Methods in Educational Leadership and Management*. London: Paul Chapman Publishing.

Cramer, D. (2003) *Advanced Quantitative Data Analysis*. Buckingham: Open University Press.

Cramer, D. and Howitt, D.L. (2004) *The Sage Dictionary of Statistics*. London: Sage Publications.

Creme, P. and Lea, M.R. (2003) *Writing at University*, 2nd edn. Maidenhead: Open University Press.

Croner (2002) *The Head's Legal Guide*. Kingston: Croner Publications.

Cross, K.P. (1981) *Adults as Learners: Increasing Participation and Facilitating Learning*. San Francisco, CA: Jossey Bass.

Cryer, P. (2000) *The Research Student's Guide to Success*, 2nd edn. Maidenhead: Open University Press.

Darlington, Y. and Scott, D. (2002) *Qualitative Research in Practice: Stories from the Field*. Maidenhead: Open University Press.

The Data Protection Registrar (1998) *The Data Protection Act 1998: An Introduction*. Wilmslow, Cheshire: The Data Protection Registrar.

Delamont, S., Atkinson, P. and Parry O. (2004) *Supervising the Doctorate: A Guide to Success*. Maidenhead: Open University Press.

Denscombe, M. (1998) *The Good Research Guide for Small-scale Social Research Projects*. Buckingham: Open University Press.

Denscombe, M. (2002) *Ground Rules for Good Research: A 10 Point Guide for Social Researchers*. Buckingham: Open University Press.

Denscombe, M. (2003) *The Good Research Guide for Small-scale Social Research Projects*, 2nd edn. Maidenhead: Open University Press.

Drew, C.J. (1980) *Introduction to Designing and Conducting Research*, 2nd edn. Missouri, CB: Mosby Company.

Duffy, B. (1998) 'Late nineteenth-century popular educational conservatism: the work of coalminers on the school boards of the North-East', *History of Education*, 27(1): 29–38.

Eggleston, J. (1979) 'The characteristics of educational research: mapping the domain', *British Educational Research Journal*, 5(1): 1–12.

Elton, G.R. (2002) *The Practice of History*, 2nd edn. Oxford: Blackwell.

Evans, R.J. (2000) *In Defence of History*, 2nd edn. London: Granta Books.

Fan, G. (1998) 'An exploratory study of final year diploma in nursing students' perceptions of their nursing education'. Unpublished MEd dissertation, University of Sheffield.

Flanders, N.A. (1970) *Analysing Teaching Behaviour*. Cambridge, MA: Addison-Wesley.

Fogelman, K. (2002) 'Surveys and sampling', Chapter 6 in M. Coleman, and A.R.J. Briggs (eds) *Research Methods in Educational Leadership and Management*. London: Paul Chapman Publishing.

Gash, S. (1989) *Effective Literature Searching for Students*. Aldershot: Gower.

Glaser, B.G. (1992) *Basics of Grounded Theory Analysis*. Mill Valley, CA: Sociology Press.

Glaser, B.G. and Strauss, A.L. (1965) *Awareness of Dying*. Chicago: Aldine.

Glaser, B.G. and Strauss, A.L. (1967) *The Discovery of Grounded Theory: Strategies for Qualitative Research*. New York: Aldine.

Glaser, B.G. and Strauss, A.L. (1968) *Time for Dying*. Chicago: Aldine.

Goodson, I.F. and Sikes, P. (2001) *Life History Research in Educational Settings: Learning from Life*. Buckingham: Open University Press.

Gray, J. (1998) 'Narrative Inquiry'. Unpublished paper, Edith Cowan University, Western Australia.

Gray, J. (2000) 'The framing of truancy: a study of non attendance as a form of social exclusion within Western Australia'. Unpublished doctoral thesis, Edith Cowan University, Western Australia.

Gudmunsdottir, S. (1996) 'The teller, the tale, and the one being told: the narrative nature of the research interview', *Curriculum Inquiry*, 26(3): 293–306.

Guttman, L. (1950) 'The basis for scalogram analysis' in S.A. Stouffer (ed.) *Measurement and Prediction*. Princeton, NJ: Princeton University Press.

Hakim, C. (2000) *Research Design*, 2nd edn. London: Routledge.

Hammersley, M. (1989) *The Dilemma of Qualitative Method*. London: Routledge.

Hammersley M. (1990) *Classroom Ethnography: Empirical and Methodological Essays*. Buckingham: Open University Press.

Hardy, M.A. and Bryman, A. (eds) (2004) *Handbook of Data Analysis*. London: Sage Publications.

Hart, C. (1998) *Doing a Literature Review: Releasing the Social Science Research Imagination*. London: Sage in association with The Open University.

Hart, E. and Bond, M. (1995) *Action Research for Health and Social Care*. Buckingham: Open University Press.

Hayes, E. and Bond, M. (1995) *Action Research for Health and Social Care: A Guide to Practice*. Buckingham: Open University Press.

Hayes, N. (2000) *Doing Psychological Research: Gathering and Analysing Data*. Buckingham: Open University Press.

Haywood, P. and Wragg, E.D. (1982) *Evaluating the Literature*. Rediguide 2, University of Nottingham School of Education.

Horne, K. (2004) 'Top ten guide to searching the Internet'. Personal communication.

Howard, K. and Sharp, J.A. (1983) *The Management of a Student Research Project*. Aldershot: Gower.

Hyatt, D. (2004) 'Writing research', in C. Opie *Doing Educational Research: A Guide to First-time Researchers*. London: Sage.

Hyland, M.E. (1996) 'Diary assessments of quality of life', *Quality of Life Newsletter*, **16**: 8–9.

Hyland, M.E. and Crocker, G.R. (1995) 'Validation of an asthma quality of life diary in a clinical trial', *Thorax*, 50: 724–30.

Johnson, D. (1984) 'Planning small-scale research', in J. Bell, T. Bush and A. Fox et al. *Conducting Small-scale Investigations in Educational Management*. London: Harper and Row.

Johnson, D. (1994) 'Planning small-scale research', in N. Bennett, R. Glatter and R. Levačić (eds) *Improving Educational Management through Research and Consultancy*. London: Paul Chapman.

Keats, D. (2000) *Interviewing: A Practical Guide for Students and Professionals*. Maidenhead: Open University Press.

Kitzinger, J. and Barbour, R.S. (1999) 'Introduction to the challenge and promise of focus groups', in R.S. Barbour and J. Kitzinger (eds) *Developing Focus Group Research: Politics, Theory and Practice*. London: Sage.

Klatzky, R.L. (1988) 'Theories of information processing and theories of aging', in L.L. Light and D.J. Burke (eds) *Language, Memory and Aging*. Cambridge: Cambridge University Press.

Korman, N. and Glennester, H. (1990) *Hospital Closure: A Political and Economic Study*. Buckingham: Open University Press.

Krippendorf, K. (1980) *Content Analysis*. London: Sage.

Lacey, C. (1976) 'Problems of sociological fieldwork: a review of the methodology of "Hightown Grammar", in M. Shipman (ed.) *The Organisation and Impact of Social Research*. London: Routledge & Kegan Paul.

Langeveld, M.J. (1965) 'In search of research', *Paedagogica Europoea: The European Year Book of Educational Research* 1. Amsterdam: Elsevier.

Laws, S. with Harper, C. and Marcus, R. (2003) *Research for Development*. London: Sage Publications.

Lehmann, I.J. and Mehrens W.A. (1971) *Educational Research*. New York: Holt, Rinehart and Winston.

Likert, R. (1932) *A Technique for the Measurement of Attitudes*. New York: Columbia University Press.

Lim, C.P. (1997) 'The effect of computer-based learning (CBL) in support classes on low-performance economics students'. Unpublished MEd dissertation, University of Sheffield.

Lomax, P. (2002) 'Action research', Chapter 8 in M. Coleman, M. and A.R.J. Briggs (eds) *Research Methods in Educational Leadership and Management*. London: Paul Chapman Publishing.

Lutz, F.W. (1986) 'Ethnography: The holistic approach to understanding schooling', Chapter 3.1 in M. Hammersley *Controversies in Classroom Research*. Milton Keynes: Open University Press.

Maimon, E. and Peritz, J. (2004) *A Writer's Resource: A Handbook for Writing and Research*. Maidenhead: Open University Press.

Marples, D.L. (1967) 'Studies of managers: a fresh start', *Journal of Management Studies*, 4: 282–99.

Marwick, A. (2001) *The New Nature of History*, 5th edn. Basingstoke: Palgrave.

May, T. (2001) *Social Research: Issues, Methods and Process*, 3rd edn. Buckingham: Open University Press.

McCulloch G. and Richardson W. (2000) *Historical Research in Educational Settings*. Buckingham: Open University Press.

Medawar, P.B. (1972) *The Hope of Progress*. London: Methuen.

Miles, M.B. and Huberman, A.M. (1994) *Qualitative Data Analysis*, 2nd edn. Thousand Oaks, CA: Sage.

Morrison, M. (2002) 'Using diaries in research', in M. Coleman, and A.R.J. Briggs (eds) *Research Methods in Educational Leadership and Management*. London: Paul Chapman Publishing.

Morrison, M. and Burgess, R.G. (1993) 'Chapatis and chips: encountering food use in primary school settings'. Paper prepared for an International Conference on Children's Food and Drink: Today's Market and Tomorrow's Opportunities, at Chipping Campden Food and Drink Association, Chipping Campden, Gloucester, on 10 November 1993.

Morrison, M. and Galloway, S. (1993) 'Using diaries to explore supply teachers' lives', in J. Busfield and E.S. Lyons (eds) *Methodological Imaginations*. London: Macmillan, in Association with the British Sociological Association.

Moser, C.A. and Kalton, G. (1971) *Survey Methods in Social Investigation*, 2nd edn. London: Heinemann.

Moyles, J. (2002) 'Observation as a research tool', in M. Coleman and A.R.J. Briggs (eds) *Research Methods in Educational Leadership and Management*. London: Paul Chapman Publishing.

Murray, R. (2002) *How to Write a Thesis*. Maidenhead: Open University Press.

Nai, C. (1996) 'Stretching the aged workforce: a study of the barriers to continuous learning among mature workers'. Unpublished dissertation submitted in part requirement for the degree of Master of Education (Training and Development) at the University of Sheffield.

Nisbet, J.D. (1977) 'Small-scale research: guidelines and suggestions for development', *Scottish Educational Studies*, 9 (May): 13–17.

Nisbet, J.D. and Entwistle, N.J. (1970) *Educational Research Methods*. London: University of London Press.

Nisbet, J.D. and Ross, L. (1980) *Human Inference: Strategies and Shortcomings of Social Judgment*. Englewood Cliffs, NJ: Prentice-Hall.

Nisbet, J.D. and Watt, J. (1980) *Case Study*. Rediguide 26, University of Nottingham School of Education.

Nyberg, L., Backman, L., Erngrund, K. et al. (1996) 'Age differences in episodic memory, semantic memory, and priming: relationships to demographic, intellectual and biological factors', *Journal of Gerontology: Psychological Science*, 51B: 234–40.

OFSTED (2003) *Handbook for Inspecting Secondary Schools*. HMI 1360. London: OFSTED.

Oliver, P. (2003) *The Student's Guide to Research Ethics*. Maidenhead: The Open University Press.

Opie, C. (ed.) (2004) *Doing Educational Research: A Guide for First-time Researchers*. London: Sage.

Oppenheim, A.N. (1992) *Questionnaire Design, Interviewing and Attitude Measurement*, New Edition. London: Cassell.

Orna, E. with Stevens, G. (1995) *Managing Information for Research*. Buckingham: Open University Press.

Oxtoby, R. (1979) 'Problems facing heads of department', *Journal of Further and Higher Education*, 3(1): 46–59.

Pallant, J. (2004) *SPSS Survival Manual. A Step by Step Guide to Data Analysis Using SPSS for Windows*, 2nd edn. Maidenhead: Open University Press.

Pears, R. and Shields, G. (1994) *Cite them Right: Referencing Made Easy*. Newcastle upon Tyne: Northumbria University Press.

Phillips, E.M. and Pugh, D.S. (2000) *How to get a Doctorate: A Handbook for Students and their Supervisors*, 3rd edn. Buckingham: Open University Press. (Updated and revised in 2004 as *Supervising the Doctorate: A Guide for Success*.)

Polit, D. F. and Hungler, B. P. (1995) *Nursing Research: Principles and Methods*, 5th edn. Philadelphia: J. B. Lippincott Company.

Pomerantz, M. (2004) 'Using ATLAS.ti', in C. Opie, ed. *Doing Educational Research: A Guide for First Time Researchers*. London: Sage.

Punch, K.F. (1998) *Introduction to Social Research: Quantitative and Qualitative Approaches*. London: Sage Publications.

Punch, K.F. (2003) *Survey Research: The Basics*. London: Sage.

Reason, P. and Bradbury, H. (eds) (2001) *Handbook of Action Research: Participative Inquiry and Practice*. London: Sage Publications.

Richardson, J.T.E. and King, E. (1998) 'Adult students in higher education: burden or boon?' *Journal of Higher Education*, 69: 65–88.

Richardson, J.T.E. and Woodley, A. (2003) 'Another look at the role of age, gender and subject as predictors of academic attainment in higher education', *Studies in Higher Education*, 28(4): October.

Roberts, B. (2002) *Biographical Research*. Maidenhead: Open University Press.

Roget, P.M. (2000) *Roget's Thesaurus of English Words and Phrases*. First published in 1982 by P.M. Roget. 2000 edition revised by Betty Kirkpatrick. London: Penguin Books.

Rose, D. and Sullivan, O. (1996) *Introducing Data Analysis for Social Scientists*, 2nd edn. Buckingham: Open University Press.

Rumsey, S. (2004) *How to Find Information: A Guide for Researchers*. Maidenhead: Open University Press.

Sapsford, R.J. and Abbott, (1996) 'Ethics, politics and research', in R. Sapsford and V. Jupp *Data Collection and Analysis*. London: Sage.

Sapsford, R. and Jupp, V. (1996) *Data Collection and Analysis*. London: Sage.

Scaife, J. (2004) 'Reliability, validity and credibility', Chapter 4 in C. Opie (ed.) *Doing Educational Research: A Guide to First-time Researchers*. London: Sage.

Schaie, K.W. (1996) *Intellectual Development in Adulthood: The Seattle Longitudinal Study*. Cambridge: Cambridge University Press.

Selltiz, D., Jahoda, M., Deutsch, M. and Cook, S.W. (1962) *Research Methods in Social Relations*, 2nd edn. New York: Holt, Rinehart & Winston.

Spradley, J.P. (1980) *Participant Observation*. New York: Holt, Rinehart and Winston.

Stanford, M. (1994) *A Companion to the Study of History*. Oxford: Blackwell.

Strauss, A.L. (1987) *Qualitative Analysis for Social Scientists*. Cambridge: Cambridge University Press.

Sutherland, V. and Cooper, C.L. (2003) *De-stressing Doctors: A Self-management Guide*. London: Elsevier Science Ltd (Butterworth Heinemann).

Talbot, C. (2003) *Studying at a Distance: A Guide for Students*. Maidenhead: Open University Press.

Thody, A. with Downes, P., Hewlett, M. and Tomlinson, H. (1997) 'Lies, damned lies – and storytelling: an exploration of the contribution of principals' anecdotes to research, teaching and learning about the management of schools and colleges', *Educational Management and Administration*, 25(3): 325–38.

Thurstone, L.L. and Chave, E.J. (1929) *The Measurement of Attitudes*. Chicago: University of Chicago Press.

Times Educational Supplement (2003) News article. 5 September.

Tosh, J. (2002) *The Pursuit of History*, 3rd edn. Harlow: Longman.

University of Manchester (1997) 'Plagiarism' (mimeo).

Verhaeghen, P. and Salthouse, T.A. (1997) 'Meta-analyses of age-cognition relations in adulthood: estimates of linear and nonlinear age effects and structural models', *Psychological Bulletin*, 122: 231–49.

Verma, G.K. and Beard, R.M. (1981) *What Is Educational Research? Perspectives on Techniques of Research*. Aldershot: Gower.

Weber, R.P. (1990) *Basic Content Analysis*, 2nd edn. Newbury Park, CA: Sage.

Wellington, J.J. (1996) *Methods and Issues in Educational Research*. University of Sheffield Division of Education: USDE Papers in Education.

Whitehead, N. (2003) 'Herbal remedies: integration into conventional medicine', *Nursing Times*, 99(34): 30–3.

Williams, G.L. (1994) 'Observing and recording meetings', Chapter 22 in N. Bennett, R. Glatter and R. Levačić (eds) *Improving Educational Management through Research and Consultancy*. London: Paul Chapman Publishing, in association with the Open University.

Wilson, N.J. (1979) 'The ethnographic style of research', in Block 1 (Variety in Social Science Research), Part 1 (Styles of Research) of Open University course DE304, *Research Methods in Education and the Social Sciences*.

Wiseman, J.P. and Aron, M.S. (1972) *Field Reports in Sociology*. London: Transworld Publishers.

Wolcott, H.F. (1990) *Writing up Qualitative Research*. London: Sage Publications.

Wolcott, H.F. (1992) 'Posturing in qualitative inquiry', in M.D. LeCompte, W.L. Millroy, and J. Preissle (eds) *The Handbook of Qualitative Research in Education*. New York: Academic Press.

Wolcott, H.F. (2001) *Writing up Qualitative Research*, 2nd edn. London: Sage Publications.

Woodley, A. (1981) 'Age bias', in D. Warren Piper (ed.) *Is Higher Education Fair?* Guildford: Society for Research into Higher Education.

Woodley, A. (1984) 'The older the better? A study of mature student performance in British universities', *Research in Education*, 32: 35–50.

Woodley, A. (1985) 'Taking account of mature students', in D. Jacques and J. Richardson (eds) *The Future of Higher Education*. Guildford: SRHE and NFER-Nelson.

Woodley, A. (1998) Review of McGivney (1996a) *'Staying or Leaving the Course: Non-completion and Retention of Mature Students in Further and Higher Education'*. Leicester: National Institute of Adult Continuing Education.

Woodley, A. and McIntosh, N. (1980) *The Door Stood Open: An Evaluation of the Open University Younger Students' Pilot Scheme*. Barcombe: Falmer Press.

Woods, P. (1999) *Successful Writing for Qualitative Researchers*. London: Routledge.

Wragg, E.C. (1980) *Conducting and Analysing Interviews*. Rediguide 11. University of Nottingham School of Education.

Wragg, E.C. (2002) 'Interviewing', in M. Coleman and A.R.J. Briggs (eds) *Research Methods in Educational Leadership and Management*. London: Paul Chapman Publishing.

Yin, R.K. (1994) 'Designing single- and multiple-case studies', Chapter 10 in N. Bennett, R. Glatter, and R. Levačić (eds) *Educational Management Through Research and Consultancy*. London: Paul Chapman Publishing, in association with The Open University.

Youngman, M.B. (1982) *Designing and Analysing Questionnaires*. Rediguide 12. Nottingham: University of Nottingham School of Education.

Youngman, M.B. (1994) 'Designing and analysing interviews', Chapter 17 in N. Bennett, R. Glatter and R. Levačić (eds) *Improving Educational Management Through Research and Consultancy*. London: Paul Chapman Publishing, in association with The Open University.

Zimmerman, D.H. and Wieder, D.L. (1977) 'The diary-interview method', *Urban Life*, 5(4): 479–99.

INDEX

WRITING AT UNIVERSITY
A GUIDE FOR STUDENTS
Second Edition

Phyllis Creme and Mary R. Lea

- What is expected of you in university writing?
- What can you do to develop and build confidence in your writing?
- How can you address the variety of written assignments you will encounter in your studies?

Writing at University is a student writing guide with a difference. It provides a deeper understanding of what writing at university is all about, with useful methods and approaches to give you more control over your academic writing.

The book explores both traditional essay and other kinds of writing that you will need to do as part of your studies. You are encouraged to build upon your existing abilities as a writer through applying practical tasks to your own work.

The second edition of this best-selling title has been completely updated with new coverage of report writing, learning journals, electronic writing and using the internet.

This book is an essential tool for anyone who wants to improve their writing skills at university or FE colleges, including both undergraduates and post-graduate students. It is key reading for students in courses that require essay, report, or dissertation writing and for students returning to study. It is also an invaluable resource for academic staff who want to support students with their writing.

Contents
You and university writing – First thoughts on writing assignments – Writing for different courses – Beginning with the title – Reading as part of writing – Organizing and shaping your writing – Putting yourself into your academic writing – Putting it together – Completing the assignment and preparing for next time – Using different kinds of writing – Using learning journals and other exploratory writing – References – Index.

160pp   0 335 21325 1 (Paperback)

THE GOOD RESEARCH GUIDE
FOR SMALL-SCALE RESEARCH PROJECTS
Second Edition

Martyn Denscombe

The Good Research Guide has been a bestselling introduction to the basics of social research since it was first published in 1998. The second edition of the book offers the same clear guidance on how to conduct successful small-scale research projects and adds even more value by including new sections on Internet research, phenomenology, grounded theory and image-based methods.

The book provides:

- A clear summary of the relevant strategies, methods and approaches to data analysis
- A jargon-free coverage of the key issues
- An attractive layout and user-friendly presentation
- Checklists to guide good practice.

Practical and comprehensive, *The Good Research Guide* is an invaluable tool for students of education, health studies, business studies and other social sciences, who need to conduct small-scale research projects as part of undergraduate, postgraduate or professional studies.

Contents
Introduction – Part one: Strategies – Surveys – Case studies – Internet research – Experiments – Action research – Ethnography – Phenomenology – Grounded theory – Part two: Methods – Questionnaires – Interviews – Observation – Documents – Part three: Analysis – Quantitative data – Qualitative data – Writing up the research – References – Index.

272pp   0335 21303 0 (Paperback)

THE STUDENT'S GUIDE TO RESEARCH ETHICS
Paul Oliver

This new title examines the ethical issues and questions which occur in university and professional research. The book helps both beginner and experienced researchers to identify ethical issues when they are conducting research, and attempt to resolve those issues.

- Examines ethical issues which arise throughout research, from the design stage through to data collection and analysis
- Investigates topical issues including consent, confidentiality, ethical questions in the dissemination of research
- Discusses ethical theories and how these may be applied in resolving ethical problems
- Provides examples of ethical dilemmas and case studies throughout the text.

Insightful, wide-ranging and accessible, this title is an invaluable tool for both undergraduate and postgraduate students and professionals who research as part of their job.

Contents
Part one: Ethics and the research process – Introduction: ethics and research – Research and the respondent: ethical issues before the research commences – Research and the respondent: ethical issues during the research – Research and the respondent: ethical issues when data collection has been completed – Part two: Ethical themes – The privacy of respondents, and restrictions on the use of data – Differences in the research context – The funding and sponsorship of research – The publication and dissemination of research – Conclusion: the role of the researcher – Index.

192pp   0 335 21087 2 (Paperback)   0 335 21088 0 (Hardback)

STUDENT-FRIENDLY GUIDES

These guides offer friendly support and straightforward guidance for undergraduates and taught postgraduates. Ideal whether you're looking for help with one particular aspect of studying or just getting stressed out!

Top-class dissertations!
- Planning and writing an extended piece of work, for undergraduates and postgraduates
- Doing the project and writing it up
- Choosing a subject and an approach, materials and methodology
- Recording findings, structuring the writing and getting the discussion right
- Turning your extended essay into a 'top-class' dissertation

136pp   Paperback

Write great essays!
Reading and essay-writing for undergraduates and taught postgraduates.

- Dealing with 'academic-speak' and monster reading lists
- Choosing and using an efficient reading and note-taking strategy
- Finding the right structure for your essay
- Avoiding accusations of plagiarism

124pp   0335 21577 7 Paperback

Sail through exams!
Preparing for traditional exams for undergraduates and taught postgraduates.

- Decoding difficult-to-understand exam questions
- Structuring top-quality answers
- Revising effectively
- Getting in the right frame of mind for exams and doing your best on the day

100pp   0335 21576 9 Paperback

Successful teamwork!
For undergraduates and taught postgraduates working on group projects.

- Allocating work appropriately
- How best to communicate and conduct meetings
- Dealing with people who are taking a 'free ride' or who try to dominate
- Making good use of your teamwork experience when looking for a job

124pp   0335 21578 5 Paperback